Neutral Europe between
War and Revolution, 1917–23

Neutral Europe between War and Revolution 1917–23

EDITED BY HANS A. SCHMITT

UNIVERSITY PRESS OF VIRGINIA

CHARLOTTESVILLE

THE UNIVERSITY PRESS OF VIRGINIA
Copyright © 1988 by the Rector and Visitors
of the University of Virginia

First published 1988

LIBRARY OF CONGRESS
Library of Congress Cataloging-in-Publication Data
Neutral Europe between war and revolution, 1917–23 / edited by Hans A.
  Schmitt.
     p.   cm.
  Includes index.
  ISBN 0–8139–1153–2
  1. Europe—Neutrality. 2. World War, 1914–1918—Influence.
I. Schmitt, Hans A.
D723.N48   1988
940.3′14—dc19   87–28724
                                                           CIP

Printed in the United States of America

Contents

Preface

    The First World War spilled more blood than any European conflict since the religious wars of the seventeenth century. At the same time it produced the greatest epidemic of civil conflict since 1848.

In the nineteenth century the immediate cause of multiple revolution had been poor harvests and widespread famine in town and country—a natural catastrophe. In the twentieth century the trigger was the break-down in international order—a human-made disaster. The motivating ideology in both instances was Liberalism—laissez-faire, the domestic quest for access to political power, and belief in a national community, claiming cultural, economic, and political sovereignty and loyal adherence from all citizens. This dynamic program ended the relative order represented by a legitimist old regime, replacing it with an unending pursuit of social and political perfection. The asserted freedom to prosper created a climate of competition in which those who failed would strive ever more desperately to succeed. The citizen's right to a voice in political counsels inaugurated perpetual debate. The claims of national sovereignty produced conflicts as irreconcilable as had the competition of dynastic interests in preceding centuries. Every nation-state continued to be surrounded by potential enemies. Every victory called the defeated to a war of revenge; every settlement left an agenda of revision. Victory validated the existing political system; defeat threatened revolution. Humankind entered a new age of perpetual war and perpetual domestic conflict.

Except for the isolated example of the Bonapartes, the belligerents of 1914 were the first to suffer the full effects of this new historical process.

Allied governments found in victory at least temporary forgiveness for past blunders. The Third Republic emerged from the war scarred but justified. The British Empire reached its maximum expansion after 1918, and the growing independence of its dominions at the peace conference was not recognized as a prelude to disintegration until the enactment of the Statute of Westminster in 1931 heralded eventual decomposition.

The same war spelled death for the Romanovs, destroyed the Habsburg monarchy, and drove Kaiser Willhelm II into exile. No matter how powerful, how well established, or how deeply rooted in history, governments could no longer survive failure to defend the national or dynastic patrimony. Even Italy's fate, lingering uneasily between triumph and humiliation, confirmed the new state of affairs.

All of this is well known and would not be worth repeating if it did not leave out of account a third element, the considerable group of European states that refused to be drawn into the conflict. Their dissenting stance spared them the loss of life and the destruction of property, but no one can say that war left them unaffected.

This should come as no surprise, for neutrality had never guaranteed immunity from the consequences of war. Saxony's attempted neutrality at the outset of the Second Silesian War had not stemmed disaster. Prussia's endeavor to remain above the battle when war resumed after the Treaty of Amiens ended catastrophically at Jena, while Austria's neutrality in the Crimean War turned out to be as costly in some ways as belligerence might have been.

We must therefore ask what position on the scale between victory and defeat the neutrals of the First World War occupied in the end. How did the echoes of battle disturb the peace they insisted on preserving within their boundaries?

Until the war separated them from the majority of their fellow Europeans, neutrals had shared with the belligerents the Liberal inheritance and the conflict-ridden interim since the French Revolution. They, too, had wrestled with the consequences of industrialization; their public places had also reverberated with the clamor for political reform. Nations as far apart, culturally and geographically, as Spain and Switzerland had fought civil wars. Belgium with the oldest industrial establishment on the continent had weathered a major constitutional crisis. The peace of restless Scandinavia had only recently been threatened by the separation of Norway from Sweden, and the solution of that crisis had deeply involved Britain, Germany, and Russia. Two former members of the Germanic Confederation, the king of Holland and the grand duke of Luxemburg, had suffered constitutional diminutions of their power as part of the modernization of state and society in their patrimonies. To varying degrees every national society bore the imprint of a hectic age. The outbreak of war could not be expected to convert the neutral polities into peaceful, static islands in a sea of conflict. Rather one would assume that the dramatic confrontations around them would at the very least increase the intensity of domestic conflict and with it the pressure to confront the remaining problems on their social, economic, and political agendas.

Reflections and suppositions of this nature have prompted the editor and authors of this volume to survey neutral responses to the war and the ensuing revolutions. The chapters examine what effect this vast conflict had on the domestic equilibrium and how the revolutions among the defeated reverberated across neutral lands. Each contribution also provides an introduction to the relevant literature.

After the evidence has been presented, an assessment is made of the extent to which neutrality reduces the effect of war in our time and to what extent neutrals become participants and victims, no matter how unwillingly.

Neutral Europe between
War and Revolution, 1917–23

1

A Civil War of Words:

The Ideological Impact of the First World War on Spain, 1914–18

GERALD H. MEAKER

A French journalist who visited Madrid in May 1917 quickly became aware of the violence of feeling that the war had aroused between pro-German and pro-Allied forces in the peninsula. "More gradually," he said,

> I recognize beneath the gloss of exterior politics the lines of interior politics. Thus the positions which [Spaniards] take in regard to this war . . . are determined by previous moral affinities. Those who fear the people go irresistibly to Germany as their model fortress, while the others persist in admiring in [the Allies] the battering ram of liberty. This is logical enough and it explains the profundity of the gulf which here separates Germanophiles from [Ententophiles]. The fact is that two families of very old passions have been awakened and set in motion by this new conflict. And such is the somber fervor that they breathe that if they had troops behind them, I ask myself if that civil war of which everyone speaks so much might not become one day a reality for Spain.[1]

Jean Breton was not the only observer who sensed the bellicosity of the Spaniards in this period. No foreigner traveling in Spain during the war could fail to recognize that although the Spanish state maintained a meticulous neutrality, the literate and political classes were not neutral at all but were instead divided into the most zealous partisans either of the Central Powers or of the Allies. It is equally clear that these two factions represented much more than merely contrasting opinions as to which side would—or should—win the war and that they reflected, rather, a deep, preexisting spiritual division within the Spanish people which the war did not create but only exacerbated. Between 1914 and 1918 this division found expression in a polemic so bitter and sustained, so filled with rancor and self-righteousness, that it had the moral quality of a civil war. It was in fact a civil war of words—a verbal clash between the two Spains which was a portent of the real civil war that still lay a generation in the future.[2]

This ideological civil war went on, moreover, against the backdrop of quasi-revolutionary disturbances in Spain, culminating in 1917, that revealed the power of the war to threaten the political and social stability of countries relatively remote from the struggle. Spain was severely tested by the forces—both economic and ideological—that the war unleashed and, despite its dogged commitment to "absolute" neutrality, was not able to remain immune to the general crisis that the growing stress of total war produced in belligerents and neutrals alike. In this period many of the symptoms of the revolutionary syndrome made their appearance: a mutinous officer corps, dissident national minorities, a radicalized proletariat, alienated intellectuals, food and raw materials shortages, sporadic bread riots, a nationwide general strike, and, beginning in the spring of 1918, growing unrest among the southern farm workers and poor peasants. There were those who, following Leon Trotsky, began to speak of Spain as "the Russia of the West" and to fear that the pressures of the war might cause the collapse of its shallow-rooted, oligarchical political system—which rested so precariously on a largely peasant social structure—and throw the country into a revolutionary upheaval à la Russe.[3]

This chapter seeks to analyze the ideological—and highly polarizing—impact of the Great War on neutral Spain by focusing on the harsh debates between pro-German and pro-Allied factions that the war ignited. The actual connection between the war and the quasi-revolutionary events of 1917 is also examined in order to distinguish among the war's ideological, political, and economic consequences. Among the collateral questions to be explored are whether the disturbances of 1917 were primarily economic in origin, as so many have asserted; whether Spain in fact experienced a true "revolutionary situation" in this admittedly somewhat turbulent period; and whether, finally, there has not been a certain amount of semantic inflation along with excessive determinism in recent historical accounts which together may have obscured important elements of contingency in the causal pattern.

For Spain the summer of 1914 began like any other. The national tempo, which could always be described as unhurried, slowed still more because of the summer heat and the taking of their annual vacations by the middle and upper classes, who departed en masse for their customary watering places—the elegant beaches and casinos of San Sebastián, Biarritz, St. Jean de Luz, and Luchon, to name a few. Madrid, a furnace in the summer, was partially depopulated. King Alfonso and the court left on June 10 for the summer capital of San Sebastián, where the king's yacht awaited him. The Cortes stayed on for a few more weeks in Madrid, listlessly and inconclusively debating. The government in power was that of Eduardo Dato, the able but unadventurous leader of the Liberal Conservative party who had come to power in November 1913 and who stood, essentially, for the politics of the status quo—for the preservation of the Restoration system unchanged. The feeling among political observers was one of futility and somnolence. A columnist for *El Liberal* wrote that "if vagueness were a goddess we would have to build her a temple here in Madrid where she is mistress and ruler of all." Everything in the capital, he said, seemed somehow blurred and ill-defined. "We are lulled to sleep by our own endless conversation. There is constant murmuring chit-chat in the cafes, in the salons, in the offices, but there are no enthusiasms and there are no idols—no great men—who might rouse us from our lethargy. Everything is discussed and nothing is accomplished. Madrid . . . is the world capital of fatalism. Events break like waves over our heads."[4]

Indeed, the greatest of all events—the European war—bore down on Spain like a tidal wave out of a quiet sea, almost unnoticed by the Spaniards until it suddenly burst upon them. The July crisis, during which European statesmen sought frantically to keep the Austro-Serbian conflict from turning into a general war, was scarcely alluded to in Spanish newspapers until nearly the end of the month. Some notice was taken of the assassination of Franz Ferdinand; but the serious goring of the great bullfighter Joselito on July 5 shook the country far more and was more earnestly debated. The trial of Mme. Caillaux in Paris for a *crime passionel* was of greater interest to most Spaniards than the tribulations of the Habsburg monarchy. Yet almost immediately there were signs that the Sarajevo killing had begun a process of polarization in Spanish society which the war would greatly accelerate. Some republicans and socialists, as well as the Basque nationalists, felt constrained to defend the assassination, while conservative Catholics, sentimentally attached to the Austro-Hungarian Empire, were outraged. Still, the armed conflict that concerned Spaniards most was the inconclusive colonial struggle they were then waging in Morocco, where approximately seventy-six thousand ill-equipped and poorly motivated peasant soldiers (out of a total Spanish army of one hundred and forty thousand) were fighting a desultory war around Melilla that had gone on since 1909 and of which the Spanish people were becoming increasingly weary—a weariness which explained in part the nation's extreme reluctance to become militarily involved in the 1914–18 war.[5]

There was another foreign event attracting the attention of Spaniards in the early summer of 1914, and that—trivial as it may seem—was the erection in Brussels by Belgian leftists of a statue dedicated to the Spanish anarchist pedagogue Francisco Ferrer, who had been shot by the Conservative Maura government as the presumed fomenter of the violent Barcelona uprising of July 1909 known as the Semana Trágica. Even moderate Catholic opinion in Spain was outraged by what it regarded as a provocative intervention in Spain's internal affairs. *El Universo* called the statue "abominable" and the "glorification of a political crime."[6]

Expressions such as these made it clear that up to the very eve of the war, Spain still lived in the shadow of the Ferrer case and of the spiritual division that it symbolized. Like the Dreyfus affair in France, this case had bitterly divided the conservative, traditional, pro-army, and Catholic elements in Spain against the liberal, antimilitarist, anticlerical, republican, and modernizing groups spearheaded by the intellectuals. The Ferrer execution upon the order of a military tribunal was, of course, little more justified than the exiling of Dreyfus to Devils Island, and Ferrer, like Dreyfus, achieved a symbolic significance which went somewhat beyond the merits of his person. In August 1914 this never-extinguished debate about Ferrer was rudely overtaken and absorbed by the even more bitter polemic between Germanophiles and Ententophiles; and the very bad impression that the Ferrer statue made on conservative-Catholic opinion in Spain helped to explain the cold indifference and even the grim pleasure with which so many Spaniards viewed the German invasion of Belgium. Since demonstrations by French leftists had also contributed to the apotheosis of Ferrer, the schadenfreude of the Spaniards extended to France also in its hour of peril. As could be expected, when the German army entered Brussels they ostentatiously pulled down the statue of Ferrer, following orders from the kaiser.[7]

It was only on July 26 that Spanish newspapers began to give the European situation front-page coverage and to convey at last to the country the impression that a crisis of immense proportions was impending. Rumors of war now flooded into Spain. The Barcelona stock exchange fell into panic and had to be closed. Catalonia, industrialized and economically linked to Europe, experienced a severe contraction of credit and was thrown into an economic crisis to which the Madrid government responded slowly and inadequately. The Madrid exchange, more somnolent and isolated from the world, remained open a day or two longer. Trains and autos were soon bringing hordes of Spanish tourists to the frontier at Hendaye as they fled from France in something close to a state of panic. Many were angry at having been unceremoniously ejected from French resort hotels converted by the government into hospitals. Pro-Allied journalists hinted darkly that this was the real origin of much pro-German feeling in Spain.[8]

While it is not the purpose of this chapter to explore the diplomacy of Spanish neutrality, it should be noted that as the war began, there was widespread anxiety in Spain that the territorial and naval agreements that Spanish goverments had entered into with Britain and France at Algeciras (1904) and Cartagena (1907) might contain clauses compelling Spain to enter the war at the side of these two powers. Indeed, some diplomatic scholars were certain this was the case. The first impulse of King Alfonso, whose wife was English and whose main ties were with the English nobility (and who appears to have made some kind of verbal commitment to Edward VII at Cartagena), was that Spain should join Britain and France in the war. There was speculation in the last days of July regarding possible Spanish intervention, and it was thought that Spain might at least permit its territory to be crossed by French troops on their way from Morocco to France.[9]

The truth is, however, that the Dato government never contemplated intervention and opted for strict neutrality from the first moment. Its declaration of neutrality on July 31—reaffirmed less than a week later—was as instinctive as the gesture of a man stepping from the path of a speeding train. It stemmed not only from the ministers' visceral awareness of Spanish political, social, economic, and military weakness but also from their understanding of the Spanish people's nearly unanimous desire to sit this war out. They were convinced, correctly, that there was a massive consensus on behalf of nonintervention—perhaps the only real consensus Spaniards had shared since the days of the Napoleonic invasion. Prime Minister Dato had little doubt that any Spanish attempt to participate in a large-scale modern war would mean the ruin of the army, the monarchy, and the country and would probably lead to civil war. To emphasize its neutrality, Spain remained the only country in Europe that did not mobilize its reservists in this period.[10]

The cabinet's decision on behalf of neutrality was also conditioned by the almost universal expectation in Spain, before the First Battle of the

Marne, that Germany would win the war as quickly and decisively as it had in 1870. This expectation helps to explain the unceremonious removal of the pro-French Spanish diplomat Francisco Villa-Urrutia from his position as ambassador to Paris when, against orders from Madrid, he insisted upon accompanying the Poincaré government in its retreat to Bordeaux while the Spanish government was expecting General von Kluck to enter Paris momentarily and the French to sue for peace. There was some feeling in Madrid that if their ambassador remained in contact with the Germans, the Spaniards would be able to play the role of mediator in bringing the war to a quick end. In any case, the Dato government was absolutely committed to neutrality and went to great lengths—including prior censorship—to ensure that Spaniards behaved with total impartiality toward both sides in the war. Spanish neutrality was thus never a bargaining position but a fervent commitment dictated by the government's unwavering conviction as to what sacred egoism truly required in Spain's case. Indeed, despite the obvious "persistence of the Old Regime" (to use Arno Mayer's term) in Spain, neither the premodern "feudal" seignorial elites nor the representatives of the emerging and modernizing capitalist sectors appear to have been in the least tempted to try to cure Spain's domestic ills with the strong medicine of foreign war. Some in the West, it may be noted, saw Spain's quick adoption of neutrality as an anti-Allied gesture. The truth is that both Dato and his foreign minister, the marquis de Lema (whom the British ambassador described as a confirmed Anglophile), in their hearts favored the Allies. In fact all the belligerents throughout the war acknowledged the sincerity and impeccability of Spanish neutrality and relied upon Spanish diplomats to handle their affairs in enemy countries.[11]

Aside from Spain's poverty and the total incapacity of its army for modern warfare, the most compelling reason behind its neutrality was the almost impenetrable indifference and incomprehension of the great mass of the Spanish people—approximately the illiterate two-thirds of the population—regarding the issues of the war and the ideological pronouncements of both sides. These submerged masses, not unlike the Russian people in 1914, were in the grip of a traditional, premodern sensibility largely untouched by modern nationalism, militarism, imperialism, or liberalism, so that the propaganda of the belligerents had virtually no resonance among them. As a collection of more or less discrete societies existing at different stages of economic development, Spain was literally without a national consciousness. Never having been forged into a true moral unity by the flames of modern national feeling, the Spanish people lacked a sense of spiritual kinship with the rest of Europe. Little that was outside of Spain had real existence for them or could win their comprehension, let alone stir their enthusiasm. Nor was there, with the possible exception of Gibraltar, an irredentist issue that could be used, as in Italy or Romania, to create an interventionist fever. And Gibraltar would not work because it implied intervention on the side of Germany, which was by no means a moral but certainly a strategic impossibility.[12]

There was, then, a strange apolitical detachment, a disengagement of sentiment which rendered the bulk of the Spanish people immune to the political passions that gripped the populations of the more advanced countries. A perceptive Spanish journalist, writing to a French colleague in 1917, said:

> Believe me, political apathy continues to dominate Spain. The immense majority are only interested in the war as in a bull-running. And they are more interested in bull-running than in the war. . . . You have already seen the accounts of the prowess of the *toreros* encroach upon the [newspaper] columns reserved for war correspondents. A week or so ago our Bellesteiros was killed by an unfortunate goring. If only you had been able to admire the magnificence of his funeral cortege passing in Zaragoza! In your country only Victor Hugo was able to inspire a similar deification. For the emotional experience of touching the coffin of the national hero, one is knocked down in the streets. Such a strong passion is overwhelming. It is hypnotic. It hardly leaves any place for really political emotions. Even in raising the famous spectre of the war, the professionals will not succeed in awakening political life in Spain.[13]

Leon Trotsky, who because of his pacifist proclivities was exiled from France to Spain in 1916, also was astonished by the cheerful indifference of the mass of Spaniards to the war and by the lack of military reports in the Cadiz papers. And more than one Frenchman recently arrived in Spain from the war zones of the north was shaken and even angered by the insouciance of the crowds that strolled the Ramblas of Barcelona and the boulevards of Madrid—so brilliantly lighted at night in contrast to the grim, blacked-out cities of Europe beyond the Pyrenees—as though the war was something happening on another planet, and as though they imagined, in their childlike ignorance, that the whole future of humanity did not rest upon its outcome.[14]

But if the masses were indifferent to the war, the elites of Spain were not. Among the literate upper third of the population, the war quickly became a matter of almost obsessive concern. For educated Spaniards the war was not merely a meaningless struggle for power between rival empires, as it was for the masses. Instead, it was almost immediately perceived as an ideological war, a war filled with meaning for Spain and for all mankind, a war with millenial overtones in which each of the warring groups came to symbolize certain transcendent ideas and values. Golo Mann once wrote that the first "betrayal of the intellectuals" in the early twentieth century was that they succumbed to propagandistic visions of the Great War and lent their eloquence to the task of endowing with transcendental purpose a war that was without meaning. This may be too harsh a judgment to level at those who raised their voices against what they perceived as a drive for German hegemony over the liberal democracies, but it is true that between 1914 and 1918 Spanish intellectuals of both the right and the left surrendered their presumed rational objectivity and detachment no less eagerly and intemperately than did the intellectuals in the warring nations. They thereby made Spain an ideological battleground in a way in which the belligerent countries—where dissenting views were largely suppressed—could not be.[15]

Thus a clear contrast between Spain and the belligerent powers of 1914–18 lay in the fact that in Spain there was no *union sacrée;* and it would not be going too far to describe the harsh debate between pro-German and pro-Allied forces as the moral equivalent of war—civil war. On one opinion only did virtually all of the political classes agree and that was that Spain should not militarily intervene in the war; but they disagreed violently as to the kind of neutrality the country should observe— whether it should be an "absolute" neutrality which was, in effect, favorable to the Germans or a benevolent neutrality calculated to favor the Allies morally and materially. In one sense, of course, Spanish neutrality was inherently pro-Entente since the overwhelming bulk of Spanish war production went to the Allies. The Spaniards would generously have produced for both sides, but Allied control of the seas necessarily limited sales to the Central Powers. On the other hand, because the government refused to pursue a neutrality which was more overtly pro-Allied, the Germans throughout the war were able, among other things, to refuel and resupply their U-boats clandestinely off the Spanish coast, and their agents—there were reported to be some eighty thousand Germans in Spain during the war—were able regularly to gather shipping information, which sent many an Allied vessel, and quite a few Spanish ones, to the bottom.[16]

All observers agreed that German propaganda and espionage activity in Spain was extremely well directed and funded and immensely superior to that of the Allies, who were late in getting started with their efforts and who were inhibited by an aristocratic embarrassment because all the wrong people—the leftists—supported the Allies. The German ambassador to Madrid, Prince Ratibor, who suffered severely from asthma, was neither the real head of the German embassy nor the true director of German diplomatic and intelligence activities. This role was played by the subtle and highly intelligent Major von Kalle, who by virtue of his courtierlike qualities developed an exceptionally close rapport with King Alfonso. Von Kalle became an almost indispensable adviser and informer to the king, to such a degree that some considered him virtually an arbiter of Spanish politics. This rapport doubtless helped to explain the evolution of the king away from *aliadofilismo* as the war went on.[17]

It would be difficult to exaggerate the depth of animosity which Spanish Germanophiles and Ententophiles felt for one another. The great debate was so quickly silenced by the ending of the war, and the postwar period was so fraught with new problems and dangers, that Spaniards by and large forgot how much printer's ink had been spilled between 1914 and 1918 and what a revelation of national disunity there had been. There were, of course, some observers even then who had premonitions of a future catastrophe. The fervently pro-Allied Unamuno regularly referred to the great polemic as a "civil war," once calling it a "civil war against the barbarians within." Ossorio y Gallardo described it as "a true civil war of minds." The French observer Paul Louis thought it a "moral civil war." And Pío Baroja compared the hatred between the Germanophiles and Francophiles to the hatred prevailing in ancient times between "moors and Christians, Jews and Catholics, Guelphs and Ghibellines."[18]

Indeed, the famous, if somewhat simplistic, concept of the "two Spains"—one Catholic, conservative, and traditional, the other freethinking, progressive, and liberal—that had confronted each other since the eighteenth century acquired a certain harsh reality in this period. Just as there were perceived to be two Europes at war, so there were two Spains—one pro-German, one pro-Allied—who saw in the war a Clausewitzian continuation of their own domestic struggles by other than peaceful means. It might even be said that the war mobilized not so much real sympathies for the warring countries as the real hatreds that one Spain felt for the other. This is to say that the sympathies of the Spanish educated classes were shaped not by abstract arguments about who had started the war but more directly by the nature of their domestic politics, by whether they belonged, in John Stuart Mill's terminology, to the "party of order" or to the "party of movement"—a political division that was itself in very large measure determined by religious views, by whether one was clerical or anticlerical in outlook.[19] As the philosopher George Santayana wrote in 1915: "The great line of cleavage which in all Latin countries cuts national life in two also creates divergent sympathies in international affairs, and quite justly, since it separates two opposite moral judgments passed on all European history and two contrary philosophies of life. . . . The liberals wish to reorganize Christian society on a pagan basis. The conservatives wish to prevent that reorganization and to restore in modern form the old moral integrity of Christian nations. It is in obedience to these opposed ideals that they take opposite sides in the present war."[20]

In fact, as between Germanophiles and Ententophiles, religious and political motives were intertwined and mutually reinforcing. Thus the Germanophiles—generally Catholic and traditional—supported Germany as a symbol of the monarchism, the authority, the hierarchical social order, the discipline, and the religious devoutness that they wished to see preserved and strengthened in Spain. The pro-Allied minority, on the other hand—instinctively anticlerical—supported the Allies as the defenders of the religious and political freedom and the social, cultural, and economic modernization that they hoped would come to Spain after the war.

What has never been sufficiently emphasized in the limited research done on the war period in Spain is the great numerical preponderance of the Germanophiles. In no neutral country did Germanophilism flourish as it did in Spain. For most Spaniards, pro-Germanism was a wholly natural and instinctive response to the war. France and England had been Spain's hated enemies for centuries and the cause of more humiliating defeats than most cared to remember. Spain's long decline and loss of empire was blamed not, of course, on the Spaniards but on their mean-spirited enemies. Thus the great Carlist orator Juan Vázquez de Mella asked rhetorically: "Who checks our legitimate aspirations in Gibraltar? England. Who prevents the absorption of Portugal in a greater Spain? England. And who, finally, destroyed our relations with the Spanish Americas? England." But France was nearly as disliked as Britain, and few things were so well remembered in Spain as the Napoleonic invasion and Murat's brutal suppression of the Madrid uprising of 1808 (Dos de Mayo), not to mention the desecration of Spanish churches by French soldiers. For conservative Spaniards the French Republic was little more than a synonym for atheism, anticlericalism, and moral corruption. Its campaign against religious institutions and on behalf of secularism was a grievance deeply felt by Spanish Catholics. Germany, though embarrassingly Protestant in its monarchy, was a young state that had had relatively little opportunity to humiliate Spain, although the Carolinas episode in the 1860s had made it clear that Germany–like the other powers—was not lacking in rapacity where the crumbling Spanish Empire was concerned. Most Spaniards, however, were refreshingly free of any substantive knowledge of Germany, and their Germanophilism reflected less a reasoned admiration for that country than a historic and ingrained hatred of France and England. Had France and England been at war with China, the majority of Spaniards would soon have become passionate Sinophiles.[21]

Thus Spanish Germanophilism between 1914 and 1918 represented the triumph of prejudices over *raison d'état*—of ideas over geopolitical and economic imperatives that really dictated support for the Allies. For Spain, after all, was entirely surrounded by Allied powers; it had a common frontier with France and Portugal; its sea-lanes were completely controlled by the Allies; the vast bulk of all its trade was with Britain and France; by far the largest portion of foreign investment in Spain was British, French, or Belgian; Spain was absolutely dependent upon British coal and American wheat to run its mills and feed its people; nearly all of its war production went to the Allied powers; and all of its interests in Morocco and the Mediterranean were dependent upon the goodwill of the French and the British. Yet against all of these imperatives, and despite the almost total lack of real congruence between Spanish and German interests, the bulk of literate Spanish opinion was pro-German and insisted for four and a half years upon a neutrality which was "absolute" and not benevolently oriented toward those Allied powers upon whom Spain was dependent for its very existence.[22]

The bitterness of the clash between the Germanophile majority and the pro-Allied minority was startling in view of the fact that Spain was, after all, a mere spectator on the sidelines of the European civil war. Fights erupted, families were divided, old friendships ruined, and innumerable angry and insulting words exchanged, all this suggesting the conviction on both sides that in this war the most crucial moral and political issues were at stake. For the Spanish masses the European war may have been just another *corrida de toros,* but for the elites it was considered decisive for Spain and for mankind.

During the first months of the war the Germanophiles were almost completely dominant. Spaniards were prone to go with the apparent winner, and as the German armies approached Paris and the French government withdrew to Bordeaux, the Ententophiles were few in number and reduced to virtual silence. It was natural, on the other hand, that the Germanophiles, fearful at first that Spain's Mediterranean agreements might carry the country into the war, would be the first to mobilize ideologically, in order to combat this possibility. At the same time their journals were jubilant over what seemed to be the impending knockout of France and England.[23]

The Germanophile majority in Spain from 1914 to 1918 was made up of the clergy, the court, the aristocracy, the army, the Carlists, and the traditional upper and middle classes. These last two groups, wrote Madariaga, "own the land and crowd the bureaucracies. They form a closely knit system of interests from banking and financial enterprises to local magistracies, from high bureaucratic positions to provincial mayorships. This system, through its nominees, controls practically all the assemblies of the country—parliament, the provincial councils, and municipal councils. It staffs the high judiciary. It is represented in every province by the civil governor, in every town and village by the mayor. It stands for vested interest and established order, it controls general elections [and all the weight of the bureaucratic machine]. This system is, of course, pro-German." These elites doubtless sensed that they were not, in fact, the true representatives of the Spanish nation but only the managers of an artificial political machine which might be shattered any day by some upheaval by the popular forces that seethed below. It was this secret fear, Madariaga thought, that made them incline toward the side of authority, that is, the side of Germany. Thus "official Spain" was pro-German while "real Spain" was pro-Entente.[24]

The vanguard of pro-German sentiment in Spain was the clergy. With relatively few exceptions, the Spanish church hierarchy was authoritarian and reactionary in outlook. Angered by the French Republic's separation of church and state and the expulsion of religious orders in the 1890s, they were prepared to endorse almost any power that would destroy the Republic and chastise the French in their godlessness. Their strong support of Protestant Germany was explained by their belief that the Lutheran Christianity of the German Imperial Household was to be preferred over the militant secularism of the French Republic. They found the religious rhetoric in which the kaiser clothed his pronouncements curiously appealing. Constantly invoking God, the kaiser was forever asking God's blessing on German arms and urging the German people to pray to God for victory. Because of the biblical sonority of his speeches he became, in the eyes of the Spanish clergy, a kind of avenging archangel whose God-ordained mission was to punish the depravity of the French as well as the insolence of the English. German agents in Spain hinted broadly that the kaiser was actually a secret Catholic who was only waiting for the end of the war to reveal himself and to make the pope once again a secular ruler over Rome as well as to return Gibraltar and Tangier to Spain. The invasion of Belgium and France led the ultra-Catholic *Siglo Futuro* to ask piously whether "this war might not be [both] a punishment and an expiation of nations which have separated from God, which have become apostates from their church and who, against the Christian constitution of nations have tried to found their [governments] on the infamous maxims of liberalism?" Three weeks later the same journal described the war as "the justice of God" and observed that "the whip of Divine justice" was punishing "with paternal anger the perversity, the rebelliousness, and the apostate iniquities of [the Allied powers]." "We find ourselves," said the journal, "in days when one seems to hear the trumpet of the final judgment, and [we now know] that God is neither blind nor deaf and that he does not ignore the currents of infernal, Luciferian rebelliousness by destructive modern states."[25]

That something more than religious feeling lay behind Germanophilism was made clear by the failure of Germanophiles to raise any protest against the ravaging of Catholic Belgium, the destruction of Catholic shrines in France, and even the execution-murder of five Spanish workers in Liège. They turned a curiously deaf ear to Belgian pleas for sympathy—partly, one supposes, because Belgian Catholicism had long been liberal and "social." Germanophiles were irritated rather than moved by stories of German atrocities, believing them to be greatly exaggerated and certainly not to be compared with what the French did to Spain during the Napoleonic occupation. They were morosely aware, above all, that France, in addition to its apostasy and atheism, was a democratic republic prone to anarchistic exaltations and hence a threat to the tranquillity of the Spanish monarchy and social order. Germany, on the other hand, appealed to them as a conservative and authoritarian monarchy characterized by a respect for order and social discipline and linked with the great Catholic Austrian monarchy with which Spain shared so many historic ties.[26]

With the exception of King Alfonso and his English wife, the Spanish court was almost wholly pro-German, taking its tone from the Queen Mother, María Cristina, who was an Austrian archduchess with close relatives in the high command of Franz Joseph and an ardent supporter of the Central Powers. The British ambassador, Arthur Hardinge, recorded the following encounter with the Queen Mother shortly after the Italian entry into the war: "She asked me, 'Ne trouvez-vous pas que ces Italiens agissent comme des cochons?' I was a good deal embarrassed, but I replied as politely as I could: 'Madame, il m'est difficile d'appliquer le terme de "cochon" aux Alliés du Gouvernement du Roi mon maître.'" Alfonso's queen, Victoria Eugenia, on the other hand, was passionately pro-Allied throughout the war and had four brothers fighting in the British army. But it was the Queen Mother who dominated the court, and it was the ladies of the court who rapturously applauded the Germanophile orations of Vázquez de Mella. The aristocracy, with few exceptions, followed the lead of the Austro-Germanophile Queen Mother.[27]

Alfonso himself—French Bourbon and Austrian archduke, admirer of the German army as well as of English culture—gradually moved away, as we have said, from his initial pro-Allied position. As the war revealed its ideological implications and the Allied cause became more and more republican in tone—especially after the March revolution in Russia and the statements of President Wilson in the spring of 1917—the king seems increasingly to have reflected upon the fact that it was, after all, the Central Powers who stood for conservative monarchy against the rising world tide of republicanism. Alfonso remained, in any event, persistently inscrutable in public regarding his sentimental attachments in the great conflict and cleverly pursued a delphic and noncommittal policy which was the perfect counterpart of the ministry's policy of "absolute" neutrality.[28]

The officer corps of the Spanish army—recruited mainly from the traditional middle classes—was almost uniformly Germanophile. The victory of Germany over France in 1870 had firmly established in the Spanish military mind a conviction of German invincibility and techno-scientific supremacy. Spanish military academies all taught the German science of war and cultivated as well the gratifying vision of a German society in which, in contrast to Spain, the role of the military was prominent and respected. Equally productive of a Germanophile outlook were occurrences in Morocco (the army's main focus of interest), where Spanish army officers frequently experienced French colonialism—and French hauteur—as the main obstacle to their own colonial aspirations. Finally, there was the general drift to the right of the Spanish officer class in the period after the 1898 disaster. Salvador de Madariaga observed in 1916 that "at the present moment, the ideas prevailing among the Spanish officers would strike Hindenburg and Ludendorff as somewhat militaristic." No small part in this process was played by the emergence of the organized workers with their class-war ideologies and the growth of the regional bourgeoisie, whose autonomist goals were viewed by the officers as a grave threat to the unity of the nation. The Germanophilism of the army during the war years, exalting not only German military prowess but also German order, unity, and discipline, was thus a natural reflection of the officers' basic concerns. It caused them, above all, to be resolutely opposed to armed Spanish intervention in the war (which, in the nature of things, could only be on the side of the Allies), and hence made it rather improbable that any Spanish government would seriously contemplate cobelligerency. *La Correspondencia Militar*—clearly fascinated by the technical aspects of new German weaponry—had no difficulty justifying the German invasion of Belgium as a legitimate manifestation of *raison d'état*. The primary reason for Spanish neutrality, said this officers' journal, was that Spain simply had "no clearly defined ideals regarding the future" and therefore did not "feel" the war and did not believe that it "should sacrifice itself to achieve a doubtful goal of problematical utility." Besides, Morocco was a "shackle" around Spain's leg; having an army in Morocco compelled Spain to be friendly with whoever controlled the sealanes, that is, with the British and French, however disagreeable this might be.[29]

The most vehement Germanophiles in Spain were the Carlists, ultra-traditionalist reactionaries, who wanted Spain to repudiate the liberal monarchy of Cánovas del Castillo and return to a medieval and populist monarchy as well as to an archaic Catholicism which would revive the Inquisition and impose religious uniformity. Their principal spokesman was the spellbinding orator and publicist-politician Juan Vázquez de Mella, whose dislike of the anticlerical French Republic was exceeded only by his hatred of Protestant and imperialist England. During the war he spoke on countless occasions before audiences composed of reactionary aristocrats and emotional women of the upper classes whom he could rouse to frenzied enthusiasm for the German cause. Vázquez de Mella was the great evangelist of the Germanophile movement in Spain, thundering out again and again on the themes of English perfidiousness, French godlessness, the grandeur of Phillip II, the moral greatness of Kaiser Wilhelm, the inspiring discipline of the German state, and, above all, the intolerable possession of Gibraltar by the British. Habitually bellicose, he was almost the only Germanophile who—at least in the early days of the war—urged Spain actually to ally with Germany and intervene militarily in the conflict.[30]

Although it was true that Carlist refugees had been warmly received in both Britain and France in the late nineteenth century and that the leader of the Carlist movement, Don Jaime de Borbón, was personally a Francophile, it was not surprising that with the outbreak of the war, Carlist sympathies went instinctively to the Central Powers. For Carlism was, as Martin Blinkhorn has said, a classic form of counterrevolution, hostile to nearly all the tendencies of the modern age: secularism, toleration, skepticism, urbanism, industrialism, liberalism, individualism, centralization. Carlists were therefore prone to see in France and England the cutting edge of a hated modernity, while Germany, though obviously a leader in science and other fields, seemed a conservative, traditional, almost premodern society. The sense of Germany as a "collectivist" and believing society and of France as a citadel of modernity, disbelief, and anarchic individualism was omnipresent in the pages of the leading Carlist newspapers, *El Correo Español* (Madrid) and *El Correo de Catalunya* (Barcelona). As between France and Britain, most Carlists hated France more—the France of Renan, Gambetta, Combes, and Dreyfus, that is, apostate and skeptical France.[31]

Finally, although it was widely held by those on the left that "all" of the intellectuals were pro-Allied, and even that one could not possibly be both an intellectual and a Germanophile, the list of Germanophile adherents also included some bona fide intellectuals who supported the Central Powers with considerable fervor. With two exceptions, none of these was really of the first rank, and many of them held official posts and were essentially members of the bureaucratic middle class. The experience of the young José Balbontín suggests that in the central region most of the university professors were Germanophile. Among the more notable pro-German savants were F. Rodríguez Marín, the respected Cervantes scholar and director of the National Library; Francisco de Carracido, director of the Cisneros Institute of Madrid; Professor Vicente Gay of the University of Valladolid, who wrote immense Germanic tomes for Spaniards about German thought and institutions and who was said, no doubt quite unfairly, to be a Germanophile because the German Embassy had agreed to buy two thousand copies of his books; Emilio Cotarelo y Morí, secretary of the Royal Academy; Professor Adolfo Bonilla y San Martín, philosopher and legal scholar; José M. Salaverría, journalist; and the novelists Ricardo Léon and Edmundo González Blanco. There were perhaps only two really major intellectual figures in the Germanophile movement—Pío Baroja and Jacinto Benevente—whose Germanophilism was the scandal of the intelligentsia of creative writers and thinkers.[32]

A survey of polemical writings in Spain during 1914–18 leaves the impression that the literature of Germanophilism may have been the more interesting of the two *filias* that competed. For whereas pro-Allied writings were usually variations on universal liberal themes, having a somewhat doctrinaire sameness about them, Germanophilism was a form of Spanish nationalism which celebrated specifically Spanish themes, interests, and traditions and had a bellicose, embittered, and defensive quality which lent it a certain reactionary charm. It was a heady brew of Catholic traditionalism, nationalism, antiliberalism, and xenophobia. By a dialectical process, the Germanophiles, having embraced Germany, inevitably moved still further to the right in the domestic sense and were soon writing eulogies of Phillip II and the duke of Alba and celebrating great old Spanish traditions such as bullfighting. They did not, of course, have a monopoly on this sport, and one finds even the bullfighting aficionados bitterly divided between Joselito, who was the torero of the Germanophiles, and Belmonte, who was pro-Allied. Germanophiles also had a rich fantasy life. The author of *España Gran Potencia* envisioned a Spanish army of sixty thousand men crossing the Pyrenees, easily scattering the army of French provincials who try to block their way, driving across France, and joining forces with the Germans at Poitiers, at which point the combined armies then crush the Allies in short order. For its contribution Spain receives Gibraltar, Tangier, a large Moroccan zone, other African colonies, and Portugal.[33]

It is difficult to generalize about the vast Germanophile literature that the war produced. Its interest lies less in what it has to say about the war than in what it says—often implicitly—about Spain, its political and social divisions, its national anxieties and aspirations. Germanophilism was not a monolithic movement but contained three basic tendencies: first, the ultra-Catholic traditionalist-reactionaries, most of whom (though not Vázquez de Mella) hated apostate France more than imperialist England; second, the moderately Catholic nationalists who, without being either especially religious or reactionary, mainly hated the British for their imperialism and military power; and third, the group of thinkers and publicists who may best be called national-regenerationists, and who hated the British, along with the French, chiefly for their economic power in the peninsula and who actually knew something about Germany and saw it as a model by which Spain might regenerate itself, emulating German science, education, and efficiency.

The first group—which had chiefly religious motives—has already been discussed in the person of Vázquez de Mella and the Carlists. The most representative figure of the second group—mainly nationalist in orientation—was the novelist Edmundo González Blanco, one of the most prolific of Germanophile writers, who published *Alemania y la guerra europea* in 1915. The leitmotiv of this work was the author's almost obsessive hatred of England, of English imperialism and domination, which he blames for Spain's prostrate condition in the world. González

Blanco was not a reactionary and claimed to be somewhat republican and even "socialist," but so consuming was his hatred of England that he gave heart and soul to the cause of Germany. His book was largely an effort to exculpate Germany for any responsibility for the war, and he provided his readers with the standard Germanophile explanation of how it began. Germany, he says, did everything humanly possible to avoid war. The kaiser loved peace. The main culprit was Russia and its mobilization, but, he adds, "let it be understood well: Russia aided by England." The Germans reluctantly reacted to the Russian threat from the east and the French threat from the west. The Germans were encircled by enemies. "Threatened in its natural territory, threatened in its influence and in its honor, there remained to Germany no other alternative than dismemberment or the invasion of continental Europe." If Germany had not invaded Belgium, the French would have. But the theme to which González-Blanco returned again and again was that Britain wanted the war for commercial reasons, in order to destroy Germany as a commercial rival. The true militarism, he said, was not that of Germany with its armies but that of England with its 549 ships which dominated the globe. Germany was the only bulwark of the continent against an English imperialism which for a century had dominated the affairs of Europe—political, economic, and financial. Was it not time for Europe to be freed forever from this domination? González Blanco ended on virtually a national-socialist theme when he suggested that Germany was the only nation capable of giving to the future European confederation "that admirable form of its socialism which lies in the potent union of authority and discipline, of political unity and imperial expansion."[34]

This latter theme is even more pronounced in the third type of Germanophilism, which has been termed national-regenerationist. The proponents of this school were not primarily *littérateurs* like González Blanco, nor were they, certainly, pious reactionaries like the Carlists. Rather they were prophets of economic nationalism (many of them were economists), whose Germanophilism derived mainly from their intense resentment of British and French economic imperialism, which they felt had turned Spain into a semicolonial country, and from their belief that a German victory in the war would break the shackles of foreign economic domination in Spain with one blow and set the country free for a new beginning.

The war had stimulated economic nationalism in all the belligerents, and the idea also gained popularity in Spain after 1914. Among the leading publications devoted to this theme was the *Revista Nacional de Economía,* founded in the spring of 1916 and associated with Emilio Ríu,

Eloy Louis André, and Vicente Gay. These men were the intellectual heirs of such regenerationist thinkers as Macías Picavea, Ganivet, Maura, and Costa and were thus trying to understand not only the sources of Spain's decadence but the means by which it could be overcome. They were impressed by the economic-centralist policies of the warring powers and also by the social "solidification"—the drawing together of classes and productive groups—that they observed in those countries and that became for them an ideal toward which Spain should strive. Their fondness for Germany sprang partly from the fact that the social discipline which Spain so sorely lacked seemed most evident there and was partly due, as mentioned, to the still low level of German investment in Spain in 1914. In contrast to the *aliadófilos,* these men were not primarily humanists and devotees of the libertarian ideals of the Enlightenment and the French Revolution; rather they were social disciplinarians, meritocrats, anticapitalists, and nationalists. The relative sophistication as well as the radicalism of their ideas show not only the diversity of Germanophile thought but also the limitations of the "two Spains" concept. For these men, in contrast to the other Germanophiles, were far from being proclerical or wedded to the existing oligarchical social and political order and might best be described as national socialists and, indeed, revolutionaries in the context of the liberal Restoration polity, which they despised.[35]

One of their most articulate spokesmen was Eloy Luis André, an eloquent and prophetic champion of the nationalizing of Spanish society and the forging of close, paternalistic links between a "new society" in which the talents and energies of the masses would be unleashed and the new "National State" which he envisioned. He hated British and French capitalism for its domination of peninsular economic life, for its close nexus with Spanish oligarchies, and—as he believed—for keeping Spain underdeveloped and in perpetual economic infancy. Thus for him the war was actually a hopeful thing which he termed a "political counterrevolution and an economic emancipation of the European continent." If the "Germanic spirit" triumphed, he said, the continent would undergo a profound transformation. The economic power of Britain would be broken, Spanish sovereignty restored, and Spain would at last be able to operate freely both internally and externally. Once foreign economic domination was ended, André's solution to the problem of production was one of almost total nationalization. No friend of private capitalism, he urged the nationalizing of the land, the subsoil resources, the railroads, credit, and electricity and a program of total state intervention.[36]

The Germanophilism of the novelist Pío Baroja bore a generic resemblance to that of the men of *Revista Nacional de Economía* but had a harsher and almost nihilistic quality. While the majority of Germanophiles (excluding, of course, the "national-regenerationists") were Catholic, proclerical, conservative, and traditional, Baroja was capable—while defending Germany—of writing anticlerical and even antireligious diatribes: "I believe," he said, "that if any country can definitively crush the Catholic Church, it is Germany. Only Germany can banish forever the old Jehova with his gang of hook-nosed prophets and their descendants, the squalid monks and the pedant priests. If there is a country that can do away with the old rhetoric, with the old Spanish traditionalism, dirty and coarse, with the Latin and Semitic scab, it is Germany. If there is a country that can substitute science, order and technology for the myths of religion or democracy, and for the force of Christian charity, it is Germany."[37] The pro-Allied journalist Julio Camba wrote the most devastating retort to this. "Baroja," he said, "is the only Spaniard who has been wrong in this matter of the European War. The militarists, the clerics, the conservatives demonstrate a certain instinct by putting themselves for a principle on the side of Germany. The republicans, the socialists, etc. are not wrong to support the Allied cause as far as possible. Only Baroja . . . among 15 million Germanophiles was [a Germanophile] for liberal and anticlerical motives. The most remote village priest, the last garrison lieutenant in the provinces saw clearly what the European war was about, and Baroja, the illustrious writer, went for four years without understanding it."[38] Needless to say, conventional Germanophiles derived little pleasure from Baroja's brand of Germanophilism and did not extend him a fraternal embrace.

Jacinto Benavente, though immensely popular as a playwright, was not really an intellectual but almost a purely literary man. Like Baroja, he was never able to articulate a coherent rationale for his Germanophilism. He had gravitated toward the Central Powers even before the war, mainly because of his patriotic, emotional reaction to the role of Britain and France in Spain's loss of great-power status. British possession of Gibraltar was endlessly galling to him. Gazing out to sea during a 1913 visit to Algeciras, he saw Gibraltar as an "enormous dreadnought" looming menacingly off the Spanish coast and felt within himself a "remote atavism" that moved him to sadness and indignation. And though he claimed affection for France, in the intense heat of the Germanophile-Ententophile debate, he was inevitably pushed toward a more overtly anti-French position, thereby alienating the same liberal intellectuals who had earlier idolized him and becoming increasingly isolated within the cultural community.[39]

Finally, it should be noted that the most agreed upon of all Germano-phile views, the common denominator of the movement, was an intense commitment to "absolute" neutrality. Germanophiles not only under-stood that such a policy perfectly suited the national mood, they also knew that, for geographical reasons, any departure by Spain from neutrality could only be against Germany—that neutralism was thus really a pro-German policy. They understood, as Madariaga said, that Spain was actually a "sleeping partner" of the Anglo-French Entente and that to awaken it from its dream of perfect neutralism could only work against the Central Powers. By the same token, the bête noire of all pro-Allied publi-cists was this same concept of "neutralism." They hated it for its pro-German implications and they expended gallons of ink trying to explain to the skeptical Spanish people how one could depart from neutrality with-out actually going to war and thereby completing the country's ruin.[40]

The pro-Allied side of the debate was slow in getting under way. Dismayed by the speed of the German advance into Belgium and France, the forces of the left fell silent, leaving the stage to the exultant Ger-manophiles who sensed a quick German victory. Before the Battle of the Marne, only three major voices spoke out on behalf of the Allies. The first of these was the leader of the Liberal party, Count Romanones, one of the very few Restoration oligarchs ever to make public his pro-Allied views. Nor was he in the mainstream of Ententophile thought, since his views were almost entirely based on realpolitik rather than on messianic ideal-ism about the war. On August 19 he stunned official Spain by publishing an article in which he denounced the neutrality policy of the Dato govern-ment and urged support for Britain and France. As a politician but also a man of large business affairs—one of the richest men in Spain—Roma-nones called the attention of the Spanish people to all those geopolitical and economic realities which he thought compelled Spanish cooperation with the Allies. He stressed that nobody loved a neutral, and that if Spain remained aloof it would not matter which side won the war, the country would still lose. The war presented Spain with an unequaled opportunity to identify itself with the Allies and thereby to revive itself as a power, to rehabilitate its army, its navy, its credit, its commerce, and possibly its colonial empire. Neutrality, on the other hand, was the rejection of a great opportunity and would, Romanones believed, sound the death knell for Spain.[41]

The Romanones article—basically an effort to stimulate public debate on the neutrality question—led to the first crisis of Spanish neutrality. Prime Minister Dato, certain that Romanones must have had the support of the king for his article, tendered his resignation in a cabinet meeting a few days later. Its acceptance was prevented by an impassioned speech by Minister of Education Bergamín, who spoke of the danger to Spain's social stability that a change in foreign policy could produce and emphasized the folly of intervening in a war in which France was already defeated. The result was that Dato's resignation was not accepted and the neutrality policy was further strengthened, becoming a fixed dogma of Spanish life that was never seriously debated in Parliament.[42]

Another major voice raised against neutralism was that of the anticlerical and extreme Francophile republican leader Alejandro Lerroux, head of the Barcelona-based Radical Republican party. Lerroux almost recklessly challenged the neutralist consensus, urging that Spain intervene militarily on the side of France because that country defended the cause of democracy and republicanism. He even drove by auto to Paris to lend support to the French cause. This so enraged the majority of Spaniards that when he returned to Spain there were angry demonstrations against him and his car was stoned. All of this prompted La Veu of Catalonia to say that the attacks proved that if Spain departed from neutrality, the result could only be civil war.[43]

Finally, in the period before the Battle of the Marne, the moderate and highly respected republican leader Melquíades Alvarez—head of the Reformist party to which so many distinguished intellectuals adhered—also spoke out against neutralism. In contrast to Romanones, he stressed the ideological significance of the war and the moral grandeur of the Allies, who were fighting for justice, liberty, and democracy against the aggressive and domineering spirit of the German Empire. A little later, in 1915, he would go so far as to assert that if Spain had an army sufficiently powerful to tip the balance to one side or the other, it should intervene on the side of the Allies, thus serving the cause of humanity by hastening the end of the war. In any event, he said, it would be better for Spain to be aligned with England and France defeated than with Germany victorious.[44]

The great upsurge of pro-Allied feeling in Spain came only after the Battle of the Marne and is interesting because of its "dialectical" quality, that is, the degree to which it was obviously a reaction to the Germanophile propaganda offensive and thus part of a polarizing process in which each side in the polemic stimulated the other side to ever-greater excesses of partisanship. Many Spaniards who might have been moderate or indifferent regarding the war were almost compelled to become fanatically pro-Allied or pro-German because their most despised social enemies had come out for the other side. The Socialist party was the most striking case in point. For years before 1914 this small, doctrinaire, and leftist party had faithfully adhered to the Marxist orthodoxy of the Second International which, ascribing all war to the effects of capitalism and imperialism, proclaimed that the workers had no fatherland and insisted that pacifism or resistance were the only proper responses of the workers in the face of military conflict. The party had severely criticized Spain's Moroccan involvement precisely on this basis. Indeed, the initial, instinctive response of the Socialists to the outbreak of war in 1914 was highly orthodox: on August 2 the National Committee issued a statement against the war impartially condemning all the belligerents and urging strict Spanish neutrality.[45]

But as German armies invaded Belgium and plunged into France—to the cheers of the conservative-clerical-military elements in Spain—the doctrinaire pacifist internationalism of the Socialists dissolved with amazing rapidity. The majority discovered that beneath the veneer of their left-wing socialism, they were actually liberal and democratic in spirit and simply could not view the collapse of the Western democracies with cold detachment but felt compelled to support them in their struggle against autocratic Germany and Austria. The majority Socialists, along with their leader Pablo Iglesias, thus became perhaps the most ardent Ententophiles in Spain, utterly opposed, for example, to all talk of a "peace without victors" for the reason that this idea had been rejected by the Allied leaders and would leave the German threat hanging over Europe. By 1917 Iglesias would assert in Parliament that if Spain were not so militarily weak, he would favor Spanish intervention on the side of the Allies. This jettisoning of the long-cherished dogmas of the Second International was conditioned above all by the tremendous upsurge of Germanophilism in Spain in the early days of the war. The often fanatical opposition to the Allies by priests, officers, bureaucrats, upper classes, and Carlists made it morally and, indeed, psychologically impossible for most Spanish Socialists to continue making doctrinaire denunciations of both groups of belligerents as "imperialists."[46]

The same kind of polarization affected other "leftist" groups and individuals. In general, the pro-Allied forces in Spain were made up of the overwhelming majority of the intellectuals (many of them German-educated), republicans of various parties, the Socialists, the Reformists of Melquíades Alvarez, the Radical Republicans of Lerroux, and the regional bourgeoisie—especially in Catalonia. Broadly speaking, Castile, in the center of the peninsula, tended to be heavily Germanophile, while the more modernized peripheral areas, Catalonia, Valencia, Vizcaya, and Asturias, counted a higher percentage of *aliadófilos*. In Spain as a whole, the pro-Entente elements were a minority voice. They were the Westernizers of a backward society who wanted to see their country put an end to its ancien régime and experience a peaceful version of the Revolution of 1789. They nourished an almost mystical faith that the victory of France and Britain would mean a victory for the democratic and progressive forces everywhere.

The heart of the pro-Allied movement in Spain during the Great War was the intellectuals. Their position was a morally difficult one, in that by supporting France and Britain, they were repudiating their country's history and traditions and embracing its historic enemies. In effect, they were choosing Europe over Spain; more precisely, they were opting for a future Europeanized Spain that would be modern, democratic, secular, and free in place of the tradition-ridden, priestly, oligarchical Spain that was. The emerging intellectual class at the time the war broke out has been called the "Generation of 1914" and was represented by a number of young intellectuals born in the 1880s and coming mostly from the ranks of the liberal bourgeoisie. They were the first generation of the "European" kind, and in contrast to their precursors they generally had more formal education and a more methodically rigorous training. They were more apt to be men of science, *universitarios,* and specialists rather than wide-ranging polymaths or brilliant autodidacts. A large number had studied abroad, chiefly in Germany and secondarily in France and England. These "new men," serious, specialized, and politically liberal, were prone to be even more impatient with *cosas de España,* with the corruption, disorganization, and general *Schlamperei* of the Restoration monarchy than their intellectual predecessors. What they wanted was something like a revolution of competency.[47]

They began in this period to acquire professorships and to put the anticlerical stamp of the Institute for Free Education on the Spanish university system. Their ideal type was no longer the literary figure in his ivory tower but rather the "engaged," technically trained intellectual-in-politics, prepared to take a "scientific" approach to the problem of backwardness. Signs of a collective consciousness among the intelligentsia began to emerge around 1909 as a result of the Ferrer case, and by 1917, according to Carlos Mainer, Spanish intellectuals at last constituted a "coherent group."[48]

It was men such as these—already conscious of their generational distance from those who dominated Spanish political and cultural institutions—whom Ortega y Gasset (born 1883) wished to summon into political life as a self-conscious renovating elite. He sought to achieve this through his writings after 1909, through the founding of the League for

Political Education in 1913, by his electrifying oration on "The Old and the New Politics" delivered in the Teatro de la Comedia in April 1914, and by establishing the intellectual review *España* in January 1915. Ortega's 1914 oration may be seen as a kind of generational manifesto, a declaration of hostilities by the younger intelligentsia against the Restoration system, which was proclaimed to be "dying," and against the older generation which persisted in supporting its moribund and presumably doomed institutions. His language was vibrant with contempt for that "official Spain" which he pejoratively compared to the "vital Spain" that the younger generation represented. There are, said Ortega, "two Spains that live together and which are perfect strangers, an official Spain which is obstinate in prolonging the ways of a past age, and another, aspiring Spain, perhaps not very strong, but vital, sincere, honorable, which, hindered by the other, has not succeeded in entering fully into history."[49]

One thus sees in Ortega's oration not merely the self-love and the self-pity so often found in a new generation seeking its place in the sun but also, on a deeper level, the patriotic bitterness of a generation born to "reflective consciousness," as he said, in the midst of the "terrible year" of 1898, which, since then, had not witnessed a single day of "glory or fulfillment, not even a day of sufficiency." His speech contained undertones suggesting a deeply wounded national pride and real anger against those oligarchs who, having led Spain into defeat and humiliation a decade and a half earlier, were still seeking to keep the country in a moribund and impotent condition.[50]

It was this element of embittered nationalism that gave Ortega's speech the extremist, root-and-branch tone that ran through it and made it less a call for reform than for revolution. Thus Ortega believed that the Restoration system was beyond repair or redemption, and that this was true not merely of the system's political parties and institutions but also of the "social structures" which coexisted with them. The abuses did not constitute mere localized illnesses; rather, "a whole Spain, with its governors and its governed, its ways and its abuses," was "in the process of dying" and could not be saved. But as a liberal intellectual and elitist, Ortega did not believe that a revolutionary mass movement would have to be organized (he seemed to favor a party of intellectuals) or that violence would have to be the midwife of the kind of political and social change he had in mind. Rather he was sure that the Restoration system was so moribund, so lacking in rational justification, that it would soon collapse of its own ineptitude and irrelevancy—especially if the intellectuals continued to carry out their critical labors.[51]

The irony here is that Ortega, speaking only three months before the outbreak of the European war, was articulating some of the basic convictions that would be expressed during the war by the pro-Allied intellectuals from whom he would so quickly distance himself: the idea (in vogue after the spring of 1917) that the Canovite system was beyond redemption, that it had to be liquidated rather than reformed, and that this could be done by means of a "revolution" which would somehow transform the country without real violence or bloodshed. Interestingly enough, Ortega himself—one of the more German-influenced Spanish intellectuals—would soon retreat into virtual silence on the issues of the war, remaining noncommittally suspended during most of the war between the inflamed partisans of the Allies and the Central Powers, both of whose polemics he seemed to regard with distaste. In sharp contrast to Ortega's uncommitted posture, the vast majority of Spanish intellectuals would almost welcome the war as the deus ex machina which, by the sheer moral force of an Allied victory, would one day crack open the great glacier of Spanish political life and "revolutionize" the country's political and social system.

The founding of the League for Political Education, along with Ortega's oration in the Teatro de la Comedia, makes it clear that the war came at a time when Spanish intellectual life was already gaining momentum and entering upon an expanded and stimulating new phase. As Tuñon de Lara says, "The review *España*, the work of Ortega, the meetings of the Atheneum, . . . the frequent visits of Spanish intellectuals to the Allied countries, and the presence in the universities of rigorously schooled, foreign-trained professors" all contributed to a "distinctive intellectual climate" in which the ideological impact of the war was very great. This is to say that the liberal, regenerationist, and Europeanizing outlook of Spanish intellectuals proved highly receptive to the increasingly democratic, republican, and somewhat messianic ideology that emanated from Allied propaganda. At the same time, their embattled, marginal situation—in which they were confronted with a moribund Spain of which they often despaired—made it almost inevitable that Spanish intellectuals would infuse the Allied cause with salvationist expectations. Thus prewar regenerationism and wartime *aliadofilismo* existed in a symbiotic, mutually stimulating relationship, nourished by the dual vision of a new Spain and a new Europe—both democratized—that would rise out of the chaos and destruction of the war. That is why Jean Breton referred to some extremely pro-Entente Spanish intellectuals as "war mystics" who, obsessed with a dream of progress through liberty, were resolved that Spain should maintain contact with the embattled Allied democracies "in order to partake of something in their spirit. . . And if a bloodbath should be needed to purchase that regeneration, well, it would not be bought too dear!"[52]

Still, it should not be forgotten that Spanish intellectuals continued to feel, on the whole, weak, inadequate, and oppressed in the face of the power of the government, the church, the army, and the ruling classes—a feeling hardly assuaged by the brusque dismissal of Spain's preeminent intellectual, Miguel de Unamuno, from the rectorship of the University of Salamanca in September 1914 or by the utter indifference of the oligarchs to all the eloquent protests made on his behalf by the intelligentsia. Above all, Spanish intellectuals—not unlike their Russian counterparts—felt depressingly cut off from the masses, half worshiping and half fearing them, knowing in their hearts that "the people" did not share their liberalism and were quite indifferent, for example, to the Allied cause. They yearned to lead and to utilize the masses on behalf of the renovation of Spain, but they also feared their reactionary-revolutionary ferocity and nihilism.[53]

It was precisely in this period that the word "intellectual" began to be used with some frequency in Spain, though it still had novel and even pejorative overtones and there were disputes between Germanophiles and Ententophiles as to what, exactly, an intellectual was. The first "manifesto" of Spanish (as opposed to Catalan) intellectuals on the war was published in the journal *España* on July 5, 1915, and was called simply "Words of Some Spaniards." Highly emotional yet moderate in tone—even though written by the intensely anti-German Ramón Pérez de Ayala—it perfectly reflected the combination of deep feeling and almost complete impotence with which the Spanish intelligentsia had perforce to observe the war, from behind the barrier of Spain's manifest weakness and its passive policy of "absolute" neutrality. For Spanish intellectuals not to speak out at this time, said the manifesto somewhat plaintively, would make it appear that Spain was "dissevered" from the course of history and "indifferent to the stirrings of the future." Not to speak out would make Spain appear to be "a nation without resonance in the bowels of the world." Hence the intellectuals wanted the world to know that whatever the policy of the Spanish government might be, the Spanish intelligentsia "participated fully, with heart and mind," in the war and declared their solidarity with the Allied powers "insofar as they represent the ideals of justice."[54]

Although this rather restrainedly pro-Allied manifesto was the last one that Ortega y Gasset would sign, the surprising thing was the alacrity with which even those intellectuals who had been educated in Germany turned against the Central Powers and in favor of the Allies—especially of France, for which there was a remarkable upswelling of sentiment. This was further evidence that, despite all their overlays of Germanic philosophy—from Krausism to Neo-Kantianism—the deepest ties of Spanish intellectuals continued to be with France and with the ideals of the Anglo-French Enlightenment and the Revolution of 1789, a fact that put them tragically at odds, of course, with the great reactionary and traditionalist mass of their own countrymen. So strong was the bond with France that in most cases it would be more accurate to speak of *francofilia* than *aliadofilia* among Spanish intellectuals, which is to say that even in the context of the powerful "dialectic" which the war produced in Spain, it was still extremely difficult for liberal Spaniards openly to speak well of Britain or to condone its possession of Gibraltar.[55]

Among the few enthusiastic Anglophiles of this era was one of the leading pro-Allied apologists, Don Benito Pérez Galdós (born 1843), the immensely popular novelist and creator of the great *Episodios Nacionales*. Full of praise for England, he said that the word "perfidious" should cease to be used to describe that country, giving way to such terms as "astute" and "ingenious." Though a devout republican of long standing, he especially admired the tolerance, flexibility, and skill with which the British Empire was governed. For France he expressed "my profound sympathy, my ardent love for [a country] which fights heroically for liberty, justice, and civilization against the Teutonic giant who seeks to crush the world under the weight of his enormous body." Above all, Galdós was anti-German, heaping his scorn on a country which had "massacred and ravaged without pity, oblivious to the desperate lamentations of the weak and the innocent." The case of Galdós illustrates the fact that all the generations of Spanish intellectuals—not just that of 1914—were virtually united in their support of the Allies and their animosity toward the Central Powers.[56]

Next to Galdós, the most illustrious *aliadófilo* in Spain was the philosopher-novelist-poet Miguel de Unamuno (born 1864), the leading figure of the Generation of 1898. The war years revealed an angry and aroused Unamuno whose outpouring of articles displayed the same passionate "engagement" found in many lesser intellectual figures. His dismissal as rector at Salamanca was not caused by his stand on the war, having to do, rather, with his too-independent posture over the years vis-à-vis the ruling parties of the *turno*, but it was a severe blow to him and unquestionably contributed to the vehemence of the pro-Allied and anti-Germanophile writings in which he ridiculed the official policy of "absolute" neutrality. As he himself said, the outbreak of the European war coincided with the start of his own personal "war" against official Spain.

Because of his early socialist proclivities and his conviction, stated in 1912, that the "main object" of the European powers was the acquisition by force or fraud of captive markets and protectorates in which to invest their surplus capital, Unamuno might have been expected to take a neutralist stance on the war, seeing it only as a struggle between imperialist states. Far from doing this, he unhesitatingly took the side of the Allies, proclaiming them to be the defenders of the highest ideals of Western civilization and protesting against those who viewed the war only as an economic struggle. In part this *aliadofilismo* reflected, as Christopher Cobb has noted, a distaste which Unamuno had long felt for German culture, which he saw as flawed by an absence of ethical content and an absorption with scientific pedantry, blind technicism, and brute power. Along with his growing religious preoccupations, expressed in his best-known work, *The Tragic Sense of Life* (1913), there were in Unamuno's thought strong populist and libertarian currents that caused him to react against the element of "hierarchical authoritarianism" in German life and to see in the Allies the champions of popular democracy and the free human personality.

The heart of Unamuno's critique of Spain's neutrality was that it was not really a policy but a nonpolicy, a kind of paralysis of the will, a sickness of the soul. It was not that he urged Spanish participation in the fighting, which he knew was materially impossible. Rather he wished to see an act of national will that would align Spain spiritually with the democratic Allies and thereby give proof that the country was not moribund but alive and on the path to its regeneration. Contemptuously he described official Spain as "terrified and paralyzed" in the face of the European war, which he called "this great world revolution" and which he believed would either bring the Spanish revolution in its train or leave Spain isolated, "like flotsam on the edge of the great river of history."

Like most Spanish intellectuals, Unamuno lived in a continual state of impotent rage during the war by virtue of the humiliations that Spain had to endure at German hands and that the official, neutralist parties of the *turno* accepted passively because the Spanish people, afflicted with a kind of spiritual sleeping sickness, could not be roused to nationalistic and patriotic anger. It was in the context of such feelings of impotence and outraged nationalism that Unamuno began to speak frequently, if not wisely, about the virtues of "civil war," by which he meant not armed conflict but a kind of intellectual struggle, rather like that between Dreyfusards and anti-Dreyfusards in France, which he appeared to believe would be the moral equivalent of civil war, that is, a beneficent polarization that would rouse Spain from its deep lethargy and, somehow, encourage the growth of a national consciousness.[57]

Also extremely active as publicists of the Allied cause were intellectuals such as Azorín (José Martínez Ruiz), who wrote for the otherwise Germanophile *ABC,* the Valencian novelist Vicente Blasco Ibáñez, Ramón Pérez de Ayala, Dionisio Pérez, Alvaro Alcalá Galiano, Ramón del Valle-Inclán, Luis Araquistaín, Ramiro de Maeztu, Emilia Pardo Bazán, Salvador de Madariaga, Felipe Trigo, Hermógenes Cenamor, and Rafael Altamira, to name only some of the more prominent figures.

In January 1917 a coalition of Castilian and Catalan intellectuals formed the Anti-Germanophile League (with Galdós as president) and published a manifesto whose harsh and somber tone contrasted with the effusions of the March 1915 manifesto. The league's purpose was to combat what it regarded as the false and pro-German neutrality of the Germanophiles and to do this not in the name of military intervention but of a beneficent, pro-Allied neutrality which would strengthen the vital ties of sympathy and historical community with the Allied powers. In contrast to the 1915 manifesto, this one (to which Ortega y Gasset did not adhere) left little doubt that a "moral civil war" was indeed being fought out in Spain and that the *aliadófilos,* just like the *germanófilos,* were anxious to delegitimize their social enemies as a kind of anti-Spain. Thus the Germanophiles were referred to as "those interior enemies of Spain" and, again, as "the worst enemies of Spain [who] lodge themselves in its very territory and call themselves Spanish citizens."[58]

Of all the signers of the 1917 manifesto, the one who perhaps best expressed the increasingly angry and revolutionary mood of the Spanish intelligentsia as the war raged on—and as the Germanophile majority kept Spain impotently in a posture of "absolute" neutrality—was the brilliant secretary of the Madrid Atheneum, Manuel Azaña (born 1880). Except for the fact that he was basically a "literary intellectual," Azaña was the archetype of the irate, embittered, pro-Allied, anticlerical Spanish intellectual of this era—the Generation of 1914.

Azaña's major pronouncement on the war was an incandescent speech, "The Motives of the Germanophiles," which he delivered to a spellbound audience in the Atheneum on May 25, 1917, at a moment when the resentment of the intellectuals against the king's neutralism was at its highest pitch. What fueled Azaña's anti-Germanophilism was obviously a kind of fury over Spain's perduring backwardness, impotence, and general unimportance in the world. For almost three centuries, he said, all the major events in world history had caught Spain unprepared. It was that recurring "national stupefaction" which was the source of all of Spain's troubles. It was, he said, "that carelessness, that abandon, that enthroned stupidity," which was the ultimate cause of "the resignation and meekness of the sad, ignorant and hungry Spanish people"—a people who, unfortunately, had never had "the spirit to rise up, rifle in hand, against their clergy and in an exemplary chastisement, impose upon them a lesson appropriate to their delinquency."

It was clear from this violent rhetoric that nothing would have pleased the bellicose Azaña more than for Spain to have had the military capacity to enable the nation to enter the war on the side of the Allies. But he well knew that behind the lack of material preparation, and ultimately responsible for it, was the profound moral incapacity from which the Spanish people suffered—a people who had somehow lost the noble capacity to be "impassioned about what is just . . . from the moral point of view." Thus the neutralist Spanish people, "because of their *incultura*, [and] by virtue of not having a sufficiently vigorous desire to find justice, has been unable to penetrate to the heart of the moral problem posed by the war, [upon which depends] the future of our civilization."[59]

One sees personified in Azaña and expressed with the relentless eloquence of a Robespierre or a St. Just the anger and despair of the Spanish intelligentsia during the years 1914–18 in the face of their status as a small, enlightened minority confronting the wickedness and incapacity of neutralist oligarchs and Germanophiles on the one hand and, on the other, the moral obtuseness of the masses who did not comprehend that Spain's whole future as a modern and democratic country was inextricably bound up with the fate of the Allied powers. Which is to say again that pro-Allied intellectuals tended to see the war as a "revolution" and to believe that its vital revolutionizing potential could only be realized if the Allies were victorious and if Spain was somehow identified with their cause. By spring 1917, this burning conviction, along with the failure of the king to come out definitively on the side of the Allies, had put the Castilian intelligentsia in what can only be described as a revolutionary mood, ready to overthrow the monarchy and set up a republic if the opportunity arose—a state of mind, it should be noted, which the intellectuals and left-wing activists of Catalonia shared completely.

No study of the ideological impact of the war on Spain would be complete without reference to the upsurge of pro-Allied sentiment in Catalonia between 1914 and 1918 and to the stimulus that the war gave to Catalan nationalism. As a frontier province with historic and ethnic links with Roussillon across the Pyrenean border—where French Catalans were going off to fight and die in defense of their country—Catalonia felt the shock of the war more acutely than any other Spanish region and responded more enthusiastically. Linguistic, cultural, and blood ties with French Catalans, along with a shared admiration for the culture and liberal political heritage of France, conspired to make Catalonia as instinctively pro-Entente as Castile was pro-German. Hence one of the earliest and warmest shows of public support for the French cause in Spain was the "Manifesto of the Catalan Intellectuals," published in their journals in March 1915, which noted that the very founding of Catalan nationality had owed to the efforts of the French Carolingian monarchs and that because part of Catalonia lay within France, "we Catalans of Spain, in the face of the new barbarian invasion, feel in our own bodies the wound through which flows the blood of [France], our historic and ethnographic *patrie*."[60]

Thus Catalonia—economically more advanced and spiritually closer to Europe—came to have a large pro-Allied majority and only a small Germanophile minority, reversing the pattern of most of the rest of the country and causing Jaime Brossa to speak of the "moral secession" of Catalonia from Spain. The pro-Allied journalist Claudi Amettla wrote some years later that the public passions accompanying this division of opinion had never before been so extreme and made it appear as though Catalonia itself were going to war. To Amettla it seemed that the outbreak of the European struggle had merely furnished a pretext for the resumption of an "interior war"—a war between two irreconcilable conceptions of Spain—which had only been in abeyance during the forty-year "slumber" of the Restoration monarchy. The European war reawakened "an old, old quarrel" which, he decided, was also the underlying cause of the civil war of 1936–39.[61]

While pro-Allied enthusiasm was very widespread in Catalonia, the spearhead of *aliadofilismo* was the region's intelligentsia. There can be no question as to the fervor and near-unanimity of Catalan intellectuals for the Allied cause or the sense of solidarity that they felt with republican France. Most of them would best be described as left-wing Catalan nationalists. Highly individualistic, they were grouped in a number of splinter parties that were committed, in varying degrees, to Catalan autonomy, democratic politics, republican government, and socialist economics. A few were out-and-out separatists and pan-Catalanists who, in 1916, formed an organization in Barcelona called "Nostra Parla" which demanded the formation of a "patria integral" out of Catalonia, Valencia, the Balearic Islands, and French Roussillon. Left-wing Catalanist intellectuals attended the Third Conference of the Union des Nationalités in Lausanne in 1916 where they bitterly attacked the Madrid government and sought to validate Catalan claims to nationhood and sovereignty.[62]

In pro-Allied journals such as *Iberia, El Diluvio, La Publicidad,* and *El Poble Català,* Catalan intellectuals poured their scorn on all those who preached the official Madrid policy of "neutralism," which in their eyes was merely dissimulated Germanophilism. As messianic about the war as their Castilian counterparts, they saw no middle ground between the pro-Allied and the pro-German positions. Like Castilian intellectuals, they had absorbed a highly ideological and idealized vision of the war, viewing it, as one of them recalled, as "a war for the liberty of men and of peoples, a war against war, the last war—nothing less!" Above all, they saw the war as a struggle for the liberation of subject nationalities. They believed that it was a struggle on behalf of democracy and self-determination against a Germanic imperialism which—almost inevitably—became identified in their minds with the "imperialism" that a centralizing Castile had long exerted over Catalonia and the other regions of Spain. One Catalanist accused the "bureaucratic caste" in Madrid of regarding the non-Castilian regions "as simple colonies destined to be exploited by the central power and to the profit only of the latter." Another said that "if we Catalans could be certain that the incorporation of Catalonia in France would . . . give us the autonomy which the Spanish government persists in refusing us, France would be able to obtain sovereignty over Catalonia with only a hundredth of the effort which she had made to reconquer Alsace-Lorraine."[63]

But there was one distinguished Catalan intellectual who rejected this pervasive *aliadofilismo* and remained stubbornly committed to a true neutralism and a broader vision of Europe. This was Eugenio d'Ors, who went against the overwhelming pro-Allied consensus of the intellectuals and articulated a position very close to that of the exiled French antiwar activist Romain Rolland—and probably not very distant from that of Ortega y Gasset, had the latter been more willing to make his views public. Angered by d'Ors's heresy, his fellow writers attributed his stance to nothing more than a perverse vanity, and d'Ors, rather like Benavente in Madrid, steadily lost influence as the war went on. Yet in the midst of the passionate "engagement" of Spanish and and European intellectuals, there was something noble and moving, even though quixotic, about the manifesto that d'Ors and a few others published on November 27, 1914. For here they took a lonely stand on behalf of "the moral unity of Europe" and sought to propound, amid the "suffocating conditions" produced by the war, the idea that the struggle was not primarily an ideological war between nations but rather a civil war within the "European Common-wealth." None of the belligerents, d'Ors felt, should be permitted to aim at the complete destruction of its opponents; nor could the "criminal hypoth-esis" be accepted that any one of the warring states might be excluded from the wider community. In this way, d'Ors sought to rally all men of goodwill on behalf of "a higher humanity and of the great traditions and rich possibilities of a unified Europe." D'Ors's hopes proved, however, to be in vain, and most of the signers of his manifestos soon drifted away. Cata-lonia became more polarized and, above all, more emphatically pro-Allied.[64]

In curious contrast to the great majority of the Catalan people, the conservative, bourgeois leaders of the Lliga Regionalista—the region's main political party—also did not succumb to the wave of Francophile enthusiasm inundating Catalonia. Francisco Cambó, the party's brilliant spokesman for national affairs, published a cold-blooded article in *La Veu* in which, without criticizing France, he refused to condemn Germany. The Belgians, he said, had been fools to resist the German advance, and if Spain was similarly attacked, the country would be wiser not to offer resistance. Sarcastically he said that a country should only go to war to attain a great national ideal and that the trouble with Spain was precisely that it had no national ideal that united all Spaniards but merely some "pseudo ideals of factions capable only of supporting civil war."[65]

Some of the Lliga's pronouncements seemed tinged with Germano-philism. Early in 1916 Enrique Prat de la Riba, the leading ideologue of Catalan nationalism, issued a manifesto titled "Por Cataluña y la grande España," asserting that if Spain did not soon achieve spiritual unity and renovation by means of regional autonomy, the country would become, in the postwar period, no more than "a large Andorra, a mere enclave in the immensity of the [victorious] Anglo-French *imperium* . . . [in which Spain would be] without influence, without personality, without force or significance whatsoever." The clear message to Madrid was that the only possible way to turn the insignificant Spain of today into a renascent "Great Spain" was for the country's rulers to come to terms with "those formidable accumulations of spiritual forces which are the nationalities," giving them autonomy and granting official status to their languages. Only thus could Spain and Portugal be saved from the grave danger of being absorbed—politically, culturally, and economically—by the emerging Anglo-French state that was preparing to assert its "hege-mony" over the world.[66]

Despite the anti-Allied tone of this and other Lliga pronouncements, the party's leaders were not in fact Germanophiles but were, rather, among the few authentic neutralists in Spain in this period—not, like d'Ors, from a nostalgic affection for Europe but rather from an egoistic passion for Catalonia. As *haut bourgeois* industrialists, they were largely immune to sentimentality regarding either the Allies or the Central Powers. Less messianic and more realistic than the intellectuals, they regarded all the belligerents a little coolly, calculating only what each side might signify for the future of Catalan autonomy. But even they were not immune to the redemptive mythology of the war, convincing themselves that its transcendent purpose—their own warnings about Anglo-French "hegemony" notwithstanding—was the freeing of all nationalities everywhere. Yet as the dominant political party in Catalonia, the Lliga largely eschewed rhetoric about the war's higher meanings and began to agitate aggressively on behalf of a whole series of Catalanist demands. While Europe burned, they focused relentlessly on the problem of Catalonia, urging in the Cortes and elsewhere constitutional changes designed to give the region almost complete autonomy in all spheres of life. Spanish public opinion was shocked by the magnitude of the Catalan demands, and the response of the government was to keep the Cortes adjourned as much as possible.

Because the clash between the Catalanist drive to autonomy and the obduracy of the centralized Restoration regime was an important causal antecedent of Spain's "revolutionary summer" of 1917, it should be emphasized that the motives of the men of the Lliga, capitalists though they were, were not merely or even primarily economic. Certainly in thinking about Spain's troubles in 1917, the economic impact of the war cannot be ignored. After the initial shocks and dislocations, Catalonia benefited greatly as a result of the prosperity—always pejoratively described by the press as a "river of gold"—that flowed from war production for the Allies and from its newfound near monopoly over Spain's domestic market. This prosperity undoubtedly stimulated the confidence of the Catalan bourgeoisie and made its members more determined than ever to win regional autonomy in order better to control their own economic destiny. The famous clash over tax policy in 1916 between the Liberal interior minister, Santiago Alba, who spoke for Madrid and for the agrarian interests, and Cambó, the champion of Catalan industrialism, dramatized the economic issues at stake. Nevertheless, one should not carry too far the image of Cambó as a purely pragmatic *homo economicus*. The impression popularized by Rovira y Virgili of the Catalan leader as a cold, cerebral, anti-ideological realist who shunned all idealisms and "erected realism into a principle" should not be permitted to obscure the profound ideological, that is, nationalist, impact of the war on Cambó and the other leaders of the Lliga nor, above all, to hide the fact that despite their calculating bourgeois mentality, these men were firmly in the grip of at least one intense and overriding idealism, this being Catalonia.[67]

At bottom the men of the Lliga were nationalists—Catalan nationalists—and it was their nationalism, greatly stimulated by the war, that primarily lay behind their "revolutionism" in the summer of 1917, not economics—a fact borne out by a reading of their parliamentary speeches and manifestos of this period, which bear the unmistakable stamp of authentic passion and idealism. The war did not, of course, create Catalan nationalism—a product of the last decades of the nineteenth century—but it did galvanize it, adding the vital ingredient of optimism, which sprang from the war-induced feeling that "great changes" were taking place in the world and that anything was possible.

Indeed, the war moved the whole program of the Lliga from mere regionalism to out-and-out nationalism. In 1914, said Prat de la Riba, Catalans were still living in the "old Europe," considered "immutable, definitive," in which it would have been foolish to think in terms of radical change. But now, after three years of war, a new "constituent Europe" had emerged in which the great powers actually paid homage to the liberty of small nations, in order that a "federalized" Europe should emerge. Catalans, he said, must therefore not feel bound by the limitations of the 1914 agreement that created the Mancomunidad, the first step toward Catalan self-government. Instead, they must comprehend "the exigencies of the new universal ambience," demand more powers, and endeavor to create a true Catalan state, albeit one within an Iberian framework. At the same time, the Madrid leaders must also move with the times toward self-determination for all the Iberian peoples or perish. Thus Prat de la Riba clearly revealed the ideological impact of the war on the men of the Lliga, articulating a vision of the postwar world as a "federation" of self-determining nationalities—a vision which at once validated and lent moral force to the efforts of the Lliga to win autonomy against the intransigence of the Madrid oligarchs.[68]

For thousands of pro-Allied Catalans fighting for France on the western front, the agitation of the Lliga must have seemed remote from the great struggle against the Central Powers. From the first moment of the war, thousands of young Catalans volunteered to serve in the French army. The large Catalan community in Paris was completely caught up in a wave of patriotic feeling which swept over France in the early days of August

1914, and many of its members went at once to offer their services to their "second *patria*" in what they assumed would be a short and glorious war. In the following months other thousands made their way through the passes of the Pyrenees to Perpignan where they were warmly greeted by the local population and sent on to Paris for enlistment. No careful count was kept by the French, but it appears that during the war as many as twelve thousand to fifteen thousand Catalans served in the French forces, fighting in all the major battles of the western front as well as in the Gallipoli and Macedonian campaigns. Catalan casualties in the war cannot have been less than three thousand and were probably a great deal more.[69]

Catalans thus constituted by far the largest body of volunteers from any of the Spanish regions. So great was their preponderance that it was widely assumed that any Spaniard fighting for France was a "Catalan," and the Castilian, Andalusian, and Basque volunteers despaired because they were certain that history would attribute their exploits to the Catalans. The journalist Enrique Gómez Carrillo labored to correct misconceptions by interviewing non-Catalan volunteers at the front and recording their experiences in a book that glorified the patriotic idealism, heroism, and high morale of all the Spanish volunteers. He largely ignored the darker aspects of their service in a war that went on far longer and proved far more brutal than anything they could have imagined in August 1914 while singing the *Marseillaise* and raising their cheers in the Place de la Bastille.[70]

Although their demonstrations in Paris had a deliberately *españolista* quality (their banner said "Les espagnols de Paris avec la France") the Catalan volunteers wanted to be constituted as a Catalan Legion. But the French government was aware of the repercussions such a step would have on relations with Madrid, and so, while welcoming Catalan manpower and manipulating Catalan sensibilities, they were careful not to encourage Catalan nationalism or separatism. Thus the Catalans were mostly taken into the Foreign Legion where they constituted the majority of the First and Second March Regiments and part of the Third and fought with great gallantry in such battles as the Yser, the Marne, Champagne, Artois, Verdun, and Lorraine.[71]

The motives that led so many Catalans to volunteer were, of course, mixed. But no one can doubt the mood of generous idealism and the sense of ideological affinity with France that prevailed. Whereas the non-Catalan Spanish volunteers were more likely to be simple apolitical workers and even peasants—swarthy, silent, and curiously unemotional, according to Gómez Carrillo—the Catalan contingents had a larger nucleus of intellectuals, writers, and artists. Thus most of the Catalans were on the left, being republicans, socialists, anticlericals, and libertarians who fought for the secular France of the great Revolution, which they identified with the liberty of oppressed peoples. Representative of this type was the young Catalan writer Pedro Ferres Costa, who came to France filled with revolutionary ardor and who cherished dreams of future societies without kings, ministers, soldiers, judges, or priests. He died bravely in battle on May 9, 1915, near La Targette in Artois, a day on which more than a thousand other Spaniards—Catalans and Castilians—also fell.[72]

But more than a few of the Catalan volunteers were good Catholics— some were even Carlists—who fought and sometimes died for a different France, a France of faith and tradition. Most of the volunteers, certainly, were Catalan nationalists who, quite apart from their inbred love of France, were guided by the feeling that the more closely Catalonia was associated with the Allied struggle against German imperialism, the better chance the region would have, when peace came, of freeing itself from subjection to Castile. Late in 1914 a Barcelona journalist observed that those Catalans who, "moved by a great impulse of the heart, have offered to France their blood and their lives, have rendered to the cause of Catalonia an immense service, [one which was] more effective, more fruitful than that of all the propagandists and politicians put together." If the present war, he said, "has, among other consequences, that of giving an international value to the nationalist movement of Catalonia, this will owe . . . to those Catalans, at once obscure and glorious, who fight at the side of the French army." The French, on the other hand, careful not to defer too much to Catalanist desires, declined to permit the Catalan flag to be displayed at the battalion or regimental level. Still, most of the Catalan companies seem to have carried their flag (white with four horizontal red stripes) when going into battle.[73]

Even though Spaniards from all regions of Spain served in the French army, nearly all the material aid and moral support for those volunteers came from Catalonia. Only in Catalonia did public opinion rally strongly behind the Spanish volunteers in the form of public contributions, banquets, and benefits of various kinds, while volunteers from other regions of Spain were largely forgotten by their compatriots. This aid was administered by an organization which arose in Barcelona early in the war, known as the Committee of Fraternization with the Catalan Volunteers. It helped not only Catalans but other Spaniards as well and was especially concerned with the wounded, the disabled, and the families of volunteers. Inspired by the Catalan example, pro-Allied figures in Madrid only much later formed a similar organization, the Foundation for the Support of Spanish Volunteers, a result of the efforts of José Subirá aided by such notables as Manuel Azaña (as secretary of the Atheneum), José María González (secretary of the Madrid Chamber of Commerce), Rafael Altamira, and the duke of Alba, who became president of the new organization.[74]

As Vicens Vives noted, the Great War exerted two fundamental types of influence on Spain, one economic and the other ideological. This chapter has dealt chiefly with the latter, seeking to analyze the response of various opinion sectors to the ideas and values that the warring powers seemed to represent. Inevitably, the focus has been more on the intellectuals—always the most sensitive receptors of ideas—and on the "civil war of words" that raged between pro-German and pro-Allied factions. Curiously enough, the most revolutionary "class" in Spain during the spring and summer of 1917 was not the officer corps, the Catalan bourgeoisie, or the workers—all of whom launched antiregime efforts—but precisely the pro-Entente intellectuals and political leftists who were the least influenced by economic factors and the most affected by ideological considerations. The immediate origin of this revolutionary state of mind went back to mid-1916 when, for various reasons, the intelligentsia began to lose their faith that King Alfonso was, at heart, pro-Entente and would sooner or later find a way to link Spain, at least in principle, with the democratic Allies. From that time, their alienation from the monarchy grew rapidly and a republican spirit took root among them. They became convinced that Spain was falling into a dangerous isolation from the western democracies. More and more they perceived the war as a "revolution—democratic and modernizing—with which it was imperative that Spain be identified if it was to profit from the coming Allied victory and be lifted out of the slough of oligarchy, *caciquismo,* and clericalism in which it had stagnated so long. The war would be the salvation of Spain, but only if it leagued itself with the proper side.[75]

It took the tumultuous winter and spring of 1917 to complete the revolutionizing of the intelligentsia. Basic to the process was the German declaration of unrestricted submarine warfare on January 31, a policy which soon led to the sinking of three or four Spanish ships per week and of some sixty-eight ships by March 1918. The failure of the government to take a sterner line with the Germans greatly antagonized the political leftists, and the culmination of their anger came on April 9, 1917, as a result of the torpedoing without warning of the steamer *San Fulgencio,* which was carrying a load of coal from Newcastle to Spain. When the

Liberal prime minister, Count Romanones, sought to send a harsh note—virtually an ultimatum—to the Wilhelmstrasse as a prelude to breaking diplomatic relations, he was forestalled by the leaders of the Cortes (Villanueva and García Prieto) and, most crucially, by the king, who could not bring himself to approve the tough language employed. This led to Romanones's resignation ten days later and his replacement by the strict neutralist García Prieto, also of the Liberal party. In this way the king, who had hitherto preserved a certain inscrutability, had his hand forced, and resentment against him on the part of the intelligentsia grew daily as they began to wonder if he was not in fact a Germanophile. Romanones did not help the king's situation by making on April 19 an angry anti-German statement which concluded by saying, "The time has come when every man of conscience must give his vote and take part in the European conflict. In tendering my resignation to the King, I voted for France."[76]

The sinking of the San Fulgencio, along with Romanones's effort to, in effect, break diplomatic relations with Germany, led to some of the most heated journalistic exchanges of the war between Germanophiles and Ententophiles, with the Carlists striking the harshest notes. The oddity of the situation was that the Spanish right—xenophobic, nationalist, militarist—whose sense of honor was so outraged by the British occupation of Gibraltar, took the ever-more-frequent sinkings of Spanish ships by German submarines with remarkable equanimity and even defended the German right to conduct such warfare, while the left—traditionally pacifist, antimilitarist, and opposed to all jingoism—was filled with patriotic outrage and something resembling a war spirit.

A month earlier, on March 8, the Russian Revolution had broken out, inevitably giving a further stimulus to the intellectuals' revolutionary mood. While the March revolution had relatively little impact on Spanish workers and peasants, who were told by the anarchosyndicalist press that it was only a "bourgeois" political movement designed to keep Russia in an imperialist war, the intelligentsia were thrilled by it precisely because they saw it—somewhat myopically—as a purely political movement in favor of Russia's continued participation in the war to end all wars. The promise of the Russian Provisional Government to hold elections for a constituent assembly proved to them, moreover, that Russia was now a democracy, and so the last nagging doubt about the ideological, that is, democratic, meaning of the war was removed. Thus in Spain during the spring of 1917, the war, viewed in highly ideological terms, took causal precedence over the March revolution, which was seen as a purely political event that merely reinforced the war's democratic meaning. The entry of the United States into the war on April 6, soon followed by a number of Latin American countries, enhanced still more the democratic and republican connotation of the war and heightened the fear of Spanish intellectuals that their country was being left in impotent isolation, losing to the United States the moral leadership over the Latin American countries to which it laid claim.[77]

The intellectuals' messianic feelings about the war and their resentment against the king reached a climax in a huge meeting of all the leftist parties held in the Plaza de Toros in Madrid on May 27, 1917. None of the somewhat inflamed speakers doubted that the war had a transcendent meaning and that it was essentially a more violent version of the same ideological struggle they were waging at home against the forces of oligarchy, *caciquismo*, and clericalism. "The war," said Roberto Castrovido, "is a revolution, and here in Spain we must make [a revolution] of our own." Menéndez Pallares added that what was occurring was "a civil war in Spain in which all the leftists must rise up against . . . reaction." But the main message of this tumultuous gathering of the intelligentsia was a thinly veiled ultimatum to the king that he must either move Spain away from absolute neutralism and toward an association with the Allies or face the loss of his throne and the creation of a republic. Because of all the evils of Spanish life, said Unamuno to the assembled multitude, it will be necessary "to shake the people, arousing them, making them feel the terrors of the war." And if, he said, the monarchy did not wish to make this needed revolution, then "we of the left will have to make it ourselves by refusing to be separatists from . . . humanity," by refusing, in other words, to see Spain continue to be neutral in this ideological war which was also a democratic revolution.[78]

This was the high-water mark of the war's ideological influence in Spain. Inspired by intense pro-Allied enthusiasm, determined to have Spain at least diplomatically aligned with the democratic western powers, and angered by the government's refusal to break with its neutralist foreign policy despite the depredations of German submarines, the intellectuals were in a thoroughly revolutionary mood. On the basis of the threatening language used in the Plaza de Toros (where the socialist Andrés Ovejero had said, portentously, to the excited crowd of leftists, "It is now or never!"), it would have been reasonable to expect them to try to launch a republican revolt without much delay, utilizing such social forces as were available, chiefly the organized workers of the Unión General del Trabajo (UGT) and the Confederación Nacional del Trabajo (CNT), who were already planning a general strike. The real anger and even recklessness of the left-wing intellectuals is revealed in a speech by Melquíades Alvarez at about this same time: responding to charges by Germanophiles that any departure from neutrality would disrupt the country, he said, "Then let this civil war come, and blessed be it if it can dissipate the errors and sweep away the phantoms."[79]

To everyone's surprise, the first revolt of the summer of 1917 came not from the political left but from essentially apolitical—and probably Germanophile—junior army officers protesting against parliamentary efforts to reform the army along meritocratic lines and against an order by the cabinet dissolving the extralegal juntas they had formed. In early June they responded to the arrest of their leaders in Barcelona with an ultimatum to the Madrid government to free the imprisoned officers immediately or face a possible coup d'état. Alarmed by the stridency of the pro-Allied and pro-republican movement that had just culminated in the meeting in the Plaza de Toros, the king felt unable to deal firmly with the officers' mutiny since he feared that he might soon be in urgent need of the army to save his throne. In this way the insubordinate officers were able to face down both king and cabinet and win a bloodless victory. The much-needed army reform efforts were ended and the *juntas militares* were sanctioned. The officers now held the balance of power in the state, and a substantial blow had been dealt to the principle, never very firmly established in Spain, of civil supremacy. Obscuring their narrow "professional" objectives under a gloss of regenerationist rhetoric, the officers had taken a major step toward the ultimate dissolution of the Restoration monarchy. Ironically, their insubordination now became the catalyst of two other antiregime movements during the summer that were far more genuinely concerned with the problem of national renewal: the "revolt" of the Catalan bourgeoisie on July 19 and the general strike launched by the socialist-led workers on August 13. A great deal has been written about all three of these movements—military, Catalanist, and labor—and space does not permit their recapitulation here in any detail. Instead, this chapter will conclude analytically with some observations on the peculiar nature of the tripartite "Spanish Revolution" of 1917 and its relationship to both the ideological and the economic influences stemming from the war.[80]

What needs to be emphasized in this context is the inadequacy of an excessively economic interpretation of events in Spain during the summer of 1917. It is difficult to escape the impression that latter-day historians have exaggerated both the adverse economic impact of the war on Spain by mid-1917 and the role of economic forces generally in producing the state-threatening movements of that year. Thus the tenor of Antonio Lacomba's excellent and useful study of 1917 is by and large economic-determinist: he believes that wartime inflationary trends, superimposed on demographic changes, such as the migration of peasants to the cities, were essentially catastrophic in their impact and inevitably produced, by a kind of spontaneous combustion, the events of the summer of 1917. He has no doubt that the causal chain ran from the economic to the social to the political. Nor does he doubt that the events of 1917 constituted a "great revolutionary upheaval," one which was marked, indeed, by social "convulsions."[81]

Such language verges on hyperbole, and a comparison with authentic revolutionary situations of the modern period would suggest a more restrained terminology. Dispassionately analyzed, the Spanish events of 1917 seem to have fallen short of constituting a true "revolutionary situation" comparable to such classic occasions as 1789, 1792, 1848, and 1871 in France, or to 1905 and 1917 in Russia, or even to 1918 in Central Europe. At most, 1917 produced in Spain a crisis of authority—a crisis, one may say, of the state and not of the people. It should further be emphasized that the causes of the events in Spain were at least as much political and ideological as they were economic and that as a consequence a strong current of contingency—as opposed to what might be called economic fatality—ran through them. Rather than being the almost inevitable result of economic, demographic, and social forces produced by the war, the three major events of 1917 prove upon examination to have been initiated rather deliberately at the top and in no case to have been ignited spontaneously by revolutionary masses from below. Nor is it difficult to imagine circumstances in which these events, so far from being the result of inexorable socioeconomic pressures, might not have occurred at all. Thus the general proposition which must brood over this discussion is that the economic impact of the war in the period from August 1914 to August 1917, while certainly substantial, had not in fact been sufficiently devastating to create a climate of mass spontaneity and widespread anti-regime anger. Let us briefly consider, then, both the contingency and the lack of revolutionary "depth" in the three major movements of the summer of 1917.[82]

Strictly speaking, the "collective insubordination" of the officers in early June owed neither to the economic nor to the ideological impact of the war but arose from an essentially defensive response by Spanish public opinion (translated into political-legislative initiatives in the Cortes) to the alarming growth in the size and technical efficiency of the European armies that were locked in combat on the western front and to the fact that the nation's security was at risk so long as the Spanish army remained unreformed and ineffectual. Thus the immediate origin of the military mutiny of 1917 lay in efforts that began under the Dato government, starting late in 1914, to push through Parliament a measure designed to modernize and professionalize the officer corps. The bill brought forward by the Conservative war minister, Echegüe, late in 1915 was moderate and, although initiating some reforms, was careful not to touch upon the highly sensitive issue of seniority. Had Dato stayed in power, this measure, if passed, would not likely have angered the officers to the point of mutiny. The crucial contingency was the unexpected fall of Dato in connection with essentially procedural questions raised in the Cortes early in December 1915. The cause of his fall was related not primarily to the war or to the economic situation or even to the pending military reform bill but, at bottom, to intraparty rivalries and rancors (endemic in both dynastic parties after about 1900), which went back, in this case, to the king's decision to pass over Antonio Maura (still under the shadow of the Ferrer case) for the premiership late in 1913 in favor of another Conservative leader, Dato.[83]

The collapse of the Dato government, which may be termed a decisive political accident, brought to power a Liberal ministry under Count Romanones which proceeded to do several things that aroused the anger of the army's somewhat bureaucratically inclined officer corps. First, Romanones (who had spoken harshly of the army and criticized the Conservative reform proposal as too moderate in the 1915 debates) lent his support to a more radical reform bill which did impinge upon the strict seniority principle so cherished by the officers. Second, the Liberals appointed "political" generals to the king's military household who, in an orgy of favoritism, proceeded to undermine a system of promotions and awards which, however bureaucratic in nature, at least had been accepted by most officers as fair. Third, the Liberals managed to humiliate a number of officers by means of competency tests and the like.[84]

The result was a rapid alienation of the junior officers, who began to organize juntas to defend their collective interests as early as the summer of 1916 when the rate of inflation was only about 6.4 percent and cannot have been a major motivating factor. The contingency, then, lay in the fact that if the unpredictable vicissitudes of factionalism had not brought down the Dato cabinet at the end of 1915, it might well have remained in office much longer—possibly throughout the war (Dato being considered the most faithful guardian of the neutrality so strongly favored by the great majority of Spaniards). In this case there would have been either no military reform or a very mild one and, in all probability, no juntas and no officers' revolt. From this basic contingency, if we are correct in so labeling it, may be deduced the contingency of the other two movements of the summer of 1917, neither of which, it seems almost certain, would have materialized—at least in 1917—if the *juntas militares* had not temporarily deprived the Spanish state of its praetorian shield and made it appear more vulnerable than it actually was. As for its revolutionary quality, the officers' revolt amounted to little more than a refusal to disband their illegal juntas and their successful defiance of the government on this point. No masses were mobilized, the rank and file of peasant soldiers were not involved, no shots were fired, no palaces or parliaments were stormed, and no one was hurt. The officers themselves conceded that they had no desire to "upset the social order" and that their movement was in fact "a revolution without revolutionaries."[85]

With regard to the Catalanist movement of July—essentially the summoning by the Lliga of an illegal constituent assembly—it is important to recognize the complexity of motives that prevailed and not simply to assume the supremacy of economic considerations. Indeed, the basic "matrix" within which other motives—economic, political, cultural— operated was a growing sense of Catalan nationality which was greatly stimulated by the war and especially by the ideological vision of the war as essentially a struggle against "hegemony" and on behalf of the liberation of oppressed nationalities. This, as we now know from the labors of the German historian Fritz Fischer, was not necessarily a mythic conception of the great conflict, and it had an energizing effect on the leaders of the Lliga as well as on the rank and file of the Catalan people. The element of contingency in the July movement lay in the fact that Cambó was no revolutionary and that the mass of the Catalan people, though aroused by the democratic and nationalist "message" of the war and supportive of the Lliga's challenge to Madrid, were not yet in a revolutionary mood. Nor would Cambó have wished them to be, since the last thing he wanted was to ignite a popular revolution whose end point no one could foresee. That Cambó suddenly turned "revolutionary" and summoned his illegal assembly—a demarche that astonished the "real" revolutionaries of the left-wing, pro-Entente intelligentsia—was solely because of the "revolt" of the officers and his quick, shrewd, opportunistic perception that the Spanish state had entered upon a period of vulnerability which he could utilize to the advantage of Catalonia. Had the officers not mutinied, it is certain that the notoriously cautious, conservative Cambó would not have taken the step he did.[86]

As it was, Cambó's revolt consisted of little more than an illegal gathering of left-wing and Catalanist deputies (about 10 percent of the membership of the Cortes), which met for a few hours in Barcelona, passed a few resolutions (their main demand was for a constituent Cortes to federally restructure the Spanish state) and then meekly dispersed when the civil governor politely asked them to. Nor could there be found any large, disorderly, revolutionary-minded crowds in the streets of Barcelona to back up the illegal gathering with violence or the threat thereof. The whole movement subsided without a shot being fired and almost without an angry word being spoken. The goal was perhaps revolutionary—at least in a constitutional sense—but the mood and the modus operandi were not.[87]

As for the general strike movement launched by the workers on August 13, it must be conceded that in its earliest origins it owed more to the economic than to the ideological impact of the war, and to that extent was "determined" rather than "contingent." Specifically, the strike originated as a response by the leaders of the socialist UGT and the anarchosyndicalist CNT to the mounting burdens placed on the workers by rising prices and other dislocations caused by the war. Thus the original purpose of the strike was not political but economic: it appears to have been a genuine effort to coerce the Romanones government into various ameliorative actions. Announced in March 1917, the strike was supposed to take place within "three months' time"; but the socialist leaders of the movement proved to be so methodical in their planning, so lacking in revolutionary impetuosity, that preparations proceeded very slowly, and there were predictions within the UGT that the strike would not actually be called until October or November.[88]

The sense of urgency became much greater after the officers' mutiny in early June, and on June 5 the impending strike movement was for the first time given a highly political objective. On that date a republican-socialist committee (made up of Pablo Iglesias, Melquíades Alvarez, and Alejandro Lerroux) proclaimed that the purpose of the strike was to put an end to the monarchy, convene a constituent assembly, and create a democratic republic. Since the three members of the committee were among the most extreme Ententophiles in Spain, it is difficult not to see here the ideological influence of the war and of the "Wilsonian" climate of the spring of 1917. Nor can it be doubted that one of the first actions of the republic, if established, would have been to terminate Spain's "absolute" neutrality in favor of a pro-Allied neutrality or perhaps even of limited cobelligerency, though all of the actual strike leaders of the UGT-CNT seem scrupulously to have avoided suggesting either possibility in order not to give the impression that the strike's real purpose was to drag Spain into the war.[89]

Though having its origin in real economic grievances, the general strike also had a strong element of contingency about it. First, the mood of the Spanish workers, despite hardships caused by inflation (still rising at a relatively modest rate in the first half of 1917), could not yet be described as revolutionary. And this left the socialist leaders relatively free to continue their plodding preparations and to make their own choice as to the timing of the strike. It also appears that the actual calling of the strike might have been delayed almost indefinitely had it not been for a clever provocation by the Dato government (too complicated to summarize here), which not unnaturally preferred to confront the workers before rather than after they were fully prepared. As a result of this provocation—and only as a result of it—the strike was reluctantly proclaimed by the UGT on August 13. The state of mind of the socialist leaders was not at all one of revolutionary optimism. Rather, they went into the strike in a mood of gloomy fatalism, knowing they were not ready but hoping for a miracle (such as support by the army) and stoically prepared for the worst. Had they known for a certainty that the recently mutinous officers would not only not aid the strike but would move against it aggressively, it is highly probable that they would not have ordered the action to begin at all.[90]

Nor can a great deal be said for the revolutionary quality of the August strike, which came close to being a debacle in which nearly all the things that could go wrong did go wrong. The strike committee was betrayed and arrested almost immediately. Coordination with the strikers in other regions broke down. Weapons were deliberately withheld from the strikers by the socialist leadership since it was imagined that the monarchy could be overthrown merely by "folded arms." The organized workers loyally and doggedly obeyed the order to strike, greeted the soldiers as "comrades"—as they had been told to do—and were shot down by army units that not only did not aid the strike but moved against it brutally in order, it would seem, to expiate the officers' own recent insubordination. The strike failed completely in Madrid and was suppressed without great difficulty in Barcelona. Only in Vizcaya and in Asturias did the tough, disciplined miners of the socialist UGT pose a challenge to the government; and even there the strike was extinguished by August 18. It is especially important to note the basically peaceful intent of the strike and that it was only the organized workers—of whom there were not more than about one hundred thousand in all Spain—who went into the streets, and not the general population. Any portrayal of this strike as an "irrepressible" upheaval of the "masses" must be less than convincing. The relatively large number of lives that were lost—about eighty—owed less to the force of the revolutionary thrust from below, which was very moderate, than to the severity of the repression from above, carried out by a government which had lost neither its nerve nor its willingness to use whatever force was necessary to preserve the Spanish monarchy.[91]

There was, then, a lack of revolutionary "depth" in all three of the movements of 1917. And while it is true that the political system of the Restoration monarchy was significantly altered—being moved away from semiconstitutionalism toward praetorianism and ultimately military dictatorship—the disarticulated events of the summer of 1917 can only be termed a quasi-revolution. A true revolutionary situation, as Lenin once observed, requires not only an "objective" set of conditions (such as the mounting tension between a narrow, oligarchical regime and a slowly modernizing society in which new social classes are demanding participation) but also a "subjective" state of mind among the masses. What was missing in Spain was precisely the subjective element of mass arousal, anger, and spontaneous antiregime activism. The economic impact of the war, though painful for the Spanish people, simply had not yet reached a critical state; and there is a question, in any case, whether sheer economic distress is as important in the genesis of revolutionary situations as, let us say, defeat in war.[92]

The government's task in the summer of 1917 was made easier, then, by the lack of widespread revolutionary feeling among the Spanish masses, both urban and rural. Interior Minister Burgos y Mazo spoke of "the general aversion of the immense majority of the country" to the disturbances of 1917 which, among other factors, "helped the regime quickly to dominate the revolt [of the workers], reduce its proportions, impede its development and . . . suffocate it." Even the manifesto of the UGT-CNT strike committee acknowledged that "during the feverish days which witnessed all these events [the rising of the military juntas and the assembly of parliamentarians] the Spanish proletariat has given proof of serenity and reflection which perhaps have been interpreted by the oligarchies . . . as manifestations of a lack of energy and of incomprehension of the gravity of the present circumstances." More recently the social historian Manuel Tuñón de Lara has confirmed this point when he said that the summer of 1917 marked "the first appearance of the masses on the primary level of events," though "not in an anarchic manner but guided by groups which aspired to the exercise of power."[93]

That the Spanish masses were not in an anarchic mood was due to several factors, such as continuing large shipments of wheat and coal from the Allies. But it owed mostly to the fact that Spain did not participate militarily in the war and hence did not suffer from the economic overstrain and loss of life that combat would have entailed. Had Spain, like Portugal, attempted to send one hundred thousand worker and peasant conscripts to fight in Flanders, then, and probably only then, would the basic indifference of the great mass of the Spanish people to the war have been dissipated and the process of politicization as a prelude to revolution have begun. As Francis Carsten has shown, military defeat was the sine qua non of revolution in Europe during and after the war. It was above all military defeat that discredited governments, caused disaffection among armies, and, most crucially, generated revolutionary turbulence and spontaneous violence among both urban and rural populations who joined forces with mutinous soldiers to bring down unpopular regimes.[94]

One sees again, therefore, the innate wisdom of the Dato government's instinctive embrace of neutrality in August 1914. Also apparent is the positive aspect of that enduring, apolitical obliviousness of the Spanish people to the war which so irritated the idealistic pro-Allied intellectuals. In that basic stupefaction in the face of the Great War lay security for the regime. If the masses had become as aroused by the war as the intellectuals, then the country might have found itself in a revolutionary situation. The irony here is that Spain was saved from the slaughter of the Great War by its very backwardness. If it had had a more modern social structure—a larger middle class, more Westernized, less traditionalist masses, a larger and more influential intellectual stratum—and a greater sense of moral kinship with Europe—it, like Italy or Portugal, might well have been drawn militarily into the war, with consequences difficult to calculate but almost certainly fraught with great peril.

Thus the heavy casualties that a Spanish Caporetto or Passchendaele would have entailed would certainly have aroused the peasantry (who made up about 85 percent of the army at this time) as the purely economic tribulations associated with neutrality had failed to do. Indeed, an excessively economic interpretation of this period is further confounded by the fact that during the years 1914 to 1917, inflation in the countryside was somewhat higher than in the cities, and yet the southern peasantry remained wholly quiescent during the summer of 1917. Most crucially, the peasant soldiers who sprang from this rural mass remained unpoliticized and loyal to the state, as was proved by their willingness—like Russian peasant soldiers in 1905—to fire on their urban brothers when ordered to do so. When, moreover, the peasants in the south did begin to rise in rebellious protest in the latter part of 1918, they did so (as I have shown in another work) more for ideological reasons having to do with the mystique of the October revolution in Russia than for economic reasons deriving from the war.[95]

The "civil war of words" went on unabated to the end of the war. Space forbids any effort to chronicle it down to the Armistice of 1918, at which time the Germanophiles, demoralized by Germany's sudden defeat, lapsed into sullen and embittered silence. Nor can the vast disillusionment that the *aliadófilos* would suffer when they learned of the harsh realpolitik of the Versailles Treaty—which made a mockery of all their wartime idealism—be dealt with here. During the final months of the war, in response to the continued sinking of Spanish ships, the Madrid government took a harder line with Germany, shifting at the very end to an essentially pro-Allied neutrality. That a complete rupture of relations was avoided was a tribute to the skill of German diplomacy.[96]

The Spanish monarchy reached its lowest point immediately after the Armistice. This was due less to the increasingly grave economic situation than to the sharp ideological upsurge of republican and pro-Allied sentiment that swept over Spain in the wake of Germany's defeat. The collapse of the Central Powers was a severe moral defeat not only for the Germanophiles but also for the Alfonsine monarchy whose undeviating support for "absolute" neutrality had caused many to view it as pro-German. Implicitly discredited by the victory of the democratic-republican and national self-determinist ideology associated with the Allied cause, the monarchy's fall was widely anticipated. In the aftermath of the Armistice, crowds of exultant young Catalans surged through the streets of Barcelona cheering President Wilson and singing *La Marseillaise, Els Segadors,* and even *Tipperary.* The sense of an impending "new era" was very strong. The extreme discomfiture of the monarchy and of the Germanophile ruling classes was clear to everyone, and for many the scent of revolution was in the air.[97]

But the revolution was still many years away. Whatever revolutionary élan had been generated in Spanish workers and people during the war had been largely dissipated as a result of the crushing of the abortive revolutionary general strike of August 1917. Now, nearly a year and a half later, Largo Caballero and the other leaders of the UGT—apparently badly shaken by that experience—made it clear that they were inflexibly opposed to any further revolutionary "adventures." While pro-Allied socialist intellectuals like Julián Besteiro and republican political leaders like Alejandro Lerroux and Marcelino Domingo were telling excited crowds in Madrid and Barcelona that the monarchy's days were numbered and that it was "now or never," the plebeian labor leaders of the

UGT—to whose masses would fall the task of actually making the revolution—were saying, in effect, "never more." And so the days and weeks of
the hopeful post-Armistice period went by and no revolutionary effort
was launched; the moment was not seized. The wave of republicanism
triggered by the Allied victory reached its climax and then subsided. Thus
did the poorly timed and premature revolt of August 1917 serve to
undermine and preempt the more promising would-be revolt of late 1918
or early 1919 when the Spanish monarchy was considerably more vulnerable than it had been sixteen or seventeen months earlier. By April 1919
the monarchy had recovered its balance. The last opportunity of the
intelligentsia to turn *aliadofilismo* into revolution had passed, and a new
era of class conflict and social struggle (1919–23), in which not the Great
War but the Russian Revolution would be the most evocative symbol, was
dawning. The "civil war of words," whose denouement was the disillusionment of both sides, would become the victim of a massive collective
amnesia.[98]

This is to say that the war had failed, in effect, to alter profoundly the
national consciousness of Spain and to engender a wider and deeper
Spanish nationalism—doing little more, in fact, than to stimulate regional
nationalism, as among the Catalans and Basques. Although both Germanophilism and Aliadophilism were forms of Spanish nationalism—one
reactionary-conservative and the other liberal-democratic—neither
proved able to penetrate the consciousness or capture the imagination of
the great majority of Spaniards, who remained as apolitically indifferent
in 1918 as they had been in 1914, greeting the outbreak of peace with the
same dazed and genial incomprehension with which four and a half years
earlier they had greeted the outbreak of war. Only participation in the war
would have roused them, but whether to a heightened national consciousness or merely to anarchic and destructive anger must remain a moot
question.

A final and crucial "ideological" impact of the war on Spain came
directly out of the republican fever of the post-Armistice period when republicans and socialists were determined not to let the monarchy strength-
en itself and thereby avoid the liquidation they felt it so richly deserved. In
a fatal misjudgment, these groups urged the left-wing Catalanists not to
cooperate with a commission set up by King Alfonso to draft a statute for
Catalan autonomy—one which promised to satisfy Catalan demands and
thereby bring Catalanism, as Stanley Payne says, into the mainstream of
the Spanish political system—something which would, of course, have
strengthened the monarchy. The left-wing Catalan intellectuals, filled with

republican hubris inspired by the Allied victory, were certain they were going to generate enough support, at home and in Paris, to enable them simply to impose their own solution to the autonomy problem; and so they foolishly rejected the proposals of the king's commission on the grounds that Catalan autonomy had to be established wholly on Catalan terms, without the intervention of "Spaniards." Mainly, of course, they and the other pro-Allied leftists just did not want to see the Spanish monarchy strengthened by the passage of such a major reform. Cambó—for pragmatic political reasons—went along with this extremism only to see within a few weeks the violent upsurge of the postwar anarchosyndicalist labor movement in Barcelona, which (inflamed by the Bolshevik Revolution in Russia) quickly began to cut the ground out from under the Catalanist movement, forcing it, because of this new and dangerous enemy on the left, to make peace with the monarchy. The monarchy survived, but Catalanism—so greatly stimulated by the war—received a serious setback.[99]

The Spanish monarchy survived in the period 1914 to 1918, one may say, because the ruling classes of Spain, though perhaps not always perfectly attuned to political and social realities, had understood one thing very clearly: participation in the war would be a catastrophe for Spain. They understood that even the "spiritual" or diplomatic alignment with the Allies so desired by the liberal intelligentsia had the potential to unleash civil war in a country where the majority was either pro-German or apolitically indifferent to the war. More than any other factor their insistence upon neutrality at any price—even at the price of honor—helped ensure that there would be no fatal parallelism between Spain's situation and that of Russia in 1917; that the war would not be permitted to produce that explosive convergence of discontents (military, urban, agrarian) that brought down the czarist monarchy. So it is that Spain during the Great War—though punished by the war's economic shock waves and seduced by its competing ideologies—offers an example of the victory of the forces of continuity over the forces of revolution, and this in a country ripe for upheaval, and in the midst of a war that seemed designed by fate to accomplish the downfall of inchoate, multinational monarchies.

Notes

The research for this chapter (which is preliminary to a larger study in progress) was made possible by a grant from the John Simon Guggenheim Memorial Foundation, to whose trustees I wish to express my sincere appreciation.

1. Jean Breton, "En mai à Madrid," *Revue de Paris* 24 (1917): 860.

2. Many observers were conscious of the "moral civil war" being waged in Spain: Paul Louis, "Les crises d'Espagne," *Revue Bleue* 55 (1917); Raymonde Lantier, "L'Attitude des intellectuels espagnols dans le conflit actuel," *Mercure de France* 113 (1916); Alvaro Alcalá Galiano, *L'Espagne en face du conflit européen* (Paris, 1917); Luis Bello, *España durante la guerra* (Madrid, 1919), p. 56; Salvador de Madariaga, *La Guerra desde Londres* (Tortosa, 1918), p. 52.

3. Tomás Eliorietta y Artaza, *El movimiento bolcheviste* (Madrid, 1919), p. 33. The phrase, though coined by Trotsky, was popularized by the Republican deputy Marcelino Domingo, quoted in François Denjean, "Le Mouvement révolutionnaire en Espagne," *Revue de Paris* 28 (1921): 739. See also *Solidaridad Obrera*, Aug. 8, 1918. José Ortega y Gasset was also struck by Russo-Spanish parallels, *Invertebrate Spain* (London, 1937), p. 71, as was Salvador de Madariaga, "Spain and Russia: A Parallel," *New Europe* 4 (1917): 198–204.

4. Fernando Periquet in *El Liberal*, July 3, 1914.

5. "Los atentados de Sarajevo," *ABC*, July 2, 1914; *El Universo*, July 5, 7, 1914; *El Liberal*, July 5, 1914; *La Correspondencia Militar*, June 29, 1914; "El proceso de Madame Caillaux," *ABC*, July 21, 1914; "Un Africanista Más," *La Guerra y el problema de Africa* (Burgos, 1914); Albert Mousset, "L'Effort militaire de l'Espagne," *La Grande Revue* 92 (1916): 126–55; *La Veu de Catalunya*, July 30, 1914.

6. *El Universo*, June 20, 1914.

7. For Ferrer, see Joan Connelly Ullman, *The Tragic Week: A Study of Anticlericalism in Spain, 1876–1912* (Cambridge, Mass., 1968), pp. 93 ff., ch. 13. For the Spanish Catholic response to the invasion of Belgium, see *Siglo Futuro*, Aug. 8, 29, 1914. On the analogy between the Ferrer case and the Dreyfus affair, see Juan Marichal, "La 'generación de los intelectuales' y la política (1909–1914)," in J. L. Abellán et al., *La crisis de fin de siglo: ideología y literatura: estudios en memoria de R. Pérez de la Dehesa* (Barcelona, 1975), pp. 25–41.

8. For accounts of the initial impact of the war on Spain, see *El Universo*, July 29, 30, 1914; Amadeo Hurtado, *Quaranta anys d'advocat: Història de meu temps* (Barcelona, 1956), ch. 12; Luis Bello, *España durante la Guerra* (Madrid, 1919), p. 59; Dionisio Pérez, *España ante la guerra* (Madrid, 1914); *Times* (London), Feb. 5, 1916.

9. Manuel González Hontoría, "Nuestra neutralidad: Contingencias e hipótesis," *ABC*, Aug. 6, 1914. For a discussion of some aspects of the diplomacy of Spanish neutrality, see Rafael Olivar Bertrand, "Repercusiones en España de la primera guerra mundial," *Cuadernos de Historia Diplomática* 3 (1956): 3–49.

10. *La Veu de Catalunya*, Aug. 7, 1914. It should be noted that Spain, next to the United States, was the largest and most important of the neutral countries. Despite its backwardness relative to the industrial powers, it was, as Paul Louis said, "the richest, the most developed in economic terms, the most active in regard to industry and commerce, . . . the most important in population and territory among the neutrals." Louis believed that if Spain had not suffered the loss of its empire in 1898, it would probably have been dragged into the war ("Crises d'Espagne," pp. 582–85).

11. Bello, *España durante*, pp. 62, 85; *El Universo*, Sept. 6, 1914; *El Liberal*, Sept. 6, 1914; Marqués Francisco de Villa-Urrutia, *Palique diplomático: recuerdos de un embajador* (Madrid, 1923); Francisco de Reynoso, *The Reminiscences*

of a Spanish Diplomat (London, 1933), pp. 217 ff.; Arthur Hardinge, *A Diplomatist in Europe* (London, 1927), p. 253; Luis Araquistaín, in *Hispania* (London), July 1, 1915; Arno J. Mayer, *The Persistence of the Old Regime* (New York, 1981).

12. Anon., "La prensa española y la guerra," *Bulletin Hispanique* 19 (1917): 125; Hans Rogger, "Russia in 1914," in Walter Laqueur and George L. Mosse, eds., *1914: The Coming of the First World War*, pp. 238 ff.; Stanley Payne, "Spanish Nationalism in the Twentieth Century," *Review of Politics* 26 (1964): 403–22; E. J. Dillon, "The Plight of Spain," *Nineteenth Century* 83 (1918): 401 ff.

13. Quoted in Breton, "En mai à Madrid," p. 861.

14. Leon Trotsky, *My Life* (New York, 1960), p. 267; Louis Bertrand, *Les pays méditerranéens et la guerre* (Paris, 1918), pp. 28 ff. For more on Trotsky in Spain, see his *Mis peripecias en España* (Madrid, 1929).

15. The extremely idealistic feeling which so many Spanish intellectuals had toward the war comes through strongly in "Les intellectuels espagnols et la guerre," *La Renaissance politique, littéraire et artistique* 3 (1915): 1332–38, which contains statements by Benito Pérez Galdós, Vicente Blasco Ibáñez, Alberto Insua, Azorín, Armando Palacio Valdés, Pérez de Ayala, Dionisio Pérez, and others. See also in this regard, "Voix Espagnols," *Pages d'histoire—1914–1915: les neutres* (Paris, 1915), pp. 3–87; Golo Mann, "The Intellectuals: Germany," *Encounter* 4 (1955), 42–49. A classic example of the surrender of objectivity may be found in Francisco Martín Melgar, *Germany and Spain: The Views of a Spanish Catholic* (London, 1916), pp. 88–89. For the mysticism of other European intellectuals regarding the war, see Roland N. Stromberg, *Redemption by War: The Intellectuals and 1914* (Lawrence, Kans., 1982).

16. On the number of Germans in Spain, see Lord Northcliffe, *At the War* (London, 1916), p. 255; and Will Irwin, *A Reporter at Armageddon* (New York, 1917), p. 23. For German impressions of Spain during the war, see P. Otto Maas, *Spanien: Eine Studienreise während des Weltkrieges* (Münster, 1921); Paul Madsack, *Vae victis: meine Erlebnisse in Spanien und Frankreich während des Weltkrieges* (Leipzig, 1918); and Herbert L. W. Goring, *Ich muss dabei sein! Als "Bachergeselle" von Spanien an die Westfront* (Berlin, 1931). On German submarine activities, see F. Vézinet, *La guerre sous-marine et l'Espagne* (Lyon, 1919).

17. For an analysis of the relative merits of German and Allied propaganda in Spain, see Jesús Longares Alonso, "La guerra de propagandas en España, 1914–1918," *Tiempo de Historia* 3 (1977): 86–89; and Ron M. Carden, "German Propaganda in Spain, 1912–1918" (unpublished paper in possession of the author). It was not until the summer of 1915 that the Allies awoke to the threat of German propaganda in Spain and finally formed the Anglo-French Institute in Madrid. For a scathing indictment of British and French propaganda efforts, see Jaime Brossa, "The Domestic and Foreign Policy of Spain," *Nation* 108 (1919): 196. One notes the evident embarrassment caused to British ambassador Hardinge by the fact that all the wrong people in Spain were pro-Ally. Thus he noted that the "extreme left," that is, the republicans, socialists, and Catalan nationalists, were "almost too embarrassingly pro-French," (*Diplomatist*, p. 259). For a discussion of German influence in Spain and the role of Major von Kalle, see P. Louis Rivière, *Un centre de guerre secrète: Madrid, 1914–1918* (Paris, 1936).

18. *Iberia*, June 26, 1914; *La Epoca*, Oct. 30, 1914; Louis, "Crises d'Espagne,"

p. 583; Pío Baroja, "Momentum catastrophicum," *Obras Completas* (8 vols., Madrid, 1946–51), 5:386.

19. The best recent treatment of the theme of the "two Spains" is the award-winning book by José María García Escudero, *Historia política de las dos Españas* 2d ed. (3 vols., Madrid, 1976). For Mill's distinction, see Arno J. Mayer, *Wilson versus Lenin: Political Origins of the New Diplomacy, 1917–1918* (Cleveland and New York, 1963), p. 4, n. 2.

20. George Santayana, "Spanish Opinion on the War," *New Republic* 15 (1915), 252.

21. There were some who took a morbid pleasure in chronicling Spain's humiliations at the hands of the French and British. See, for example, Ramón Resa, *España, víctima de Francia e Inglaterra: recopilación de datos históricos* (Seville, 1917). See also E. Schultz, *England und Spanien* (Hamburg, 1915). Juan Vázquez de Mella is quoted in Sanford Griffith, "The German Myth in Spain," *Outlook* 116 (1916): 364. Most ultra-Catholic Carlists were especially bitter toward France. See for example, "La libertad jacobina y el estado-blasfemia" in *El Correo Español*, Sept. 3, 1914.

22. For a discussion of some of the geopolitical and economic realities of Spain's situation, see Charles H. Cunningham, "Spain and the War," *American Political Science Review* 11 (1917): 421–47.

23. Bello, *España durante*, pp. 56 ff.; "La derrota de la república," *El Correo Español*, Sept. 16, 1914.

24. Salvador de Madariaga, "Spain's Home War," *Contemporary Review* 114 (1918): 382; Madariaga, "Don Quixote Is Not Neutral," *New Europe* 1 (1916): 299.

25. *Times* (London), Sept. 8, Dec. 18, 1915; *Siglo Futuro*, Aug. 8, 1914. The Carlists were certain that a German victory would mean the restoration of the French monarchy: "La restauración de la monarquía," *El Correo Español*, Sept. 20, 1914. It should be noted that the clerical picture was somewhat different in Catalonia where by 1916, according to E. Cortade, a majority of the clergy (led by Francophile bishops) had swung over to a pro-French position (*Catalunya i la gran guerra* [Barcelona, 1969], p. 22).

26. *El Universo*, Sept. 18, 1914; *Siglo Futuro*, Oct. 17, 1914; *La Vanguardia*, Nov. 14, 1914, quoted by Christopher Cobb in the introduction to *Miguel de Unamuno, Artículos olvidados sobre España y la primera guerra mundial* (London, 1976), p. xxi. For a Spanish view of Belgian Catholicism, see *El Universo*, June 18, 1914. For an analysis of the problem of Spanish Catholic Germanophilism, see Raymonde Lantier, *La propagande française en Espagne* (Paris, 1916); "Les raisons doctrinales de francophobie," in Louis Arnould, *Le duel Franco-Allemand en Espagne* (Paris, 1915); A. Morel-Fatio, "Les néocarlistes et l'Allemagne," *Le Correspondant*, July 25, 1915.

27. Hardinge, *Diplomatist*, p. 260; Sir Charles Petrie, *King Alfonso and His Age* (London, 1963), ch. 8.

28. Petrie, *King Alfonso*, pp. 121–22; Brossa, "Domestic and Foreign Policy," p. 518. The king was very active in humanitarian endeavors with respect to the war. See G. Reval, "L'oeuvre humanitaire de S. M. Le Roi d'Espagne," *Revue des Deux Mondes* 35 (1916): 842–63. A recent study based on German Foreign Office archives reveals, correctly or not, a more Germanophile king than has been

commonly assumed. Alfonso is quoted as saying to Prince Ratibor that he hoped Germany would win the war, since it would give him a free hand in Portugal, Gibraltar, and Tangier (Lillian Galos de Vaz Ferreira, *Die Neutralitätspolitik Spaniens während des Ersten Weltkrieges* [Hamburg, 1966], p. 48).

29. Madariaga, "Spain's Home War," p. 381. The main journal of the officers was *La Correspondencia Militar*, which, in the early stages of the war, took only a moderately pro-German line and reported the news quite objectively. It, too, urged "absolute" neutrality and was mainly concerned with the effect of the war on Morocco (Nov. 21, 1914). More pro-French was *Ejército y Armada*, which was a mouthpiece for noncommissioned officers—this suggesting still another "dialectic" in Spain, that between Germanophile officers and Francophile noncommissioned officers and enlisted men ("La guerra y el derecho," Aug. 4, 1914).

30. Griffith, "The German Myth," p. 364. The core of Vázquez de Mella's doctrine is found in his *Discurso íntegro de "los tres dogmas nacionales"* (Madrid, 1941), which was delivered in the Teatro de la Zarzuela on May 31, 1915.

31. Martin Blinkhorn, *Carlism and Crisis in Spain, 1931–1936* (Cambridge, 1975), ch. 1. The Carlists admired the "federative" qualities of both the German and Austrian monarchies, which they compared with the centralist tendencies of the French Republic ("Monarquías federativas y república centralizadora," *El Correo Español*, Sept. 19, 1914). One should also contrast the Carlist sense of Germany as a traditional society with the belief of many non-Carlist Germanophiles that Germany, as Edmundo González-Blanco said, represented in the world a "dynamic, revolutionary, and progressive ideal" (*Iberismo y Germanismo: España ante el conflicto europeo* [Valencia, Buenos Aires, 1917], p. 130).

32. For unflattering portraits of the various Germanophiles, see Luis del Olmet, *Los bocheros: la propaganda teutona en España* (Madrid, n.d.). An ex-Germanophile, the author wrote about such pro-Germans as Pío Baroja, J. Salaverría, Benavente, Rodríguez Soriano, F. Carracido, Vázquez de Mella, Vicente Gay, Calvo Sotelo, and others. See also Vicente Gay, *El pensamiento y la actividad alemana en la guerra europea* (Madrid, 1916), and F. Martín Caballero, *Vidas ajenas* (Madrid, 1914), pp. 17–41. González-Blanco argued that in fact the vast majority of what he called the "cultivated classes" (scientists, lawyers, professors, businessmen) were Germanophiles and should even be considered "intellectuals," while most of the *aliadófilos* were actually not intellectuals (masters of science and philosophy) but mere *literatos*. He argued, not unpersuasively, that not all writers are thinkers (*Iberismo*, pp. 134 ff.). A very clear impression of the extremely wide support for Germanophilism among the "cultivated classes" in Spain may be gained by perusing the long lists of names (broken down by cities) in *Amistad Hispano-Germana* (Barcelona, 1916). Ricardo León, a Germanophile not unsympathetic to France, was a novelist. See his *Europea trágica: ironías de un téstigo de la guerra 1914–1918* (Madrid, 1945). To sample the thought of the Germanophile José M. Salaverría, see his *La afirmación española: estudios sobre el pesimismo español y los nuevos tiempos* (Barcelona, 1917).

33. José María Requeña, *España gran potencia* (Madrid, 1915), quoted in Griffith, "The German Myth in Spain," p. 365. The verve of much Germanophile writing is revealed in the pioneering study by Fernando Díaz-Plaja, *Francófilos y germanófilos: los españoles en la guerra europea* (Barcelona, 1973). This work is arranged topically rather than chronologically and contains a vast number of

fascinating, well-selected quotations. Some Germanophile titles are: P. Iglesias Hermida, *España alemania: no hay conflicto* (Madrid, 1916); Juan Español, *Los esclavos del mar y nuestros amigos los ingleses* (Madrid, 1917); Juan M. López, *La razón y la ciencia están de parte de Alemania* (Seville, 1915); Sidi-Guatzemelem, *Inglaterra usurpadora: Gibraltar y España* (n.p., n.d.); Domingo Cirici Ventalló, *El secreto de Lord Kitchener y el desastre de Inglaterra (fantasía)*, 2nd ed. (Madrid, 1915); Joaquín Argamasilla de la Cerdá, *La explosión de mentira* (Madrid, 1917).

34. Edmundo González-Blanco, *Alemania y la guerra europea* (Madrid, 1915), pp. 9, 23–31. See also his *El origen de la guerra europea* (Madrid, 1916).

35. Santiago Roldán López, "La consolidación de la vía nacionalista del capitalismo español durante la 1 guerra mundial," *Anales de Economía* 2 (1971): 17–56.

36. Eloy Luis André, "Los problemas de España y la guerra europea," *Nuestro Tiempo* 16, no. 208 (1916): 17–32; André, "Hacía una política exterior en sentido nacional," *Nuestro Tiempo* 16, no. 212 (1916): 137–50. An effective rebuttal to André's argument, stressing the immense material benefit to Spain of Allied capital investments, was made by "X," "Quelque points de vue espagnols sur la guerre," *Mercure de France* 128 (1918): 37 ff.

37. *España*, Feb. 28, 1915.

38. *El Sol*, No. 13, 1918, quoted in Díaz-Plaja, *Francófilos*, p. 45.

39. For a perceptive analysis of Benavente's Germanophilism, see Robert Louis Sheehan, *Benavente and the Spanish Panorama, 1894–1954* (Chapel Hill, N.C., 1976), pp. 77–100. For an example of Benavente's somewhat diffuse views on the war and neutrality, see his introduction to *Amistad Hispano-Germana*.

40. Salvador de Madariaga, "The Future of Spanish Neutrality," *New Europe* 3 (1917): 144.

41. *Diario Universal*, Aug. 19, 1914.

42. Bello, *España durante*, pp. 73–75.

43. *La Veu de Catalunya*, Sept. 9, 1914. For Lerroux's views on the war, see *La Verdad a mi país: España y la guerra* (1915).

44. Bello, *España durante*, pp. 75–76; Maximiano García Venero, *Melquíades Alvarez: Historia de un liberal*, 2d ed. (Madrid, 1974), pp. 318, 322.

45. *El Socialista*, Aug. 2, 1914. The Dato government, in support of its policy of "absolute" neutrality, prohibited all public meetings at this time. This angered the socialists because it meant canceling a "gran mitin" against the war which they were going to hold on Aug. 2 (*Siglo Futuro*, Aug. 2, 1914); but within a short time the socialists' attitude changed dramatically.

46. *El Socialista*, Aug. 30, Dec. 6, 1914; see also "La simpatía de los clericales": "The clericals have given all their sympathy to those countries whose systems are more in harmony with their reactionary views and their phobia against liberty and progress" (ibid., Aug. 14, 1914). The change in Socialist thinking appears to have come within the first two weeks of the war, for on Aug. 15, the party voluntarily canceled a twenty-four-hour strike they had planned against the Moroccan war because of "the grave circumstances which have been created by the war provoked by Austrian and German imperialism" (ibid., Aug. 15, 1914).

47. Some of the best studies of Francophilism in Spain were made by French observers: J.-Félicien Court, *Chez les neutres: en Espagne* (Paris, 1916); Louis Bertrand, "Mon enquête en Espagne," *Revue des Deux Mondes* 31 (1916): 241–

80; Bertrand, *Les pays méditerranéens*, ch. 11; [St. C.], "L'Espagne francophile," *Bulletin Hispanique* 19, no. 3 (1917): 134–56; Lantier, "L'Attitude des intellectuels," pp. 40–54. See also Alvaro Alcalà-Galiano, *L'Espagne en face du conflit europeen*, tr. Alfred de Bengoechea (Paris, 1917), chs. 8, 10; "X," "Quelques points de vue," pp. 16–42; Azorín, *Entre España y Francia: páginas de un francófilo* (Barcelona, Paris, 1916); and Fernando Díaz-Plaja, *Francfilos*, chs. 1, 2, 5.

48. For a radical right-wing critique of the Spanish intelligentsia which emphasizes its anticlerical propensities, see Enrique Suñer, *Los intelectuales y la tragedía española* (San Sebastián, 1937).

49. A useful survey of the history of the Spanish intelligentsia will be found in Francisco B. Villacorta, *Burguesía y cultura: los intelectuales españoles* (Madrid, 1978). For background, see also J. López-Morillas, *El Krausismo español: perfil de una aventura intelectual* (Mexico, 1956); V. Cacho Víu, *La Institución Libre de Enseñanza* (Madrid, 1962); Alberto Jiménez Fraud, *La Residencia de Estudiantes: visita a Maquiavelo* (Barcelona, 1972), pp. 9–88; J. L. Abellán et al., *Crisis de fin de siglo* (Barcelona, 1975); Gonzalo Sobejano, *Nietzsche en España* (Madrid, 1967). See also Jean Becarud and Evelyne López Campillo, *Los intelectuales españoles durante la II república* (Madrid, 1978), ch. 1.

50. Manuel Tuñon de Lara, *Medio siglo de cultura española: 1885–1936*, 3d ed. (Madrid, 1977), ch. 8; Juan Marichal, *La vocación de Manuel Azaña* (Madrid, 1968), pp. 65 ff.; Villacorta, *Burguesía y cultura*, ch. 5.

51. José Ortega y Gasset, *Obras Completas* (Madrid, 1956), 1:267–308. On Ortega as the leader of the Generation of 1914, see the fine essay by Robert Wohl in *The Generation of 1914* (Cambridge, Mass., 1979), ch. 4. Also extremely useful on the Generation of 1914 is Marichal, *Azaña*. See also Marichal's "La 'generación de los intelectuales' y la politica (1909–1914)," in Abellán et al., *Fin de siglo*, pp. 25–41. For more on the Generation of 1914 see: Tuñon de Lara, *Medio siglo*, chs. 7–11; José-Carlos Mainer, *La edad de plata (1902–1932): ensayo de interpretación de un proceso cultural* (Barcelona, 1975); Paul Aubert, "Los intelectuales y la crisis de 1917," in [Anon.], *VIII Coloquio de Pau: la crisis del estado español, 1898–1936* (Madrid, 1978), pp. 245–317; Mainer, "Una frustración histórica: la aliadofilia de los intelectuales," in his *Literatura y pequeña burguesía en España* (Madrid, 1972), pp. 141–64; Juan Marichal, "La signifación histórica de Juan Negrín (1892–1956)," in Manuel Ramírez, *Estudios sobre la II República española* (Madrid, 1975), pp. 187–202.

52. Tuñon de Lara, *Medio siglo*, p. 147; Wohl, *Generation of 1914*, ch. 4; Breton, "En mai à Madrid," p. 860.

53. Ramiro de Maeztu, *La revolución y los intelectuales* (Madrid, 1911), pp. 39 ff.

54. For the debate on the meaning of the term "intellectual," see Edmundo González-Blanco, *Iberismo*, pp. 129 ff. The text of the manifesto appeared in *España*, July 9, 1915. Among the signers were: Gumersindo de Azcárate, Adolfo Buylla, Américo Castro, Manuel B. Cossío, Enrique Díez Canedo, Luis de Hoyos, Gregorio Marañon, Ramón Menéndez Pidal, José Ortega y Gasset, Adolfo Posada, Fernando de los Ríos, Luis Simarro, Miguel de Unamuno, Gabriel Alomar, Luis Araquistaín, Manuel Azaña, "Azorín," José Carner, Manuel Ciges Aparicio, Francisco Grandmontagne, Eduardo Gómez de Vaquero, Ignacio Iglesias, Antonio Machado, Ramiro de Maeztu, Gregorio Martínez Sierra, Armando Palacio Valdés, Benito Pérez Galdós, Ramón Pérez de Ayala, and Ramón de Valle-Inclán.

55. The French writer Albert Mousset challenged the belief that the majority of Spaniards studying abroad resided in Germany, noting that the records of the treasury of the *Junta para ampliación de estudios* showed that in 1911, sixty-five students opted for Germany, while ninety-one went to France, forty-three to Italy, thirty-six to Belgium, and twenty-three to England ("L'Espagne dans le conflit actuel," *La Grande Revue* 19, no. 2 [April, 1915]: 26). González-Blanco was astonished by the tendency of German-trained Spanish intellectuals to become *aliadófilos* (*Iberismo*, p. 138).

56. "Les intellectuels espagnols," p. 1333.

57. Miguel de Unamuno, *Obras Completas*, 10: 382–83, 461; Cobb, *Miguel de Unamuno*, pp. xii, xiii, xv; Vicente González Martín, introduction to Miguel de Unamuno y Jugo, *Crónica política española (1915–1923): artículos no recogidos en las obras completas* (Salamanca, n.d.), pp. 18, 21–22; Luis Urrutia Salaverri, ed., in introduction to Miguel de Unamuno, *Desde el mirador de la guerra* (Paris, 1970), pp. 11–82; Miguel de Unamuno, "En Salamanca, notas de un testigo," *España*, Oct. 25, 1917; Stanley Payne, "Unamuno's Politics," in J. Barcía Rubia and M. A. Zeitlin, eds., *Unamuno, Creator and Creation* (Berkeley, Los Angeles, Calif., 1967), pp. 203–47.

58. "Manifiesto de la Liga antigermanófila," *España*, Jan. 18, 1917. Among the signers of this document were: Gabriel Alomar, Américo Castro, Gustavo Pittaluga, Leopoldo Alas, Luis Araquistaín, Manuel Azaña, E. Díaz Reitg, Enrique Gómez Carrillo, Ignacio Iglesias, Roman Jori, Antonio Machado, Manuel Machado, Pérez Galdós, Pérez de Ayala, Antonio Rovira y Virgili, Miguel de Unamuno, Melquíades Alvarez, Alvaro de Albórnoz, Gumersindo Azcárate, Roberto Castrovido, Pedro Corominas, Marcelino Domingo, and Rodrigo Soriano.

59. Manuel Azaña, *Obras Completas* (Madrid, 1966), 1:140–42 ff. See also his account of his visit to the western front in October 1916 as part of a Spanish delegation: "Nuestra misión en Francia," *Bulletin Hispanique* 19 (1917): 26–47.

60. "Le manifeste des intellectuels Catalans," *Voix Espagnols*, pp. 78–80.

61. Brossa, "Domestic and Foreign Policy," p. 198; Claudi Amettla, *Memòries polítiques, 1890–1917* (Barcelona, 1963), pp. 335 ff.

62. Antonio Rovira y Virgili, *El nacionalismo Catalán: su aspecto político: los hechos, las ideas y los hombres* (Barcelona, 1917), pp. 208–9.

63. Conférences des nationalités . . . , *IIIme Conférence des nationalités*, Lausanne, 27 Juin, 1916: étude du problème des nationalités en vue du Congrès des Puissances après la guerre. Documents préliminaires (Lausanne, 1916); Union des nationalités, Office central, Lausanne, *La nation Catalane: son passé, son présent et son avenir* (Lausanne, 1916); Amettla, *Memòries*, p. 122; Union des Nationalités, *La question Ibérique: mémoires et déclarations présentés par les délégués Basques et Catalans a la IIIme conférence des nationalités*, pp. 11–18. For Catalan nationalists the "message" of the war was that "in a general way, the present conflict is a rising against hegemony—a rising against imperialistic tendencies—and the statesmen of the Entente have . . . declared many times that in the Europe of tomorrow, there cannot be anything but free peoples" (*La Nation Catalane*, pp. 137–38). See also Union des nationalités, *La Solidarité Catalano-Basque et la réorganisation de l'Espagne* (Lausanne, 1917), p. 7; *La Nation Catalane*, p. 145.

64. "Manifesto of the Friends of the Moral Unity of Europe" in Romain Rolland, *Above the Battle* (Chicago, 1916), pp. 122–26.

65. *La Veu de Catalunya*, Aug. 20–24, 1914.

66. Maximiano García Venero, *Historia del nacionalismo catalán 1793–1936* (Madrid, 1944), pp. 377, 379 ff., 575 ff.; *La Nation Catalane*, p. 143.

67. The definitive study of Cambó's initiatives in this period is Jesús Pabón, *Cambó, 1876–1930* (2 vols., Barcelona, 1952), 1:446 ff. Amettla notes that as a result of the war "there was more money, well-being increased, comfort was more widespread in Catalonia," (*Memòries*, p. 340). It is difficult to accept Rovira y Virgili's charge that Cambó's nationalism was merely "tactical" (*El Nacionalismo Catalan*, p. 267). For the fervor of his nationalism, see the texts of Cambó's speeches to the Cortes on June 7–8, 1916, in García Venero, *Historia del nacionalismo Catalán*, pp. 379–402. Pabón confirms Cambó's sincerity, referring to his Catalanism as "an ideological and sentimental reality, initial and permanent" (*Cambó*, 2:5). In an interview late in 1916 Cambó, noting that the fate of Catalonia had always been decided by international conflicts, said, "I believe that Catalonia can expect the solution of its national problem from [the World War] which can only be resolved by the consolidating of the principle of nationalities" (*La Nation Catalane*, p. 148).

68. Enrique Prat de la Riba, "Als diputats de la mancomunitat de Catalunya," in Díaz-Plaja, *Francófilos*, pp. 356–59.

69. Cortade gives the figure of 15,000 (*Catalunya i la gran guerra*, p. 59). S. Albertí says that the estimates run from 12,000 to 15,000 Catalan volunteers (*El republicanisme català i la restauració monàrquica, 1875–1923* [Barcelona, 1972], p. 381). Cortade speculates that perhaps as many as 12,000 Catalans died in battle (p. 74), and José María Poblet argues that the "major part" of those Catalans who fought died on the field of battle (*El moviment autonomista a Catalunya del anys 1918–1919* [Barcelona, 1970], p. 7). Jaime Brossa stressed the fighting qualities of the Catalan volunteers and claimed that out of 14,000 only 2,000 survived the war ("Domestic and Foreign Policy," pp. 519–20).

70. E. Gómez Carrillo, *La gesta de la legión: los hispanos-americanos en la guerra* (Madrid, 1921), pp. 12 ff., ch. 11; Cortade, *La Catalunya y la gran guerra*, pp. 55 ff.

71. Cortade, *La Catalunya y la gran guerra*, pp. 56–58. For information on the war experiences of Spanish and Catalan volunteers, see Jose Subirá, *Los españoles en la guerra de 1914–1918* (Madrid, 1919), and Gómez Carrillo, *La gesta*, chs. 1–10.

72. Gómez Carrillo, *La gesta*, pp. 110–11; *Patronato de voluntarios españoles: memoria de su actuación, 1918–1919* (Madrid, n.d.), p. 57.

73. Quoted in Gómez Carrillo, *La gesta*, pp. 90–91; Cortade, *La Catalunya y la gran guerra*, p. 63.

74. *Patronato de voluntarios*, pp. 1–5; Gómez Carrillo, *La gesta*, p. 89; Subirá, *Los españoles*, 3:12, 16–17.

75. Jaime Vicens Vives, *Approaches to the History of Spain*, 2d ed., tr. Joan Connelly Ullman (Berkeley, Calif., 1971), p. 148; Société des amis de l'Espagne, "La situation en Espagne," introduction, p. 13 (mimeographed MS, dated July 12, 1917, in Hoover Institution, Stanford, Calif.); Luis Araquistaín, *Entre la guerra y la revolución* (Madrid, 1917), ch. 3.

76. Interview in *Petit Parisien* quoted in "Germany's Victory in Spain," *Literary Digest* 54 (1917): 1587. For Romanones's resignation speech to the Cortes, see *Correspondencia de España*, April 19, 1917; Sanford Griffith, "The Recent Crisis

in Spanish Neutrality," *Nation* 104, no. 271 (1917): 731. For a detailed discussion of Spain's neutrality diplomacy in this period, see "Kritische Phasen der Neutralität" in Vaz Ferreira, *Die Neutralitätspolitik*, pp. 42–80. The angry, eloquent manifesto of the Reformist party (probably written by Melquíades Alvarez) conveyed the response of all the pro-Allied intellectuals to the crisis caused by German submarine warfare and the refusal of king and Cortes to approve breaking diplomatic relations with Germany. It demanded an immediate diplomatic break with Germany as something required by both pride and honor. Not to do this would brand Spain as a vile and weak country and would probably bar it from the inevitable peace conference and expose it to the danger of demands by the victorious Allies for "compensation" or even "repartition." The manifesto also reveals two illusions which gripped the intellectuals in the spring of 1917 and which encouraged them to revolutionary action: first, that the "immense majority" of the country supported the aliadophiles and, second, that the army's sense of honor would turn it against Germany and in favor of a diplomatic break (*Heraldo de Madrid*, April 26, 1917, quoted in "L'Espagne francophile," pp. 135–39).

77. The Paris-based *Bulletin des presses espagnoles* said on March 31, 1917, that the March revolution in Russia created a "profound sensation" in the pro-Allied press in Spain, convincing the *aliadófilos* that the world war had definitively acquired its true meaning as an "ideological confict." See also Madariaga, *La guerra desde Londres*, pp. 49 ff. What is being suggested is that the March revolution, while it served to arouse and revolutionize the pro-Allied intelligentsia, did not have a significant effect on the three quasi-revolutionary movements in Spain in the summer of 1917, including the general strike of Aug. 13. For a contrary and somewhat romanticized view, see Luis Araquistaín in *España*, Oct. 25, 1917. For a more complete discussion of the effect of the March revolution on Spain, see Gerald H. Meaker, *The Revolutionary Left in Spain, 1914–1923* (Stanford, Calif., 1974), pp. 46–49. In his resignation speech Romanones said: "Spain is the custodian of the spiritual patrimony of a great race. She aspires to preside over a moral federation of all the nations of our blood, and she will definitely lose this role if, at an hour so decisive for the future . . . Spain and the races that have issued from her shall seem divided" (*Correspondencia de España*, April 19, 1917).

78. For an edited and somewhat softened version of Unamuno's rather threatening speech, see Fernando Díaz-Plaja, *El siglo XX: la historia de España en sus documentos* (Madrid, 1960), pp. 352–55. For an unexpurgated version of the speeches given in the Plaza de Toros, see *El Socialista*, May 27, 1917: here it will be seen that the sense of patriotic outrage over Germany's treatment of Spain is strongest in the speech of Melquíades Alvarez. For excellent summaries of the speeches see also "L'Espagne francophile," pp. 134–56. An American observer claimed that there were street demonstrations in Barcelona in the early summer of 1917 in favor of intervention in the war on the side of the Allies (*Survey* 38 [1917]: 489).

79. *El Socialista*, May 27, 1917; Breton, "En mai à Madrid," p. 869.

80. On the military juntas, see Carolyn P. Boyd, *Praetorian Politics in Liberal Spain* (Chapel Hill, N.C., 1979), chs. 2–5; Stanley G. Payne, *Politics and the Military in Modern Spain* (Stanford, Calif., 1967), chs. 7–8; Juan Antonio Lacomba, *La crisis española de 1917* (Madrid, 1970), ch. 4. Still useful on all three

movements is Fernando Soldevilla, *Tres revoluciones (apuntes y notas)* (Madrid, 1917).

81. Lacomba, *La crisis española*, pp. 15–33.

82. Lacomba's picture of the war's economic impact on Spain seems somewhat overdrawn. Thus the rise of prices through most of 1917 was less than "meteoric": based on 1913 as 100, prices rose from 107 in September 1914 to 123 in March 1917, when the real planning for the general strike began, and to 136 in August 1917 when the strike was declared, to 145 in March 1918. Thus from the start of the war to the time the strike was agreed upon, prices rose less than 15 percent; and in the period up to August 1917 they rose 27 percent—a substantial but not catastrophic average rise of about 7 percent per year (Instituto de Reformas Sociales, *Encarecimiento de la vida durante la guerra: precios de subsistencias en España y en el extranjero, 1914–1918* [Madrid, 1918], p. 82). It should also be recalled that on the average money wages rose by about 10 percent up to March 1917, according to Boyd, *Praetorian Politics*, p. 49, and that many workers—especially in Catalonia, the Basque Provinces, and Asturias—received even higher wage raises from employers anxious to avoid strikes in a time of high profits. Thus the *Informes de los inspectores del trabajo sobre la influencia de la guerra europea en las industrias españolas* (Madrid, 1918) suggests that the wages of Catalonian workers had risen between 20 and 50 percent by 1918 (p. 91). On the other hand, one recent study posits that the real wages of Spanish workers may have declined by 10.8 percent between 1914 and 1917 (Santiago Roldán and José Luis García Delgado, *La consolidación del capitalismo en España* [Madrid, 1973], 2:203). But even this (an average decline of 2.7 percent per year) does not seem the stuff that revolutions are made of. Actually, the analysis of Roldán and García Delgado—although economic-determinist in nature—tends to cancel out that of Lacomba, for they believe that the "revolutionary" events of 1917 were the result not of an economic slump and hard times but of a vigorous war-induced prosperity which, ironically, tended to accentuate rather than minimize the various "contradictions" within Spanish society (ibid., pp. 71 ff.). It should also be noted that the number of strikes and strikers in Spain—a rough index of economic discontent—stayed well below the level of 1913 clear up to 1918 (Alberto Balcells, *El sindicalismo en Barcelona, 1916–1923*, 2d ed. [Barcelona, 1968], p. 181). Moreover, the severity of inflation in Spain did not match that in either the warring or the neutral powers of Europe. Thus, while the price level in Spain in October 1917 was 141, in Germany it was 209, in Britain 204, in France 184, in the Netherlands 188, in Norway 261, and in Sweden 181. Demographic changes should also not be exaggerated and would not seem to have had the revolutionary effect that Lacomba claims for them in 1917. Thus we see that in the whole period between January 1914 and January 1919 the population of Madrid grew only by 12 percent and that of Barcelona and Bilbao by only 10 percent, with about half this rise being attributable to natural population growth (Instituto Nacional de Estadística, *Principales actividades de la vida española en la primera mitad del siglo XX* [Madrid 1952], pp. 9–10). These figures are borne out by a population study made of the city of Barcelona in 1918 which indicated that the excess of immigration into the city over emigration between 1914 and 1917 averaged only a little more than 7,000 per year (presumably mostly peasants) which, for a city with a

1917 population of 628,000, would not seem to have extremely revolutionary implications, since it amounts to an average 1 percent gain per year. The highest immigration, it should be noted, was in 1915 (12,290), while the figure for 1917 was only 6,284 (Manuel Escudé Bartoli, "La población de Barcelona," *Estudio* 7, no. 76 [1918]: 31–32). The points I have made here represent a partial modification of views I myself set forth in *The Revolutionary Left in Spain*, chs. 2–3, where, though I argued against an excessively economic interpretation of the events of 1917, I, too, exaggerated, as I now believe, the "revolutionary" quality of the events of that year. Since so much of Lacomba's analysis depends on the demographic image of an "avalanche" of peasants crowding into the industrial zone and creating, by 1917, almost inexorable revolutionary pressures, it may be well to add one further demographic datum: the loss of rural population in Spain between 1910 and 1920 (which, by the way, would include both emigration abroad and internal migration to the cities) was only 9 percent, which would be an average loss of rural population of less than 1 percent per year; conversely, the industrial sector gained only 3.14 percent in this same ten-year period (*VIII Colloquio de Pau*, p. 19).

83. For an example of this patriotic response to the army's condition vis-à-vis the war, see the remarks of the archbishop of Tarragona in "St. C.," "Le main de l'Allemagne en Espagne," *Bulletin Hispanique* 19 (1917): 5. For the genesis of the army reform efforts, see Boyd, *Praetorian Politics*, chs. 2, 3; and Salvador Canals, "Crónica de política interior," *Nuestro Tiempo* (Oct.–Dec. 1915): 345–63, (April–June 1916): 230–36. *El Imparcial* (Oct. 21, 1915) quoted the Parisian daily *Le Journal* as saying that the cabinet crisis was "above all an interior crisis" which revealed the difficulty of survival of a government whose "congenital weakness" was notorious. By the fact of not calling Maura to power in 1913, the Conservative government found itself divided. Abandoned, in effect, by many of his own party, Dato had survived only by the "tolerance" of the opposition. The war weakened an already weak government and hence a "budgetary incident" was sufficient to bring the government down. The handling of the army reform measure in Parliament is discussed in detail by Salvador Canals and the essentially procedural nature of the crisis is clearly shown ("Crónica, pp. 346–63). This is confirmed by *El Imparcial*, Nov. 12, Dec. 7, 1915. Economic influence on the crisis is called into question by the remark of the editor of *El Imparcial* on Nov. 3, 1915, that "we admit that, in fact, the consequences of the war have not been as evident in the economic life of Spain as in the belligerent nations and even in [the neutrals] which have had less *fortuna* and today suffer a dangerous crisis." My emphasis on the "contingency" of the Spanish "revolution" of 1917 is not to suggest that there were no "structural" aspects to the Spanish crisis but only that the nature and timing of the events were not determined by irrepressible economic forces. My point is similar to the one made by R. V. Daniels in *Red October: The Bolshevik Revolution of 1917* (New York, 1967) in which he argues against post hoc deterministic interpretations of the Bolshevik seizure of power and insists upon its contingency. See the restatement of his position in the *American Historical Review* 88 (1983): 1137–38, and an effort at rebuttal by R. G. Suny, pp. 1139–40.

84. Canals, "Crónica de política interior," pp. 350 ff.; Madariaga, "Spain and

Russia," p. 200; Anon., "The Spanish Crisis," *New Statesman* 9 (1917): 294. See also Canals, "Crónica," pp. 376 ff., for further discussion of the Liberal camarilla and the manner in which it alienated the officers.

85. Soldevilla, *Tres revoluciones*, p. 16.

86. Amettla, *Memòries*, pp. 380 ff. On the eve of the July 19 meeting, the Lliga issued a circular urging the Catalan people to avoid all public demonstrations, to stay in their work places, to avoid gathering in the streets, and "not to offer *gritas* or *vivas* of any kind" (Pabón, *Cambó*, 1:513). Fritz Fischer, *Germany's War Aims in the First World War* (New York, 1967).

87. Pabón, *Cambó*, 1:517; Soldevilla, *Tres revoluciones*, pp. 124–28.

88. For a detailed discussion of the genesis of the strike, see Meaker, *The Revolutionary Left in Spain*, pp. 76–98.

89. All the manifestos issued by the strike leaders scrupulously avoided any reference to the question of modifying the neutrality policy or intervening in the war in any way (Andrés Saborit, *La huelga de agosto: apuntes históricos* [Mexico, 1967], pp. 52–55, 70, 72–74). Yet García Venero is probably not wrong when he says that the defeat of the general strike was also a defeat for the idea that Spain should enter the war—toward which it was being pulled by the "aliadophile vehemency of the leftists" (*Historia de las internacionales* [Madrid, 1956], 2:268).

90. Manuel Cordero, *Los socialistas en la revolución* (Madrid, 1932), p. 32. At some point the Socialist strike leaders apparently agreed that the strike would not be called until November. Its outbreak on Aug. 13 was regarded by the workers themselves as a violation of an agreement made by Llargo Caballero (Miguel Maura to Gabriel Maura, Aug. 18, 1917, in Díaz-Plaja, *El siglo XX*, p. 378). In the Cortes, after the strike, Julián Besteiro said that after the officers' uprising in June, it "seemed absolutely impossible that they should throw themselves against any type of sedition." He acknowledged ruefully that nevertheless "we should have had some guarantee that at least a part of the army [would be] on our side" (*La huelga de agosto en el parlamento: discursos de Julián Besteiro, Indalecio Prieto, Andrés Saborit, Daniel Anguiano, Largo Caballero y Marcelino Domingo* [Madrid, 1918], p. 179).

91. Unamuno, "En Salamanca," *España*, Oct. 25, 1917; Dillon, "The Plight of Spain," p. 399.

92. V. I. Lenin, *Collected Works* (Moscow, 1964), 21:213–14; Walter Laqueur, "Revolution," *Encyclopedia of the Social Sciences*, 13:501–7.

93. Manuel de Burgos y Mazo, *Páginas Históricas de 1917* (Madrid, 1917), p. 219; Saborit, *La huelga*, p. 72; Tuñon de Lara, *Medio siglo*, p. 188. A. F. G. Bell wrote in September 1917 that "what is certain is that there is no widespread antidynastic feeling [in Spain]" ("Spain in the World's Debate," *Contemporary Review* 112 [1917]: 266). Paul Aubert halfway concedes the revolt's contingency when he writes, "The crisis had a structure but the revolution did not" ("Los intelectuales y la crisis de 1917," *VIII Coloquio de Pau*, p. 276).

94. Francis Carsten, "Revolutionary Situations in Europe, 1917–1920," in Charles L. Bertrand, ed., *Revolutionary Situations in Europe, 1917–1922: Germany, Italy, Austria-Hungary* (Quebec, 1977), p. 31. Writing in August 1917, Salvador de Madariaga said, "If Spain had been a belligerent, there would be today in Madrid a Provisional Government with a Spanish Kerensky at its head" ("Spain and Russia," p. 198). On the events of 1917 see also Octavio Ruiz Manjón, *El Partido Republicano Radical, 1908–1936* (Madrid, 1976), pp. 113 ff.

95. Meaker, *The Revolutionary Left in Spain*, ch. 5; IRS, *Encarecimiento*, p. 82.

96. Hispano-German diplomacy during 1918 is covered in considerable detail, albeit from a somewhat pro-German perspective, in Vaz Ferreira, *Neutralitäts-politik*, pp. 62–85. See also Ronnie Melbourne Carden, "German Policy toward Neutral Spain in World War I" (Ph.D. diss., University of New Mexico, 1980), which is also based on German Foreign Office archives.

97. Poblet, *El moviment autonomista*, pp. 12 ff. The British observer A. F. G. Bell noted the upsurge of revolutionary republicanism after the Armistice and feared that the republicans might try to overthrow the monarchy in the name of the Allied victory ("Spain and the Allies," *Contemporary Review* 115 [1920]: 62–66).

98. *El Sol*, July 14, Oct. 7, 1918.

99. Stanley Payne, "Catalan and Basque Nationalism," *Journal of Contemporary History* 6 (1971): 29–30.

2

The Swiss National General Strike of November 1918

HEINZ K. MEIER

The general strike in Switzerland of November 1918 brought to a climax decades of mounting conflict between the growing labor movement and the prevailing social and political structure of the country. The dominant bourgeois class and its political parties received a shock that imprinted the general strike on its memories for decades as a national crisis and a moment of grave danger to its values. For organized labor and its political arm, the Social Democratic party, the general strike was only one in a series of events leading to social and political equality.

The 1918 general strike assumed special significance because of its timing. Triggered by the economic hardship World War I created even in peaceful Switzerland, the strike seemed to have also been inspired by foreign forces that wanted to use the chaos and turmoil of the decade to carry the communist revolution into Central Europe. This presumed international dimension of the strike played a considerable role in frightening the Swiss bourgeoisie and giving the events a significance they otherwise would not have had.

Accounts, analyses, and interpretations of the events of November 1918 in Swiss historiography are voluminous. This chapter organizes the volumes of available material in three stages. It begins by providing the basic chronological sequence of events beginning in November 1918, when a partial mobilization of the Swiss army led to the call for a general strike, and ending with the trial of the strike leaders in spring 1919.

A discussion of the background issues of the general strike follows, with an analysis of the motivations of the leaders in the conflict. The chapter concludes with a review of the impact of the general strike on both the international sphere and the domestic developments of Switzerland in the 1920s and 1930s.

On Tuesday, November 5, 1918, the Swiss Federal Council, the highest executive office in the country, ordered the mobilization of two infantry regiments and two cavalry brigades from the cantons of Luzern and Thurgau for the purpose of maintaining peace and order in the city of Zurich. The next day it mobilized four additional units.

The Federal Council explained this measure to the Swiss people as having been made necessary by the presence of certain elements, mainly foreigners living in Zurich, who wanted to misuse the nation's political and economic crises to transplant anarchic and revolutionary experiments from Russia to Switzerland. The mobilization was designed to prevent disturbances before they could erupt. The Federal Council counted on all Swiss to support its effort and to work together for democracy and social justice.[1]

The united Zurich labor organizations immediately protested the measure taken by the Federal Council. They accused the authorities, in both Zurich and Bern, of establishing a military dictatorship. The mobilization of the troops was a provocation of the working class; an investigation of the situation in Zurich would prove, they claimed, that the contentions of the Federal Council were not founded on facts.[2] At the national level the Olten Action Committee, a group of leaders of the Swiss Social Democratic party, the Swiss Labor Union Council (Gewerkschaftsbund), and the Social Democratic members of the National Council, issued a similar protest.

The Olten Action Committee had been founded by Robert Grimm in February 1918 at a meeting in Olten, Canton Solothurn, and had become recognized as the leadership organ of its constituent groups. The action of the Federal Council took the committee by surprise. Grimm and his fellow leaders had just completed a relatively successful round of negotiations with the Federal Council concerning the economic and social improvement of the workers in Switzerland. They had received sufficient concessions and promises to put aside the various protest measures they had considered in the course of the year. Hastily convened in Bern on November 7, just three days after the Federal Council's mobilization, the Olten Action Committee made plans to stage a twenty-four-hour strike in nineteen Swiss industrial centers against the unnecessary and undeserved provocation. The limited strike was to be an explicit warning to the federal authorities. If the authorities did not listen to the voice of reason, a general strike would show them that the workers were no longer willing to suffer misery and injustice in silence.[3]

Since the strike was ordered for November 9, a Saturday, only half a workday was lost. But not all cities selected for the protest strike actually participated in it. Labor leaders in Biel, Lausanne, and Geneva informed the Olten committee that they had not had sufficient time to prepare the union membership to ensure a successful execution of the order.[4] In Zurich, on the other hand, labor and party leaders who had previously been critical of the Olten committee for being too cautious, decided, with the enthusiastic support of their members, to continue the strike beyond the twenty-four-hour deadline. They declared that the siege of Zurich forced them to continue the fight, and they vowed that they would not give up until the troops were withdrawn.[5]

Division Commander Colonel Emil Sonderegger, charged by the wartime commander of the Swiss army, General Ulrich Wille, to maintain peace and order in Zurich, had stationed his troops in and around Zurich. Even though the ranks of his soldiers were weakened by the devastating Spanish influenza epidemic, the presence of helmeted cavalry on the Bahnhofstrasse and the Paradeplatz and the appearance of heavy machine gun nests near the Hauptbahnhof and other strategic places were shocking and unnerving.

Sunday, November 10, was the day planned by the Zurich proletarians to celebrate the anniversary of the Bolshevik October revolution. It was also a day when news of the collapse of the German Imperial Army, the overthrow of the Hohenzollerns, and the revolutions in Germany in all their stunning significance stirred the minds of the Zurichers.[6] Colonel Sonderegger had issued stern warnings against staging any public demonstrations. He carried out those warnings when he ordered his troops to disperse the crowd that had assembled on the Fraumünsterplatz. Four civilians were wounded and one soldier was killed in the disorders that ensued. When the people reassembled on the Milchbuck, cavalry with drawn sabers sent them fleeing across the fields and into the streets of Oerlikon and the city.[7]

The events in Zurich and the refusal of the Federal Council to withdraw the troops forced the hand of the Olten Action Committee. At a long and turbulent meeting, of which no minutes were kept, the assembled members called for a national general strike to begin at midnight on Monday, November 11. They hammered out a proclamation *To the Working People of Switzerland* that called for a new federal government and contained a program demanding the immediate reelection of the National Council

on the basis of proportional representation; the right of women to vote
and hold political office; the introduction of a general duty to work; the
introduction of the forty-eight-hour workweek in all public and private
enterprises; the reorganization of the army into a people's army; the
guaranteed supply of food in cooperation with the farmers; the creation of
an old-age and disability insurance system; the establishment of state
monopolies for import and export; and the payment of all goverment
debts by the propertied class.[8] Special directives went to the railroad
workers, exhorting them to join the other workers in an act of solidarity.[9]

The reaction of the Federal Council was swift and firm. It informed the
Swiss people that it had no choice but to reject the demands of the Olten
Action Committee. Although willing to entertain proposals for social and
political change, it could not approve of measures that were taken in
violation of existing political and legal procedures. Attempts to bring
about changes by threats and violence had to be stopped at their inception.
The Federal Council urged the Swiss citizens to help save the fatherland by
supporting the government in this grave crisis. It further announced that
all federal employees, including public transportation workers, were now
subject to military law and would be punished if they participated in the
strike.[10] In order to guarantee order and security, the council ordered the
mobilization of a large number of additional military units. Some 110,000
soldiers—almost one-third of the strength of the total Swiss army—were
under arms in November 1918.[11]

The Federal Council also decided that the time had come to expel the
Soviet mission which had been in Bern since May 1918. On November 12
mission chief Jan Berzin and thirty-two mission employees were loaded
into automobiles and driven under military escort across strike-ridden
eastern Switzerland to the German border near Kreuzlingen, where they
disembarked after a tiring, uncomfortable, and tense trip that lasted more
than twenty hours.[12]

The first day of the national general strike, Tuesday, November 12,
passed without incident. In Zurich and Basel the strike order was carried
out with enthusiasm. In most of the industrial areas of northern and
eastern Switzerland, work came to a halt. Even those workers inclined to
go to work were prevented from doing so because the trains had stopped
running. The strike was less successful in French-speaking Switzerland,
the Romandie. Robert Grimm and the Olten committee did not have
much support there. The Romands accused Grimm of having pro-German
sentiments, and the strike interfered with their mood of jubilation over
the victory of the Entente powers.[13] Even in Zurich and Bern, public life

did not come to a standstill. The University of Zurich, for example, did not close its doors. Leonhard Ragaz, professor of theology and a prominent religious socialist, continued to lecture, even though he was upset that his students "openly sided with the bayonets and money bags."[14] The Bern city council, in which the Social Democrats had a majority, issued an urgent request to all city employees "to appear punctually at work and to fulfill their duty in their usual manner."[15]

On the same Tuesday, the Federal Assembly, the national legislature consisting of the Council of States and the National Council, was meeting in special session. Some of the parliamentarians had to be brought to Bern by military transport. The sixteen Social Democrats in the National Council found that none of the other councillors supported them during two days of debates. In motion after motion they were voted down, and the measures taken by the Federal Council to break the strike were endorsed 136 to 15.[16] Strengthened by this show of support and by reports that the troops were in control of local situations all over Switzerland, the Federal Council gave the Olten Action Committee an ultimatum to call off the strike by 5 P.M., November 13.[17] By 2 A.M., November 14, the Olten committee, complemented by the Social Democratic national councillors, had decided to accept the ultimatum and ask the workers to resume work on Friday morning. Only Grimm and the Basel labor leader Friedrich Schneider voted against this decision.[18]

The broadside announcing the termination of the general strike told the workers the reasons for the capitulation. Even though the strike had been a success in many localities, in Switzerland as a whole, the Olten committee stated, it had not had the desired response and impact. Many railroad workers had sabotaged their unions and union leaders and had continued to work, thus preventing the transportation system from being crippled. Furthermore, the mobilized troops, rather than putting down their arms and joining the strikers, were disciplined and obeyed the orders of their commanders. Finally, the strike order had not been carried out well in most of French- and Italian-speaking Switzerland. All of these factors forced the committee to conclude that adhering to the strike was futile. Its continuation would have led to a bloody confrontation in which all the advantages were with the armed forces of the government.[19]

Only after the call for the strike's termination had gone out across the country did the major incident of the whole general strike take place. In Grenchen, Canton Solothurn, demonstrating workers who tore up the railroad tracks were fired upon by soldiers of a Vaudois batallion. Three of them were killed and several wounded.[20] In Basel and Zurick the striking workers did not believe the news from Bern announcing the termination of the strike. Schneider had to go in person to Basel to convince the assembled workers that the decision indeed had been made and that it was in their best interest to obey it.[21] In Zurich, Ernst Nobs, fiery editor of the Social Democratic daily *Volksrecht,* denounced the decision as a betrayal of the Swiss labor movement. But after a heated debate, cooler heads prevailed, and a majority of the Zurich labor leaders voted to accept the termination of the strike.[22] Not all unions resumed work the next day; some factories were back to normal only by the following Monday (November 18).

In the meantime, the victors of this crisis wanted to savor their moment of triumph. On Saturday, November 16, General Wille in person reviewed the army units that had guarded Zurich. The many spectators along the lakeshore applauded the soldiers marching past them and showered them with flowers. The commander of the Bern forces, however, declined to stage a similar event. Corps Commander Colonel Eduard Wildbolz reported to his general that serious medical reasons spoke against a parade. The flu epidemic that had decimated the ranks of the soldiers served as a pretext for omitting a gesture that could be nothing but offensive and humiliating to the defeated opponent.[23]

The effect of the general strike reverberated through Switzerland for a long time. At the second General Swiss Labor Congress in Bern on December 22–23, 1918, the Olten Action Committee was sharply criticized for having stirred up the masses with revolutionary slogans which they themselves did not believe. The radical wing of the labor movement, represented by party secretary Fritz Platten, was told to recognize that the Swiss workers were not interested in a violent overthrow of the government. Reform, not revolution, was the prescription for Switzerland, and a future national general strike was to be launched only with the express approval of the labor congress.[24]

In spring 1919 twenty-one strike leaders were brought to trial before a military tribunal. The procedures gave them a chance to describe once again the plight of the working class during the war years and to condemn the unwillingness of the bourgeoisie to respond to their justified demands for improvements of the social, economic, and political conditions of the laboring masses.[25] Robert Grimm, Friedrich Schneider, and Friedrich Platten (in absentia) were found guilty of the charge of incitement to mutiny through the publication and distibution of the November 11 pamphlet, *An das arbeitende Volk,* that contained a passage calling for soldiers to form soviets and to disobey orders to shoot at their fellow citizens. Ernst Nobs was found guilty of incitement through a subversive editorial in the *Volksrecht*. The first three were sentenced to six months' imprisonment, the minimum penalty available to the court, and Nobs to four weeks. Together they had to bear almost half of the trial costs, some 1,100 francs. The rest of the cost was paid by the court. The other seventeen accused were found not guilty.[26]

When the Federal Assembly refused to grant amnesty, the four served their sentences in different parts of Switzerland. Since the tribunal had expressly stated that they had not acted from "personal, greedy, or dishonorable motives," their political rights were not suspended.[27] Grimm continued serving in the National Council and was elected its president in 1946. Nobs became mayor of Zurich and the first Social Democratic federal councillor in 1943 and president of the Swiss Confederation in 1948.

The national general strike of 1918 stirred deep emotions in Switzerland, and it is still considered a major event and turning point in the history of the modern Swiss state.[28] The strike had created a moment of severe crisis and had posed apparent danger to the established democratic order of the country. It raised the possibility of class warfare and the violent overthrow of the government at the very moment when such upheavals rocked other European countries. The issue debated then and for decades to come was whether the strike indeed had been an attempt to stage a revolution according to the Russian Bolshevik example, or whether it was basically a protest by the Swiss workers against the harshness of their living conditions. If it was the former, then it must have been planned and conducted with the guidance and under the influence of external forces. If the strike was primarily a domestic event, it was brought about by the provocations of the ruling elements in the country.[29]

The Swiss bourgeoisie was convinced that the socialists wanted a revolution. Typical of many statements to that effect is that of Walter Boveri, twenty-four years old in 1918, son of a prospering Baden industrialist. In his autobiography he wrote: "Later it was often claimed that the strike was merely a struggle for the improvement of the working class and not an attempt to overthrow the political and social structure of the country. Those who lived through those times, however, cannot doubt that the leaders of the movement aimed at the destruction of the existing system. . . . For many people it was difficult to forget that the revolution had been really planned."[30]

What aside from class differences and deep-seated resentments toward the rising labor movement were the reasons that induced such firm convictions?[31] They can be found in some of the events and developments that took place in Switzerland during World War I.

At the outbreak of the war the Swiss Social Democratic legislators, like their comrades all over Europe, had joined their bourgeois counterparts in approving the measures that gave the government the emergency powers to prepare the country for war. Those were the days of the *Burgfrieden,* the *union sacrée*—the sacred union in support of the fatherland in times of danger.

The euphoria of those days did not last long. As early as December 1914 some of the leading Social Democrats, among them Robert Grimm, argued that the party should withdraw its support of the war-mongering classes. The Federal Council, in their view, used the special war powers it had received to control the economy of the country only to help industrialists, war profiteers, and farmers at the expense of the employees and blue-collar workers.[32] Grimm invited socialists from European countries to a conference in Switzerland to discuss a socialist program and socialist tactics in response to the madness of the war. The conference of September 5–8, 1915, held in the village of Zimmerwald near Bern, brought together thirty-eight persons whose names read like an honor roll of world revolutionaries. The official result of the conference, the Zimmerwald manifesto *To the Proletarians of Europe,* was relatively innocuous, inasmuch as it was a compromise of conflicting viewpoints among the participants. More significant was Lenin's move toward reconciliation with Leon Trotsky and his discovery in Karl Radek of another radical who openly advocated world revolution.[33]

The so-called Zimmerwald Left around Lenin came with its own program to the second conference (also organized and chaired by Grimm), held April 24–30, 1916, in Kiental, Bernese Oberland. Lenin clashed openly with Grimm, whose strong personality was a roadblock to Lenin's undisputed leadership. The Swiss Social Democratic party was officially represented; it was the only European party that had adopted the Zimmerwald program at its party congress. Even though the proceedings at the conferences were secret, enough information filtered out to alert the public to significant and potentially dangerous conspiratorial developments. Furthermore, the participants could not contain their animosities and revealed their competing programs in the socialist newspaper press.

The Zimmerwald Left developed a strong propaganda activity in Zurich. Lenin and Radek both tried to convince their Swiss friends to oppose openly the concept of Swiss national defense and to break with those Social Democrats who were unwilling to vote against further military expenditures.[34] Rallies by the Socialist Youth under the German deserter Willi Münzenberg culminated in the demonstrations against the army on Red Sunday, September 3, 1916, in several Swiss cities.

Lenin's influence did not seem to diminish after his departure, in the famous sealed railroad car, for Stockholm in April 1917. The news of the Bolshevik victory in the October revolution was hailed by the Swiss socialist press as the dawn of a new day. The more radical element within the Social Democratic party, especially in Zurich, called for a revolution at home. Grave incidents in Zurich, which cost the lives of four persons and during which the labor leaders lost control over their wilder comrades, seemed to be a clear indication of Bolshevik agitation.[35] Even though right-wing and moderate segments of the party condemned these activities and opposed such talk—they were denounced by Lenin and his followers as social patriots, opportunists, defectors to the bourgeoisie, and worse— the bourgeoisie registered with growing concern how foreigners and foreign ideas radicalized the working-class movement.[36]

This concern was greatly heightened by developments that involved national defense and the army. In the extraordinary party meeting in Bern on June 9–10, 1917, a majority of the delegates (227 to 77) voted not to support the national defense effort any longer. This act, which created grave conflicts of conscience for many party members, was received by the nonsocialist compatriots as a kind of treason, a withdrawal from the community of *Eidgenossen* in times of danger to the country.[37] Furthermore, the army itself seemed to become an object of defeatist infiltration. Private First Class Walther Bringolf of Schaffhausen founded the first soldier's club in September 1917 with the goal of improving the treatment and feeding of the troops.[38] The idea proved to be popular; before long some five thousand soldiers joined the Swiss Soldiers' Alliance (Schweizerischer Soldatenbund). General Wille watched this development with disgust and suspicion. He suspected the organization to be a front for soldiers' soviets and asked that the Federal Council order its dissolution.[39]

At their regular 1917 meeting of October 9, 1917, the Social Democratic party delegates openly discussed an active program for a general strike. Later the Olten Action Committee worked out a plan which foresaw the possibility of an unlimited general strike that would lead to civil war and aimed at the overthrow of the bourgeois class system, but shied away from advocating such an approach as its first priority.[40] Grimm's leadership was opposed by some of the unions and the moderate leaders of the party who saw in the Olten committee an usurper of their authority.[41] But the General Labor Congress in Basel on July 27–28, 1918, endorsed the actions of the Olten committee and directed it to take the necessary steps for the preparation of a general strike.[42]

Still another factor that contributed to the suspiciousness and apprehension was the presence of the Soviety mission in Bern. On May 19, 1918, a mission of the Russian Soviet Socialist Republic headed by the Latvian Jan Berzin took up residence in Bern. After evicting the chargé d'affaires of the old Russian government from the legation building on Schwanengasse, Berzin deployed his employees in the many activities which a diplomatic mission is supposed to carry out. Before long rumors were widespread that the Bolsheviks engaged in active propaganda work aimed at fomenting revolution in Switzerland and in the neighboring Entente countries and that they had considerable sums of money to buy the services of agitators and traitors.[43]

The event that brought home to the bourgeoisie the danger of the situation took place in Zurich in early fall 1918. On September 30 the employees of all major banks went on strike to protest their salaries which, they maintained, did not allow them a decent existence in the face of steadily rising prices. Such an action by white-collar workers who belonged neither to the Swiss Cartel of Unions nor the Social Democratic party was unprecedented. Organized labor in Zurich immediately staged a sympathy strike out of solidarity with their suffering brothers. The dual action proved effective. The bankers, who had closed their ears to the many petitions submitted previously, now granted the demands of their employees. Salaries were doubled, and the employees' organization was officially recognized by the banking syndicate.

When the workers of Zurich called off the strike on October 1, they could celebrate a substantial victory. The bourgeoisie, however, vowed to be prepared the next time. Chief of General Staff Theophil von Sprecher deplored that the troops had not been used to break the strike: "What has happened on October 1 in Zurich is no more and no less than the capitulation of bourgeois government to the revolutionary mass. Whether the bank employees were right to strike or not is absolutely no concern of the army. We do not hinder those who want to strike, but lawful order under the control of the troops may not be toppled. Not even for one day."[44]

Under the pressure of these developments the Federal Council made a number of preparations for the eventuality of further and more serious disturbances. It created a national strike commission that submitted a secret report on the measures to be taken in response to a nationwide upheaval. The report was adopted by the Federal Council on October

29.[45] The central staff of the Swiss army worked out plans for counter-measures in the event the revolutionaries succeeded in arresting the members of the federal and cantonal governments.[46] General Wille asked that he be given authority to intervene in emergency situations without prior invitation by the cantonal governments, but the Federal Council felt that it could not give the general such blanket powers.[47]

Wille, upset by the decision, repeated his request. He pointed out to the Federal Council that it did not make sense to prepare secret measures for a counterrevolution without doing everything in one's power to prevent the revolution in the first place. In a long memorandum of November 4, 1918, the general expressed the view that Swiss particularism was one of the major causes for the danger in which the Confederation found itself. The local authorities did not want "foreign" troops—units from other cantons—in their communities and underrated the efficiency and dangerousness of the well-prepared Bolsheviks. The Zurich government in particular had demonstrated that it was unable to act as decisively and firmly as was needed to put an end to disturbances and to prevent bloodshed. Neither the argument that a mobilization would be provocative nor that the flu epidemic forbade the assembly of large numbers of young men weighed much in view of the seriousness of the situation. Declaring himself willing to assume responsibility for the consequences of such a step, Wille again asked for the mobilization of additional troops.[48]

Labor was getting ready to celebrate the anniversary of the Bolshevik October revolution. The executive council of the Social Democratic party issued a proclamation calling upon its members to honor their Russian comrades by staging public mass rallies: "The approaching revolution is reddening the sky over Central Europe. The redeeming conflagration will envelop the whole rotten bloody structure of the capitalist world."[49] A cache of bombs was found in Seebach on the outskirts of Zurich. Reports of preparations for an attack on military installations in Zurich circulated widely and were passed on to Bern. Events on the battlefronts of the war, the impending collapse of the Central Powers, and the revolutionary stirrings in Germany further contributed to the widespread apprehensions. The Zurich government urged the Federal Council to be ready to strengthen the troops in Zurich at a moment's notice.[50]

The Federal Council was under pressure to act not only from the general of the Swiss army and his staff and from an increasingly insecure cantonal government but also from foreign governments. Both France and Italy took steps through diplomatic channels to warn the Federal Council against the consequences of Bolshevik disorders in Switzerland. The

French minister in Bern, Paul Dutasta, officially complained that the preventive measures taken by the Federal Council against the Bolsheviks had no teeth and threatened that France would close its border with Switzerland in order to keep the poison from spreading westward. The Italian government let it be known that it was displeased that the Federal Council allowed Angelica Balabanoff to prepare the revolution while living in Switzerland.[51] The American president and his secretary of state, who were considering Switzerland as the venue for the upcoming peace conference, wrote that it was "saturated with every poisonous element and open to every hostile influence in Europe" and "the headquarters of Bolsheviks and other revolutionaries."[52] Rumors circulated in Bern that units of the American Expeditionary Force were assembling at the French border to invade Switzerland.[53]

Late on Tuesday, November 5, members of the cantonal government of Zurich met with members of the Federal Council and the general and his chief of staff. They had come to Bern to ask for military protection of the city of Zurich. The danger of revolution in the neighboring countries, the agitation of the *Volksrecht,* the upcoming anniversary celebration, the ties of the socialists with the Russian soviets, all convinced the Zurich magistrates that the time had come to take this fateful step. General Wille firmly supported them, except in their wish to use Zurich battalions. He thought that the peasants from central and eastern Switzerland could be better trusted to make use of their weapons in case of need than the Zurich soldiers.[54] The next morning the Federal Council endorsed the decision to mobilize troops and sent them to Zurich.[55]

There can be little doubt that the responsible governmental authorities acted from a sense of reluctant necessity in what they perceived to be the interest of the country. The Federal Council had refused to be stampeded into hasty decisions either by the general or foreign diplomats or prominent citizens. Consistently it had rejected complaints and accusation as unfounded rumors and had asked for concrete substantiation. It also had kept the lines of communications open with the Olten Action Committee and negotiated in good faith with it.

General Wille and his military advisers, on their part, made neither unreasonable suppositions nor exaggerated demands. The only maneuver that might be interpreted as having a Machiavellian design was Wille's order on November 4 to move the Neuchatel battalion that had been guarding Zurich to the Austrian border. For some hours Zurich was without the protection of troops, which helped to scare the Zurich government into asking for increased mobilization the next day.[56]

Considering how socialist and union rhetoric in the press, books, broadsides, posters, and speeches had contributed to the climate of uncertainty and apprehension and taking into account Social Democratic election victories and strikes during 1917 and 1918, it is understandable that an important segment of the Swiss population believed that the country was in danger of a revolutionary upheaval. Yet when all the known facts and factors are taken into account and weighed, the conclusion still has to be that the national general strike of November 1918 in Switzerland was provoked rather than planned, and that it was primarily an act of protest triggered by domestic causes rather than a revolutionary attempt in response to foreign influences.

Underlying the widespread labor dissatisfaction and unrest was not so much foreign-inspired socialist propaganda as the very real distress of the working class in wartime Switzerland. Prices of daily necessities such as pork, bread, butter, potatoes, and coal doubled and then tripled between April 1914 and March 1919. Wages were lowered at the outbreak of the war and never kept step with the rising living costs. Real wages dropped by about 30 percent, and thousands of people depended on welfare support to feed their families. One-fourth of the population of Zurich and 692,000 of the 3.8 million Swiss were in that situation in 1918.[57] They watched the privileged owners and stockholders of the chemical, metal, and food industries flourish and make rich profits year after year.

The farmers, organized in an influential lobbying group, also did very well during the war. By 1918 the average daily income of a farmer, except that of the mountain peasants, was twice that of a blue-collar worker. The farmers were important allies of the bourgeoisie and could be counted upon to oppose the workers and their Social Democratic leaders stubbornly and unwaveringly. Grimm as editor of the Bern *Tagwacht* and Nobs at the Zurich *Volksrecht,* among others, frequently and strongly denounced the injustices of the economic system and called for much-needed reforms. The Olten Action Committee bargained with the Federal Council for the amelioration of these conditions, with some success, notably on the issue of the price of milk in April 1918.[58]

Under the influences of the expanding distress, Swiss workers became better organized. Membership in the Social Democratic party increased from 33,230 in 1914 to 52,160 in 1919, and union membership jumped from 69,990 in 1915 to 223,500 in 1919.[59] These increases gave the workers strong governmental representation in the major cities but did not create tangible political influence at the national level. The Olten Action Committee at least gave the semblance of a united front. A personal creation of Robert Grimm, the committee, without initial authorization of the component parts of its members, the party, the cartel of unions, or the Social Democratic members of the federal Parliament, spoke on behalf of the entire Swiss labor force. It was a convenient forum for the representatives of the various labor groups and a useful body for the federal government to negotiate with. Its authority and power, however, were limited, as was proved when it called for the protest strike of November 9 and even more when neither the French- nor the Italian-speaking workers joined in the general strike on November 12.

The labor movement did not have much cohesion even during the hard times of the war. The right wing of the party, the social-patriotic Grütli association, was expelled from the party in fall 1916.[60] Moderates, such as veteran socialist "Papa" Herman Greulich, were ridiculed by the radicals when they warned against undisciplined behavior and loose talk of general strike and revolution. Yet the rank and file tended to elect moderates to office. Neither the Social Democratic Bern mayor Gustav Müller, a lieutenant colonel in the Swiss army, nor the Social Democrats in the Zurich city council favored violent means to gain their ends. Most of the Social Democrats in the National Council spoke out against and voted down radical motions at the party congresses. Even though outvoted there, they would continue their protests while carrying out their mandates. Even stranger, the voters did not hold their actions against them and sent them right back to Bern. It is no wonder that Lenin despaired of the Swiss socialists.[61]

The left wing of the party was divided in its turn. At the core of that division was the incompatibility of the two strong personalities of Grimm and Lenin. Grimm overshadowed Lenin at the Zimmerwald and Kiental conferences, and Lenin left Bern for Zurich because he had no chance of gathering a following on the home turf of Grimm.[62] But Grimm's shadow was present even in Zurich. Platten and Nobs, Lenin's most prominent Swiss supporters, caught Lenin's scorn for agreeing with Grimm on some tactical and procedural matters at the Zurich party congress in November 1916. The "scoundrel" Grimm was accused by Lenin of deceiving the others, and Nobs and Platten were labeled "completely characterless guys (if not worse)" who "feared Grimm more than fire. . . . Shame, shame! And these want to be leftists!"[63] The party congress demonstrated convincingly that Lenin had little influence, even though he participated in it. His attempt to use left extremists either to split the party or to commit it to a straightforward revolutionary program failed. Their motion was opposed by Grimm, and when Nobs and Platten gave in, it was defeated 82 to 32.[64]

Two other factors made it difficult to create a united labor movement in

Switzerland. The unions, with some notable exceptions, were on the whole less doctrinaire and more practically oriented than the party. Their leaders did not relish the heated debates over theoretical dogmas and therefore often put a damper on the revolutionary fervor of the radicals. The federalist structure of Switzerland, where every canton and every major city had its own party organization, proved to be a serious obstacle for any would-be national leader. At the decisive moment, working-class solidarity did not materialize. Of the 800,000 wage earners, only 250,000 participated in the national strike.[65]

Most ironically, neither Grimm, nor the Olten committee, nor anybody else in the Swiss labor movement had planned for a general strike to start when it did. The Olten committee had just been assured that the Federal Council would give serious consideration to most of its demands and was by no means preparing for a major coup. The committee, like everybody else, was surprised by the announcement of the mobilization of troops for the "protection" of Zurich and other cities. That was the action that determined the next weeks' events.

Whether or not a national strike would have taken place in Switzerland without that fateful decision by the Federal Council is a question that cannot be answered. That the Federal Council made its decision on the flimsiest of grounds, however, is amply documented; there were no urgent concrete reasons for it to abandon its course of moderation and concilia-tion. Neither the protestations of the general nor the diplomatic pressure by foreign governments established a firm basis for action. And the argu-ments used by the Zurich magistrates (without having been checked with the city government) were derived from such events as anonymous tele-phone calls, professorial letters, and the apprehension of bankers. All the contentions that the Social Democrats had plans for an uprising in Zurich around November 10 were rumors that no researcher has been able to substantiate.[66]

Another issue debated since the general strike is whether the strike hurt or helped the absorption of the Swiss working-class movement into the mainstream of the social and political life of Switzerland. There can be no doubt that the national strike left a deep feeling of animosity and suspi-cion toward the socialists among the farmers and the bourgeois classes of the cities. Of course, none of these groups was well disposed toward labor even before the strike. They were not willing to forgive and forget quickly. Already during the strike, voluntary citizen defense groups organized in many towns to combat the socialists. Now they demanded federal guaran-tees against the recurrence of a national strike. Neither the Federal Council nor the top echelon of the army was enamored with their actions and ideas. Leaders of these groups formed the center of the later frontist fatherland movement that was to have its day during the early 1930s.[67]

For the workers, the strike had no direct impact. The year 1919 saw many more work stoppages, including new general strikes in Zurich and Basel. However, the workers, with the exception of a relatively small segment that formed the Swiss Communist party, realized that they had to fight for their demands within the established constitutional framework and according to the ground rules of the prevailing political processes. The Federal Council, which had been willing to negotiate with the Olten Action Committee right up to the ultimatum of November 13, conceded the justification for some of labor's demands and felt obligated to attempt to implement them. New elections for the National Council on the basis of proportional representation were called for October 1919, a year earlier than planned. The outcome was a disappointment for the Social Democrats. Instead of winning 50 to 60 seats, as expected, they received only 41 (out of 189). The Liberals lost the dominant position they had held since the founding of the modern Swiss state in 1848. But since most of the seats were lost to the Catholic Conservatives and the newly founded Peasant party, the real victors under the new system, the bourgeois bloc, was as strong as it had been before.[68]

The next demand of the Olten committee was for a forty-eight-hour workweek. After the necessary fact-finding and legislative process had taken place, a federal law was enacted on January 1, 1920, that made the legal workweek forty-eight hours. The Federal Council also submitted a proposal for old-age and disability insurance to the Federal Assembly in summer 1919 with a plan of how to finance such a social security system. The deliberations were difficult and protracted, and the insurance scheme was not enacted into law until after World War II. However, the legislators agreed to create a Federal Labor Office in 1920, and in 1924 they passed a law providing financial contributions to unemployment insurance. The road to woman's suffrage was rockier still. It took a full half century until that basic political right was adopted at the federal level.[69]

The depressions of the early 1920s and the middle 1930s were not conducive to the improvement of the living and working conditions of the working class. By 1935, however, political developments in neighboring Germany had made clear the need for all major Swiss parties to pool their resources to prepare for resistance to the growing threat from abroad. The Social Democrats gave up their opposition to military expenditures and came out in support of national defense. In 1937 the path-breaking peace

agreement between the workers in the metal industries and their employers established procedures for the resolution of conflicts through
binding negotiations at the bargaining table rather than by disruptive
strikes.[70]

The outbreak of World War II found the Swiss Confederation much
better prepared than it had been in August 1914. The lessons of World
War I had been learned; the social and economic needs of all segments of
the population received great attention from the federal government, and
the supply of food was well regulated. By 1943, finally, the time was right
to admit the first Social Democrat to the Federal Council. The Social
Democrats now participated in the national government, and even though
their expectations about the results of that participation differed considerably from those of their bourgeois counterparts, the end effect amounted
to a confirmation of the political system which, a quarter century earlier,
they had seriously endangered through their national general strike.

Notes

1. Minutes of the Meeting of the Federal Council of Nov. 6, 1918, Doc. no. 69
in Willi Gautschi, *Dokumente zum Landesstreik 1918* (Zurich, 1971), pp. 186–
87; Appeal of the Federal Council of Nov. 17, 1918, to the Swiss People, Doc. no.
73, ibid., pp. 196–98.

2. *Volksrecht* (Newspaper of the Social Democratic party in Zurich), Nov. 7,
1918, Doc. no. 72, ibid., p. 195.

3. Minutes of the 21st meeting of the Olten Action Committee, Nov. 7, 1918,
Doc. no. 76, ibid., pp. 203–4; Broadside of the Olten Action Committee, Nov. 7,
1918, Doc. no. 77, ibid., pp. 204–6. For a listing of the membership of the Olten
committee and its meetings from February 1918 to September 1919, see Willi
Gautschi, *Der Landesstreik 1918* (Zurich, 1968), pp. 396–98.

4. United Union Leaders, Biel, to the Olten Action Committee, Nov. 8, 1918,
Doc. no. 84, Gautschi, *Dokumente*, pp. 227–28.

5. Broadside of the Workers' Union to the Workers of Zurich, Doc. no. 88,
ibid., pp. 234–35.

6. The turbulent era of World War I, culminating in the general strike of
November 1918, inspired a number of Swiss writers to create major literary works
whose characters are set against the background of that time. Among them are
Charles-Ferdinand Ramuz, *Les signes parmi nous* (Lausanne, 1919); Jakob Boss-
hart, *Ein Rufer in der Wüste* (Leipzig and Zurich, 1921); Meinrad Inglin, *Schwei-
zerspiegel* (Leipzig, 1938); and Kurt Guggenheim, *Alles in Allem, Zweites Buch,
1914–1919* (Zurich, 1957).

7. Speech by Hermann Greulich in the National Council, Nov. 12, 1918, *Steno-
graphisches Bulletin* of the Federal Assembly, National Council (Bern 1918), pp.
442–47, Doc. no. 133, Gautschi, *Dokumente*, pp. 286–88.

8. Broadside of the Olten Action Committee, Nov. 11, 1918, Doc. no. 91, ibid., p. 238.

9. Leaders of the Cartel of the United Railroad Personnel Organizations to the Railroad Workers of All Categories, Nov. 11, 1918, Doc. no. 92, ibid., pp. 240–41.

10. Proclamation by the Federal Council of Nov. 11, 1918, to the People of Switzerland, Doc. no. 93, ibid., pp., 244–45; Announcement concerning the Measures against the Threat to and Disruption of the Domestic Security of the Swiss Confederation, Bern, Nov. 11, 1918, Doc. no. 42, ibid., pp. 245–47.

11. Gautschi, *Landesstreik*, p. 245.

12. Report about the departure of the Russian Soviet Mission for Germany, Nov. 12–15, 1918, for the Political Department by Dr. V. Jacob, Bern, Nov. 20, 1918, Doc. no. 135, Gautschi, *Dokumente*, pp. 347–62. See also Alfred Erich Senn, *Diplomacy and Revolution: The Soviet Mission in Switzerland, 1918* (Notre Dame, Ind., 1974).

13. Senn, *Diplomacy*, pp. 288–89. Constant Frey, in *La grève générale de 1918. Légendes et réalités* (Geneva, 1969), includes material from French-speaking Swiss cities in his general account of the strike. The Basel situation is described in great detail by Markus Bolliger, *Die Basler Arbeiterbewegung im Zeitalter des Ersten Weltkrieges und der Spaltung der Sozialdemokratischen Partei* (Basel, 1970). Thomas Rohr's *Schaffhausen und der Landesstreik von 1918* (Schaffhausen, 1972) does the same for the city on the Rhinefall.

14. Markus Mattmüller, *Leonhard Ragaz und der religiöse Sozialismus* (Zurich, 1968), 2:416–18.

15. City Council of Bern to the Employees and Workers of the City Administration, Nov. 11, 1918, Handbill, Doc. no. 102, in Gautschi, *Dokumente*, pp. 263–64; Fritz Marbach, *Der Generalstreik 1918: Fakten, Impressionen, Illusionen* (Bern, 1969), p. 50.

16. Gautschi, *Landesstreik*, pp. 308–12; speeches by Felix Calonder, Hermann Greulich, and Robert Grimm, Docs. nos. 108, 113, 115, Gautschi, *Dokumente*, pp. 270–76, 280–92, 293–307.

17. Federal Council to Robert Grimm for the Olten Action Committee, not dated (Nov. 13); Facsimile of ultimatum in Gautschi, *Landesstreik*, p. 311.

18. Gautschi, *Landesstreik*, pp. 318–21.

19. To the Workers of Switzerland, Broadside, Bern, Nov. 14, 1918, Doc. no. 125, Gautschi, *Dokumente*, pp. 320–21.

20. Gautschi, *Landesstreik*, p. 328.

21. Bolliger, *Die Basler Arbeiterbewegung*, pp. 118–19.

22. Ernst Nobs editorial, "The Swiss General Strike," *Volksrecht*, no. 267, Zurich, Nov. 15, 1918, Doc. no. 126, Gautschi, *Dokumente*, pp. 322–24; Gautschi, *Landesstreik*, pp. 327–28.

23. Gautschi, *Landesstreik*, pp. 330–31.

24. Ibid., pp. 342–49.

25. Statement by Robert Grimm at the National Strike Trial, Doc. no. 147, Gautschi, *Dokumente*, pp. 418–27.

26. Sentencing of the Strike Leaders, April 10, 1919, Doc. no. 149, ibid., pp. 431–32.

27. Paul Schmid-Ammann, *Die Wahrheit über den Generalstreik von 1918: Seine Ursachen, sein Verlauf, seine Folgen* (Zurich, 1968), pp. 346–47.

28. Marc Vuilleumier, "Le mouvement ouvrier en Suisse pendant et après la première guerre mondiale: Bilan historiographique," *Le mouvement social* 84 (1973): 97.

29. The traditional "official" historiography consistently emphasizes the international, revolutionary aspects of the general strike, most recently Erich Gruner, ed., *Die Wahlen in den Schweizerischen Nationalrat 1848–1919* (Bern, 1978), 1:1079. After the fiftieth anniversary of the strike this emphasis changed: the key work is Willi Gautschi's *Der Landesstreik 1918* and his *Dokumente zum Landesstreik 1918*. Schmid-Ammann's *Die Wahrheit über den Generalstreik von 1918* covers much the same ground. The general strike appears as an episode of varying significance in the autobiographies and biographies of many persons who lived through that event. Examples of such works, among many others, are Walther Bringolf, *Mein Leben: Weg und Umweg eines Schweizer Sozialdemokraten* (Bern, 1965); Walter Boveri, *Ein Weg im Wandel der Zeit* (Munich, 1964), vol. 1; Jules Humbert-Droz, *Mon évolution du tolstoïsme au communisme, 1891–1921* (Neuchâtel, 1969); Hermann Böschenstein, *Bundesrat Edmund Schulthess: Krieg und Krisen* (Bern, 1966); J. R. von Salis, *Giuseppe Motta: Dreissig Jahre eidgenössische Politik* (Zurich, 1941); Mattmüller, *Leonhard Ragaz und der religiöse Sozialismus*, vol. 2. In addition to significant local studies, such as Bolliger's and Rohr's on Basel and Schaffhausen, Christine Nöthiger-Strahm's *Der deutsch-schweizerische Protestantismus und der Landesstreik von 1918* (Bern, 1981) and Martin Fenner's *Partei und Parteisprache im Politischen Konflikt: Studien zu Struktur und Funktion politischer Gruppensprachen zur Zeit des schweizerischen Landesstreiks, 1917–1919* (Bern, 1981) address still other neglected aspects of the history of the period.

30. Boveri, *Ein Weg*, 1:327–32.

31. For an authoritative and detailed description of the working-class movement in Switzerland before World War I, see Erich Gruner, *Die Arbeiter in der Schweiz im 19. Jahrhundert* (Bern, 1968). The documentary volume *Schweizerische Arbeiterbewegung: Dokumente zu Lage, Organisation und Kämpfen der Arbeiter von der Frühindustrialisierung bis zur Gegenwart* (Zurich, 1975) gives a more abbreviated and partisan overview of the struggles of the Swiss workers during the last two centuries.

32. Schmid-Ammann, *Die Wahrheit*, p. 34.

33. Ernst Kux, "Zimmerwald und der internationale Kommunismus," *Neue Zürcher Zeitung*, Sept. 14, 1965. Alfred Erich Senn's *The Russian Revolution in Switzerland, 1914–1917* (Madison, Wis., 1971) gives an account of the intrigues and maneuverings of competing groups of Russian émigrés in neutral Switzerland, and Alexander Solzhenitsyn's *Lenin in Zurich* (New York, 1976) presents a realistic and convincing picture of the life of the exiled revolutionary.

34. Karl Radek to Nobs and Platten, July 30, 1916, and Lenin to Arthur Schmid, Dec. 1, 1916, Docs. nos. 7 and 9, Gautschi, *Dokumente*, pp. 39–42, 46–48, 376.

35. Gautschi, *Landesstreik*, pp. 4–5, 60–61.

36. Ibid., pp. 68–69; Lenin's "Farewell Letter to the Swiss Workers," Doc. no. 86, *Schweizerische Arbeiterbewegung*, pp. 174–75.

37. Gautschi, *Landesstreik*, pp. 74–75.

38. Bringolf, *Mein Leben*, pp. 53–54.

39. Gautschi, *Landesstreik*, p. 82.

40. Minutes of the meeting of the Olten Committee, Bern, March 1–3, 1918, Doc. no. 22, Gautschi, *Dokumente,* pp. 68–74.

41. Paul Schmid-Ammann, *Emil Klöti, Stadtpräsident von Zürich: Ein schweizerischer Staatsmann* (Zurich, 1965), pp. 102–3.

42. Schmid-Ammann, *Die Wahrheit,* pp. 130–39.

43. Gautschi, *Landesstreik,* pp. 156–62. See also Senn's *Diplomacy and Revolution.*

44. Quoted in Schmid-Amman, *Die Wahrheit,* p. 186. The story of the strike of the Zurich bank employees is in ibid., pp. 176–86.

45. The Chief of the Justice and Police Department on behalf of the National Strike Commission to the Federal Council, Bern, Oct. 7, 1918, Doc. no. 49, Gautschi, *Dokumente,* pp. 137–45.

46. Army Staff, Instructions for the Chiefs of Staff of the Divisions and Army Corps, Bern, Nov. 1, 1918, Doc. no. 57, ibid., pp. 159–61.

47. Wille to Calonder, Nov. 1, 1918, and Minutes of the Meeting of the Federal Council, Nov. 1, 1918, 9:30 P.M., Docs. nos. 59 and 60, ibid., pp. 162–65.

48. Wille to Federal Councilor Camille Decoppet, Nov. 4, 1918, Doc. no. 62, ibid., pp. 167–75.

49. *Volksrecht,* Oct. 31, 1918, Doc. no. 55, ibid., pp. 155–57.

50. Council President Gustav Keller to President Calonder, Oct. 31, 1918, Doc. no. 56, ibid., pp. 157–58.

51. Minutes of meeting of Federal Council, Nov. 4, 1918, Doc. no. 63, ibid., pp. 175–76; Gautschi, *Landesstreik,* pp. 211–13.

52. See Heinz K. Meier, *Friendship under Stress: U.S.-Swiss Relations 1900–1950* (Bern, 1970), pp. 106–7.

53. Edgar Bonjour, *Geschichte der schweizerischen Neutralität* (Basel, 1967), 2:714–18, and Hans Beat Kunz, *Weltrevolution und Völkerbund: Die schweizerische Aussenpolitik unter dem Eindruck der bolschewistischen Bedrohung 1918–1923* (Bern, 1981), pp. 65–66.

54. Minutes of the Conference on the Situation in Zurich, Nov. 15, 1918, Doc. no. 68, Gautschi, *Dokumente,* pp. 183–85.

55. Minutes of the Meeting of the Federal Council, Nov. 6, 1918, Doc. no. 69, ibid., pp. 186–87.

56. Schmid-Ammann, *Die Wahrheit,* p. 215.

57. *Schweizerische Arbeiterbewegung,* pp. 159–60. For the description of the situation in a particular locality, see Rohr, *Schaffhausen,* pp. 29–35.

58. Gautschi, *Landesstreik,* pp. 60–61.

59. *Schweizerische Arbeiterbewegung,* pp. 403, 398.

60. Gautschi, *Landesstreik,* pp. 60–61.

61. Lenin to Inessa F. Armand, Zurich, Feb. 7, 1917, Doc. no. 13, Gautschi, *Dokumente,* p. 55. Hans-Ulrich Jost's *Linksradikalismus in der deutschen Schweiz 1914–1918* (Bern, 1973) is the authoritative work on the left radicals and their colorful, yet divided and divisive, movement during the war.

62. Solzhenitsyn, *Lenin,* p. 86.

63. Lenin to Armand, Jan. 8, Feb. 14, 1917, Docs. nos. 11 and 13, Gautschi, *Dokumente,* pp. 51, 54–55.

64. Ibid., p. 56; Gruner, *Die Wahlen in den schweizerischen Nationalrat,* 1: 787.

65. Gautschi, *Landesstreik,* pp. 296–97.

66. The flimsiness of the basis for the decision of the Federal Council to send troops to Zurich is confirmed by Documents nos. 50 and 51 (editorial by Professor Fritz Fleiner in the *Neue Zürcher Zeitung* of Oct. 20, 1918, and letter of Fleiner to President Caloner, Oct. 25, 1918); Doc. no. 62 (Memorandum of Wille to Federal Councillor Decoppet, Nov. 4, 1918); Doc. no. 67 (Report about a plan for an uprising in Zurich by Otto Heusser, extraordinary prosecutor, Nov. 5, 1918); Doc. no. 68 (Minutes of the meeting of the Federal Council with members of the Zurich [cantonal] government, Nov. 5, 1918); and Doc. no. 69 (Minutes of the meeting of the Federal Council of Nov. 6, 1918), all in Gautschi, *Dokumente*, pp. 145–50, 167–75, 182–87.

67. Gautschi, *Landesstreik*, pp. 366–68.

68. Hektor Ammann and Karl Schib, eds., *Historischer Atlas der Schweiz* (Aarau, 1951), p. 36; *Handbuch der Schweizer Geschichte* (2 vols., Zurich, 1972–77), 2:1140–41.

69. Gautschi, *Landesstreik*, pp. 374–77; and Frey, *La grève générale*, pp. 185–88.

70. See Association for Historical Research in Economics, *Swiss Pioneers of Economics and Technology*, vol. 2: *The Peace Agreement in the Swiss Engineering and Metal Working Industries* (Zurich, 1967).

3

Denmark, 1918

CAROL GOLD

There was no revolution in Denmark in 1918. There was revolution to the north in Finland, to the east in Russia, and to the south in Germany, but nonbelligerent Denmark followed instead the pattern of the victorious democracies to the west.

There were, however, people in Denmark who thought the country was on the verge of revolution. Revolutions elsewhere, high unemployment, a decline in real wages, and an escalating series of street riots in Copenhagen led some to hope or fear that Denmark's turn was next. Many viewed the syndicalists, the largest group on the revolutionary left, as the instigators of the riots and as the leaders of any forthcoming revolution. A recent Danish historian, Erik Rasmussen, claims that in the months following the armistice, "the country came closer to revolutionary conditions than at any time in the preceding 400 years."[1]

Operating against revolution were not only those four hundred years without a revolutionary tradition but also the Danish history of slow, gradual change which had given most Danes a political and economic stake in the system. Also operating against revolution was the absence of a revolutionary leadership; the syndicalists failed to take advantage of the situation. They never called for the "social general strike" that they believed to be the mechanism for overthrowing the existing economic and political system.

This chapter examines the reasons for the absence of revolution in Denmark in 1918, beginning with a description of the events that led people to wonder whether revolution was at hand, discussing the role of the syndicalists, and explaining why the situation was not really a pre-revolutionary one.

In any discussion of revolution, the terminology and concept of revolution must be clarified. The traditional usage of the term, at least among American commentators, implies violence. Political change, no matter how radical, that takes place through the mechanism of parliamentary debate and legislation is not a "revolution." This means that revolutions carry with them a measure of illegality as well as violence. One may approve of the goals of a revolution, while still noting that its methods were not legal within the context of its own time and place. Crane Brinton, in *Anatomy of Revolution,* defines revolution as the "drastic, sudden substitution of one group in charge of the running of a territorial political entity by another group hitherto not running that government. There is one further implication: the revolutionary substitution of one group for another, if not made by actual violent uprising, is made by *coup d'état, Putsch,* or some other kind of skullduggery."[2]

On November 4, 1918, German sailors in Kiel rebelled, setting off a revolution in Germany which was to topple the German kaiser. Until 1864 Kiel had belonged to the Danish king, and the revolution that started there spread rapidly through the former Danish provinces of Schleswig and Holstein. Within a week, workers' and soldiers' soviets had been established throughout the area. On November 8 *Politiken,* the largest Danish newspaper, reported "workers' soviets throughout south Jutland" and two days later that "the reds control all of Schleswig-Holstein."[3] This was of particular interest to the Danes not only because it was just to the south of their border (in fact the only land border which the Danes have) but also because Germany's defeat once again gave Danes hope for the return of north Schleswig, or south Jutland, an area still ethnically Danish.

With workers' soviets springing up so close to home, would it be long before they crossed the border and came north to Denmark itself? In fact, the soviet movement in Schleswig-Holstein turned out to be neither very radical nor very effective. It was an overwhelmingly German phenomenon, but this was not yet obvious in November 1918.[4]

There was some feeling in Denmark that the moment of revolution had indeed arrived. Revolutions in Russia, Finland, and Germany had led the way. Denmark's turn was next. Marie Nielsen, a founder of the Socialist Workers party, welcomed the moment: "As the red flag waves over Schleswig, revolution has come as close to Denmark's borders as possible. One more step and 'the goddess' will cross the border and then we *will have* revolution here. . . . We *know* that it will come and we *know* also that the bourgeoisie, with all its confused preventive measures, will not be able to stop it."[5]

That there was some fear of this revolution is also true. The Danish government initially sent troops south to protect the border against penetration by foreign revolutionaries, but then quite suddenly, in November and December 1918, most of this "security force" was sent home. According to Rasmussen, "The officers were afraid that revolutionary feelings would take control of the men." Better to disband the military than to risk their joining a revolution.[6]

As a nonparticipant Denmark, of course, lost no men fighting in the world war. But the Danish economy was severely jolted by its effects. For some, this "jolt" brought high profits. Danish agricultural products were much in demand by both sides, and a new group of nouveau riche "goulash barons" emerged, named after the canned foods that were their major export. As Danish industry capitalized on belligerent needs, unemployment declined to 5 percent in 1916, half the 1914 figure. But the unlimited submarine warfare of the Germans and the tightened control of the Allied blockade shut off Danish imports and curtailed the prosperous times. Goods grew scarce (potatoes disappeared from Copenhagen for several months), their quality declined, and rationing was introduced in 1917 on staples such as flour and bread.

Agriculturally self-sufficient, Danes did not face large-scale starvation, but with the supply of raw materials cut, industrial production dwindled and unemployment rose to a record 18 percent in 1918. The expansive extension of credit, particularly to the Central Powers to finance their purchases in Denmark, the shortage of goods, and foreign inflation all helped to drive up prices. As inflation cut into wages, real incomes in 1917 dropped to 85 percent of their 1914 level,[7] and a new group of homeless people emerged. These were Danes put out on the street either because they could not pay their rent or because they were unable to find a place to live because of the severe housing shortage. The construction industry was one of those hit hardest. There were "barracks" for the homeless, but any acceptance of "poor help" resulted in the loss of certain civil rights, such as the right to vote (which had recently been extended to include women). Some preferred homelessness to exclusion from the community of responsible citizens.

Danish workers were not completely helpless in the face of this decline in their standard of living. They were highly organized, probably the most organized working class in Europe before the war. Unions increased dramatically during the latter part of the war. Membership in the Danish

Trade Union Federation, De samvirkende Fagforbund (DsF), grew by 42 percent in 1918 alone. By 1919, 54 percent of all Danish workers belonged to a union.[8] That unions administered unemployment benefits undoubtedly explains their high membership but does not negate the fact that workers were organized.

Not only did absolute union membership grow, but workers were now joining the more radical unions. Membership in the syndicalist unions reached a high point of ten to fifteen thousand during the immediate postwar period. Bang et al. estimate that syndicalist unions accounted for 20 percent of union membership in 1919. Circulation of the weekly syndicalist newspaper, Solidaritet, increased from three thousand in 1914 to fifteen thousand in 1918, at which time it was actually making a profit.[9] In 1919 syndicalists even organized their own federation of unions, Føderalistisk Sammenslutning, as a radical alternative to the more moderate Danish Trade Union Federation. This would seem to indicate a growing radicalization of workers, who were no longer content with the gradual reformism of the "establishment" unions. According to a recent historian of the syndicalist movement, Therkel Stræde, "The precondition for the tremendous growth which syndicalism experienced during the war years was the massive immiserization which took place. Shortage of goods, inflation and profiteering ate away at wages."[10]

But perhaps the most dramatic, and obvious, manifestation of dissatisfaction and potential revolution was the seemingly endless series of demonstrations and riots which took place throughout 1918. On May 26, 1918, the conservative paper Nationaltidende in an article headlined "Syndicalist Riots," exclaimed, "It is about time that a thorough and serious stop was put to the more or less pernicious riots that a swarm of syndicalists are organizing around the city. The list of the diversions these gentlemen are allowing themselves has finally grown too long." The article goes on to list these "diversions"—the storming of the stock exchange, the coercion of landlords and businessmen, violent behavior at Social Democratic meetings, and attempts to prevent workers from taking jobs in England and Germany, resulting in riots at hiring offices and railroad stations. The article concludes: "This is enough. . . . It must not be allowed to reach the stage where a crowd of syndicalists set themselves up as a kind of tribunal of terror." Nationaltidende was obviously fed up and perhaps a bit worried, as its reference to a "tribunal of terror" might indicate, but two of the biggest demonstrations were yet to come—one in August and another in November.

The 1918 demonstrations were not all organized by the syndicalists, although some were, but they all did get syndicalist support and considerable attention in the syndicalist newspaper, *Solidaritet*. It was characteristic of all these events that no matter how peacefully planned, they all became somewhat unruly and ended in street battles between demonstrators and police, which sometimes lasted for days and were carried out with a violence quite uncharacteristic of Danes. Mindful of the Russian Revolution, which began as a peaceful demonstration in recognition of International Women's Day, March 8, 1917, but then exploded into a riot which eventually toppled the czar, some Danes must have wondered if their turn was next.

Although *Nationaltidende* started its list with the storming of the stock exchange in February, the demonstrations had actually begun some weeks earlier. On January 29 a procession of unemployed workers marched on Parliament demanding a doubling of weekly benefits, from 14 to 30 kroner. Unemployment benefits, although issued by the unions, were determined by the state. The handbill announcing the demonstrations called for "a march to Parliament once again—and for the last time peacefully—to make Parliament and the government understand that the demands of the unemployed must be satisfied if misery and its attendant disorder are not to replace peaceful conditions!" According to *Politiken*, a liberal Copenhagen daily, fifteen thousand people gathered at Grønttorvet, an outdoor marketplace, and listened to speeches from syndicalists and conscientious objectors. Some seven thousand then marched to Parliament and waited while a deputation met with the parliamentary committee on unemployment. Much of the march then disbanded, but some groups milled around the area of the royal palace and the main shopping street, Strøget, and tangled with the police.[11]

The "storming of the stock exchange" two weeks later aroused considerably more concern. On February 11, Fagoppositionens Sammenslutning (FS), the syndicalist organization, held two simultaneous meetings in Copenhagen to discuss the issue of unemployment. The meetings were quite emotional, and both groups decided, by secret prearrangement of the organizers, to march to the wholesale meat market and plunder it, as a visible demonstration of their need. According to two of the FS leaders, Laurits Hansen and Andreas Fritzner, the meat market idea was just a decoy because they feared infiltration by police spies. The real target was to be the stock exchange, which was to be closed with a sign on the door, "Gambling den closed by order of the unemployed."[12]

After the meetings, the two groups marched through the streets of Copenhagen, joined, and held an impromptu open-air meeting at Kultorvet. There they were told by the organizers to follow an anonymous "man with the red cloth," who led them to the stock exchange instead of the meat market. They caught the stock exchange completely off guard. An advance group of three walked past the guard to hold the door open for the rest of the demonstrators. By all accounts, they had no difficulty getting into the building, where they frightened and chased out the stockbrokers and vandalized much of the interior. According to *Social-Demokraten,* some people were hurt, but none seriously.[13]

The general newspaper reaction was one of shock and amazement. *Politiken* reported in a front-page caption that "from all over the city people crowded in to witness these disorders, the most serious one can remember in Copenhagen." The headlines of *Ekstra Bladet, Politiken*'s afternoon tabloid, read, "Bloody Riots Today!" But *Berlingske Tidende,* a conservative Copenhagen newspaper, the oldest and fourth largest paper in Denmark, downplayed the significance of the event: "We cannot identify the hooligans and yesterday's hooligan riots with Danish workers . . . or even with unemployed workers. . . . What happened yesterday was not an unemployment demonstration; it was a bubble from the morass which is to be found in every big city." "Although the demonstrations were not the manifestation of a movement," *Berlingske Tidende*'s editorial put the responsibility squarely on the shoulders of the syndicalists for stirring up masses they could not control.[14]

Shortly after the storming of the stock exchange, an organization of unemployed workers, De arbejdsløses Organisation, was formed with the help and encouragement of the syndicalists, many of whom were also active in its ranks. This organization engaged in the "direct action" often advocated by the syndicalists and deplored by *Nationaltidende,* the coercing of landlords and businesspeople. When families were evicted for nonpayment of rent, or furniture was repossessed because payments fell behind, groups from the workers' organization appeared. Sometimes they would pay a symbolic amount, but not always. They would reappropriate the furniture or apartment and by their very numbers "convince" the reluctant landlord or furniture dealer to come to some agreement with the tenants or customers. Another commonly used tactic was for large numbers of unemployed to demonstrate at the private residence of the businessperson or landlord in question.

Demonstrations and riots also broke out during the summer at employment offices that hired workers to go to England and Germany. Syndicalists objected to the hiring of Danes for foreign jobs, saying that every Dane who worked in a belligerent country allowed an Englishman or German to fight in the war. They tried to stop the actual hiring process by blocking

offices and occasionally even went to the central railroad station to prevent Danish workers from boarding trains. The syndicalists, intensely
antimilitarist, cooperated closely in these activities with an organization
of conscientious objectors, Foreningen for konsekvente Antimilitarister,
founded in 1915.

When war broke out in 1914, Denmark had immediately declared its
neutrality and called up its security forces, sixty-four thousand men, most
of whom were stationed in Copenhagen. As the war dragged on and the
fronts stabilized, there was growing dissatisfaction with the idea of keeping so many men in the army. It was expensive and an unfair burden on the
individual men and their families, and discipline deteriorated as the danger seemed to pass. In 1915 fifteen thousand men were sent home, and in
1916 the force was again reduced, to thirty-two thousand men.[15] But even
that did not satisfy many of the conscripted soldiers, several of whom
simply took matters into their own hands and deserted. The most common method was to hang up one's uniform on a light post and go one's
way.

On August 9, 1918, such a uniform was found hanging from a light post
on Åboulevarden, just outside an unemployment control office. The long
lines of unemployed waiting outside the office to go inside and have their
"control cards" stamped were attracted by the uniform. People started
milling about. Two police officers appeared and, fearing a riot, called for
reinforcements. These appeared very quickly in a new police car acquired
after the stock exchange affair for just such emergencies. The police had
been criticized in February for having taken too long to reach the stock
exchange and hastened to avoid further accusations of inefficiency. Tem-
pers flared and a battle ensued that lasted on and off for the next five days.

On August 10 a meeting to protest police violence organized by De
arbejdsløses Organisation and the Socialist Workers party was held in
Fælledparken, a traditional meeting place and the scene of previous violent clashes between workers and police. Although speakers apparently
called for a peaceful protest petition, someone thought he spotted a police
informer in the crowd; there was a rush to the speakers' platform, which
collapsed under the crush, and chaos ensued.

On August 12 *Berlingske Tidende* reported that these had been the
worst riots since the end of the previous century. *Nationalitidende* on
August 12 again exclaimed that "now it is enough!" only to have to keep
reporting on the "syndicalist riots" for the next two days. On August 13
the papers published a detailed catalog of destruction, with shop names,
addresses, and amounts, and on August 14 they reported that "Nørrebro-
gade resembles a battlefield." This time the fighting centered on Nørrebro,

a working-class district of Copenhagen adjacent to Fælledparken. No one was seriously injured—and certainly no deaths occurred—but by Danish standards this was unusual violence.

"Finally," according to some, on August 13, four of the FS leaders, including Christian Christensen, editor of *Solidaritet,* were arrested, presumed responsible for the disorders. Danish law at the time had no stipulation about speedy trials, and prisoners sometimes waited months for their cases to be heard. Nor did this time necessarily count toward the reduction of an eventual sentence. One way to get alleged ringleaders off the streets was simply to arrest and hold them in jail.

Inspired by the growing revolution in Germany, FS called a meeting for Sunday, November 10, 1918, to protest the continued jailing of their leaders. They demanded the release of all syndicalists by 6 P.M. the following day, or they would call a twenty-four-hour general strike for Wednesday, November 13. Since the government refused to release the men, a strike was called and another protest meeting was scheduled for November 13 at Grønttorvet. The strike flopped, but the meeting was large. Andreas Fritzner, FS member, reported the crowd numbered between thirty and forty thousand people.[16] The police were there, of course, and the meeting again turned violent. This time people had to be hospitalized. *Klassekampen,* the Socialist Workers party newspaper, reported that 150 men, women, and children were admitted to the municipal hospital, Kommunehospitalet; Ejnar Mellerup, a police officer (later to become chief of police), related that more than 100 policemen were wounded at the "Grønttorvet riots."[17]

This event again spawned running street battles with the police that lasted for several days. On Friday, November 15, Ove Rode, Radical Liberal minister of the interior, recorded in his diary: "The disturbances seem to have stopped for the present. Whether they will start again depends on events in Sweden and Germany." And on the next day: "There is now complete calm in the city."[18]

This was to be the last of the big demonstrations. Several more syndicalists and members of the newly formed Socialist Workers party (including Marie Nielsen) were arrested. Trials were finally held—Christian Christensen's in March 1919 and Marie Nielsen's in December 1919. Most of the convictions were for inciting to violence against the police; some were for vandalism. Sentences ranging from three months to two years were passed down. Christian Christensen and Marie Nielsen each received eighteen months. The "troublemakers" were off the streets.

The year 1918 seemed to be filled with escalating episodes of destruction and violence. Scarcely was the town quiet after one clash when a new one broke out. When finally the demonstrations in November coincided—not by accident—with the uprisings in Germany, the threat of revolution must have seemed very great.

Yet the demonstrations, which turned to riots, never became a revolution. Part of the explanation for this can be found in the absence of a revolutionary organization or leader. While it is certainly true that revolutions can break out spontaneously (witness St. Petersburg in March 1917), they have not been successful without some sort of leadership, however hesitant. (The 1789 French National Assembly, for example, seemed at times to be pushed, rather than to take the lead, but it did remain a center of power.)

There was one group in Denmark in 1918 whose ideals, goals, and rhetoric could have turned it into the leader of a revolution. This was the syndicalists, organized as the United Trade Union Opposition, Fagoppositionens Sammenslutning. They claimed to be working for the complete overthrow of existing society by means of the "social general strike." Yet their one call for a "general strike" in November 1918 was a complete failure, and they never tried again. (In comparison one might note that the failure of the July revolt in Petrograd, no matter who started it, did not stop Lenin from another effort in November.)

Who were the syndicalists and what happened to them in 1918? Fagoppositionens Sammenslutning was founded in 1910 by a small group of manual laborers and construction workers. From its modest beginnings of 34 members, it grew to between 300 and 400 in 1914, 600 in 1917, reaching a highpoint of 4,000 in 1919. The source of these figures, Carl Heinrich Petersen, is very probably exaggerating, but more accurate figures are not available.[19]

FS was undeniably syndicalist and probably took much of its inspiration from the American Industrial Workers of the World (IWW), the French Confédération générale du travail, and the Swedish syndicalists. Certainly FS showed an awareness of and interest in these foreign models, whose activities were regularly reported in *Solidaritet* and whose manifestos were translated into Danish. Syndicalists believed, even more consistently than Marxist socialists, that economics formed the basis of society; political and social structures merely reflected the existing economic base. Thus Parliament was a bourgeois phenomenon, and to the extent that the Social Democrats participated in it they had been co-opted by the capitalists. Obviously then, anything done by Parliament merely reflected the interests of the ruling capitalist class. The only way to achieve true change was for the workers to seize the means of production.

Eschewing political activity, FS concentrated exclusively on organizing within the trade union movement. Only trade union members could belong. Until 1919 FS worked to take over already existing unions, rather than trying to establish their own. They agitated for the establishment of industrial rather than craft unions, which would join together in "one big union." Eventually, by means of "the social general strike, the working class would eliminate the present wage slavery and conquer the means of production." In the meantime, they would educate the working class and concentrate on short-term improvements, such as a shorter working day and higher wages. These would be achieved by means of "direct action"— wildcat strikes, obstruction, sabotage, boycotts, and sympathy strikes, which would not result in property damage. The revolution would not be brought about through street violence but rather through control of industry.[20]

After the general strike brought the capitalist society to a grinding halt, the trade unions, having led the strike, would take on leadership roles and organize the new society. At this point, the utopia becomes a bit vague, but one can assume that with workers owning the means of production, there would be a more equitable distribution of income. One point is clear— syndicalists were firm believers in local, decentralized control. They casti- gated the DsF unions for practicing what in a different context might be called "democratic centralism." That is, too many decisions were made at the top and passed down to the rank and file. FS fought constantly, and often won, to submit all decisions to a democratic vote of the entire union membership. Local branches ran their own affairs, and the "one big union" was to be only an administrative, non-decision-making, umbrella organization.

There is no question that FS's popularity grew during the First World War. Workers turned to it as a radical alternative in desperate times. But did this make all FS members syndicalists? Probably not. Christian Chris- tensen, editor of *Solidaritet* and one of the major forces in the syndicalist movement, admitted as much in a front page article on January 6, 1917, titled "Who We Are and What We Want!": "There is a great danger for workers, and . . . for our movement, if we gather a membership who see us only as an ordinary opposition movement, whose goals and activities are limited to reforms within the old trade movement." Because of the addi- tion of large numbers of new members during the past year who might not be aware of the true meaning of syndicalism, Christensen outlined its methods and objectives in the article.

If, then, the new members were not really syndicalists and did not fully understand or accept the revolutionary goals of the movement, who were they and why did they join? Christensen gives one of the reasons—FS was the only organized opposition within the labor movement. If one was dissatisfied with the somewhat creaky, hierarchic functioning of DsF, then FS was the place to go.

FS spoke out and agitated in support of some of the less secure members of the working class, such as the homeless and the unemployed. Although refusing to engage in parliamentary political activity, its members did take political stands, for example, in favor of conscientious objectors, whom they supported wholeheartedly and openhandedly, often collecting money for imprisoned objectors and their families. FS was militantly antimilitary, believing that the army was simply a branch of the capitalist state set up to defend the state against workers, not against other capitalist states. This belief did not change with the coming of the war; on the contrary, it was strengthened. Why should Denmark, a nonbelligerent, call up even more men, if not to put down the workers' revolution that the war would surely bring on?

FS openly supported birth control. *Solidaritet*, as early as 1911, regularly carried advertisements for condoms. Christian Christensen's only book-length publication (during his lifetime) dealt with birth control, *Arbejderne og børneflokken* (*Workers and Large Families*, 1910). He maintained that workers' large families were directly responsible for their poverty. If they could control the number of children and the timing of their births, they would be able to improve their economic situation. And, while it was hardly feminist, because it was rather patronizing, FS did try to enlist women in its activities.

For all these issues FS was the best place to go. It was the oldest, largest, most organized and vibrant group to the left of the Social Democrats. There were indeed other leftist, socialist parties, but they were all short-lived and received little support. Indicative of the strength of the syndicalists was that whenever there was any trouble, the newspapers inevitably attributed it to "syndicalists." Not for another year or so did "Bolsheviks" become the bogeymen.

In analyzing FS's popularity, the role of Christian Christensen, the driving force behind the organization, must be considered. Carl Heinrich Petersen, who knew him, speaks of his "almost hypnotic ability to influence others" and quotes Richard Jensen, a union leader: "When Chr. Christensen spoke to a gathering he could get them to turn their pockets inside out and contribute everything they had with them."[21]

That DsF and the Social Democrats also worried about Christensen's drawing power is evident by their changed tactic from trying to ignore the syndicalists to sending a representative to public meetings at which Christensen was speaking in order to counter his arguments. As Christensen stumped the provinces in 1914, Peder Hedebol, a Social Democratic politician, followed, attending the same meetings and trying to neutralize Christensen's effect.[22]

Most of Christensen's writing is to be found in *Solidaritet* where, under numerous pseudonyms, he wrote much of the paper. There are the theoretical articles, long, ongoing accounts of the meaning of syndicalism, and reports of syndicalist activities in Denmark and abroad. These articles speak mainly to the "converted." It is the short, admittedly semifictional vignettes that are the most gripping—cautionary tales about alcohol, charity, and overpopulation, descriptions of the homeless, visits to a jail, and of a mother forced into infanticide. Christensen's writing made vivid the conditions which his readers knew existed, illuminating the frustrations that would drive a man to beat his wife or a woman to murder her child. Without condoning these actions, he explained them and held out a solution.[23]

But while Christensen could drum up support for FS, would he have been able to lead it into a revolution? Christensen seemed unable to keep close friends for long and apparently alienated many of his co-workers, so most accounts of him are negatively biased. Carl Heinrich Petersen, for instance, with whom Christensen inexplicably broke off relations, says that Christensen kept very few friends. "It was almost a natural law that it [friendship] ended with open and hateful enmity on his side."[24]

Nonetheless, two somewhat contradictory points can be made. The first is that he did not call for the "social general strike" at any point in 1918 (as distinguished from the "twenty-four-hour general strike" called in November for the release of syndicalist leaders). Whether he did not recognize the moment or did not believe it was the moment, at no point in 1918 was there a call for revolution from the leader (nor anyone else, for that matter) of the most likely "vanguard." The other point is that in 1920, when the Social Democrats did call for a general strike, FS initially refused to join. But Christensen, who had been serving a jail sentence for the 1918 demonstrations and had just been released, convinced FS that it had to support the general strike call, which it then did. Christensen had the ability to turn his organization around; in 1918, he apparently saw no reason to do so.

Erik Rasmussen, who feels Denmark was closer to revolution in 1918 than at any time during the preceding four hundred years, believes it was quick thinking on the part of the government that averted revolution.

Potential leaders were arrested, potentially dissident soldiers were sent home, and the pot then was sweetened by giving additional responsibility for social issues to the one Social Democratic minister in the government, Thorvald Stauning.[25]

But how close to revolution was Denmark in 1918? Christensen obviously did not believe the moment had come. Nor did the Danish press. Although well aware of revolution elsewhere, newspaper editors did not exhibit a sense of its impending arrival in Denmark. Certainly, many columns of newsprint were devoted to events in Germany. It was good press. *Politiken* ran a daily map which charted the course of the revolution. On November 10 its caption read, "Half the German Empire has joined the revolution. . . . The revolutionary movement in Germany spreads like fire." *Aftenbladet*, a democratic liberal paper, under the headline "Revolution in Berlin," on November 14, also ran a smaller caption reading: "Many reforms instituted immediately. . . . The revolutionaries are trying all means to restore order." *Berlingske Tidende*, less restrained, screamed in a front-page banner headline on November 12 that "Germany is under the sign of pure Bolshevism. . . . Socialist dictatorship in Germany." This may have distressed readers who drew their own conclusions. However, neither in their news reports nor in their editorials did these papers imply that Denmark was next, or indeed had anything to fear. *Berlingske Tidende*, in fact, concentrated most of its coverage on the fate of the German imperial family, rather than on the revolution itself, and all of the papers seemed primarily concerned with the effects of the Spanish influenza which was ravaging Denmark.

These large nonsocialist Copenhagen dailies—*Politiken, Aftenbladet,* and *Berlingske Tidende*—tended to lump the Russian and German revolutions together as fights against autocracy. *Aftenbladet* noted on November 8, 1918, that there had been no revolutions among the western powers. "The reason for this must surely be found in the fact that they are citizens in a free, democratic society, where autocracy disappeared long ago." Since Denmark was also a "free, democratic society," *Aftenbladet* saw no reason to fear revolution there. It even seemed to welcome the German revolution as improving the chances for a return of north Schleswig. "Now in Germany's hour of freedom, will Germany's leading revolutionaries see that freedom also rings for the south Jutlanders? We have reason to believe so."[26]

There was a certain smugness in the Danish newspapers when reporting on events in Germany. They warned the Germans to beware of the Russian example, while implying that Denmark had little to fear. *Politiken,* more cautious, did conclude its November 8 editorial by advising: "However little one believes in the possibility that something similar could happen [here], caution demands that one be on guard against it." This was hardly a flaming call to arms against revolution.

Social-Demokraten, understandably, welcomed what they initially referred to as "the German peace and popular movement." (Later they would also use the term *revolution.*) Its purpose, according to a November 9 article, was to end the war and "to convert the old Prussian military system into a popular democratic one." *Social-Demokraten* hoped that the Entente powers would now allow the "reborn German people" to join equally in the family of nations.[27]

What these newspaper accounts all reflect is the sense that revolution would not be successful in Denmark because it was a modern, democratic nation. There was no soil for it to grown in. What they also reflect is the tradition of the absence of revolution in Denmark. Recent research has turned up some evidence of peasant uprisings, but none since the Count's Feud of 1536.[28] And even if more recent uprisings should be uncovered, it remains true that most Danes believed, indeed still believe, in their non-revolutionary tradition.

The processes that introduced absolutism in 1661 and removed it in 1848 were peaceful. When Frederik III turned himself into an absolute monarch in 1661, he first wrote a Fundamental Law (*Kongeloven*) listing all his powers, stating precisely what he could and could not do, and then circulated copies for his nobles to sign. None objected. There was no Fronde in Denmark, no Cromwell, no analogue to the Swedish Freedom Era, no echoes of the French Revolution. In 1848 when revolutions again swept the European continent, Danish liberals marched to the palace to demand a constitution and were met by a king who had already acceded to their demands, convened a constituent assembly, and proclaimed himself a constitutional monarch. There was no violence, no blood, not so much as a black eye. The revolution that did take place occurred in the Danish duchies of Schleswig and Holstein, centered on Kiel, but never moved north.

There are two aspects to the lack of a revolutionary tradition worth noting. One is that the absence of prior revolutions or violent uprisings, successful or unsuccessful, may tend to eliminate consideration of violence as a feasible option; people would simply tend not to think in those terms. The other equally if not more potent force at work in Denmark was the realization that violence was not necessary to achieve change. The political structure was growing steadily more democratic; the system was not stagnating.

The constitution promised in 1848 was promulgated on June 5, 1849, and contained several liberal features. The right to vote for the lower house (Folketing) of the new Parliament was granted to virtually all independent men over the age of thirty—excluding felons, imbeciles, and those receiving poor help, although the right to receive such poor help was also guaranteed by the constitution. The vote was direct and equal. Any Danish male citizen over the age of twenty-five, with the same exceptions as for the franchise, could be elected a member of the Folketing. The age for office-holding was lower than that for voting to allow individual exceptional men to hold office. In 1915 the franchise was extended to include women.

Although the liberal Agrarian party (Venstre), representing independent farmers, controlled the Folketing from 1872 on, they did not achieve control of the government until the introduction of responsible parliamentary government in 1901, the so-called change of system. This change too, occurred peacefully and was the culmination of half a century of parliamentary compromise and maneuvering. By 1918 there was even a Social Democratic cabinet member, brought in during the war with the creation of a "national government." There was thus a legitimacy to the Danish government. It worked. At no point did "the moral bond of stable government snap" (R. R. Palmer's phrase in reference to the 1905 revolution in Russia).

Turning from the political to the economic sphere, we see a similar pattern of gradual change. In the 1780s wealthy Danish landlords, encouraged and subsidized by the Danish crown, began selling their land to the peasants who worked it. Peasants received outright ownership to their land, free and clear of the residual "feudal" encumbrances which French peasants were to abolish in 1789. At the same time (1788) male peasants who had been tied to their place of residence were released from these bonds and allowed to move freely. Female peasants had never been so constrained under the theory that where the men were, the women would stay. Besides, their labor was not considered as valuable.

One result of the eighteenth-century agricultural reforms was to split the peasantry into a smaller group of independent farmers with title to sufficient land to support themselves (about 40 percent), and a larger group of agricultural workers with little or no land (about 60 percent). Whereas the independent farmers rapidly became self-sufficient and improved their landholdings, the landless group began to feel shut out from any possibilities of improving their situation. There was thus a growing demand during the nineteenth century for land for agricultural workers and smallholders (husmænd). By the late nineteenth century the government was again offering low-interest loans to smallholders to enable them to purchase farms, thus appearing to address this land problem as well. The claim of reform was bolstered by the makeup of the government since 1901, formed by a coalition of Agrarians and Radical Liberals (Radikale Venstre), the latter a party of smallholders and artisans.

At the time of the First World War, Denmark was still an overwhelmingly agricultural society. Agriculture (including such related fields as fishing and forestry) accounted for 32 percent of the gross national income, industry only 10 percent, and skilled craft work 7 percent. The remaining 51 percent of the gross national income was divided among sales and service (24 percent), transportation (7 percent), construction (5 percent), the liberal professions (2 percent), and public assistance (7 percent). Some 39 percent of the workforce was engaged in agriculture.[29] Not until 1957 would industrial exports exceed agricultural exports.

During the mid-nineteenth century Danish agriculture had converted from grain to animal farming and in the process became modernized and mechanized. However, farming remained a family concern. In 1905, 90 percent of Danish farms were owned by the people who worked them; 70 percent were from 1 to 16 acres. Danish farming was big business. Some 88 percent of Danish exports in 1912 were agricultural products.[30] Farming was no longer simply for subsistence; it was for sale on an international market. Independent farmers thus had a considerable stake in the system.

Industrialization came gradually to Denmark and in two waves—one in the mid-nineteenth century and the other in the 1890s. The pattern that emerged was one of small, craft-oriented workshops rather than large concentrations of workers in factories. Yet, these workers were highly organized. The trade union association, DsF, with its close ties to the Social Democratic party, was very moderate—the voice of reform and not of revolution.

Danish trade unions were legal and part of the system. For nineteen weeks in 1899 employers and workers had squared off against each other in one of the longest lockouts in Danish history. The resulting "September Compromise" formed the basis of subsequent relations between the two groups. By the terms of the compromise, employers recognized the existence of unions, and the unions in turn agreed to abide by certain rules regulating strikes and work conditions and to control their workers. Employer-employee relations took on a formalized pattern. FS campaigned fiercely against the September Compromise, which, it said, tied workers' hands. But most workers were apparently satisfied with the security that the compromise provided; 80 percent did not join the syndicalist unions.

The Social Democrats prided themselves on this slow, gradual change. F. H. J. Borgbjerg, a Social Democratic member of Parliament, claimed in 1908 that the social revolution "is being prepared by reform after reform, by continually more extensive and radical reforms. . . . We are revolutionary Social Democrats, . . . but we are also the most zealous reform party in the country."[31]

Still, these changes were only political and did not address themselves to the basic socialist, or syndicalist, demands for worker ownership of the means of production, distribution, and exchange. Surely here was basis for dissatisfaction at the lack of "progress." And that, indeed, was what the syndicalists and assorted left revolutionary parties claimed. But the Social Democrats insisted that they had not abandoned economic objectives; these would come by means of gradual, political, and parliamentary reform. Gustav Bang, a Social Democratic politician, wrote that "one could imagine that the conditions were so arranged by capitalism that only a parliamentary law would be needed to expropriate the concentrated capital."[32]

There is no question that the Danish Social Democratic party was one of the least radical socialist parties in Europe. It had worked closely with the Agrarian party in the successful fight for the introduction of responsible parliamentary government in 1901. When a group split off the left wing of the Agrarian party to form the Radical Liberal party, the Social Democrats provided parliamentary support for Radical Liberal governments. In 1918, when the wartime coalition government was dissolved as Conservative and Agrarian members withdrew so that they could campaign against the Radical Liberals, the Social Democratic minister, Stauning, remained in the government and was even given expanded responsibilities. According to historian Niels Finn Christiansen, these working relationships had a decisive impact on the Social Democrats. "The fact that the labour movement came into being at the same time as it established the democratic alliance with a petite bourgeoisie [of independent farmers] that was extraordinarily progressive . . . made a lasting impression on the Danish working class. This can be seen not only in the way the working class identified democracy with bourgeois parliamentary democracy, . . . but also in the fact that the working class to a great extent defined its social interests as dependent on the continued existence of the petite bourgeoisie's agricultural production."[33]

In the elections held on April 22, 1918, the Social Democrats received

28.7 percent of the votes, making them the second largest party, after the Agrarians. Their election partners, the Radical Liberals, polled 21 percent of the votes. Together the two government parties received almost half the votes cast. The Socialist Workers party received 0.1 percent, and the syndicalists, refusing to engage in political activity, did not run.[34] Quite obviously the Social Democrats despite (or because of) their moderation received considerable support.

Thus the working class, which was to be the revolutionary rank and file according to syndicalist and socialist rhetoric, was instead represented and active in the political process. Not only was there a Social Democratic minister in the government after 1916, but their election partners, the Radical Liberals, actually formed the government from 1913 to 1920. This also meant that the Social Democrats had an active part in determining the shape of the new welfare state that was slowly emerging. The social legislation dating back to the 1890s (health insurance, old-age pensions, and poor help), which was to evolve into one of the most extensive welfare states in the West, was already beginning to ease some of the insecurity of day-to-day living. The unemployment demonstration held in January 1918 demanded, not new benefits, but an increase in those that existed. The principle of government responsibility for its citizens had already been accepted; the discussion was about the level of support.

The absence of a revolutionary tradition combined with a history of peaceful change in a democratic direction was a powerful force militating against recourse to violent revolution. Theoretically, of course, there could still be a revolution if the circumstances were right. And times certainly were not good. Two groups were especially hard hit—the urban poor, particularly the unemployed, and the rural smallholders. Whether or not their problems would have led them into open revolution is a matter of interpretation, but the indications are against it.

However, assume for the moment that there was the potential for revolution in 1918. This is where the syndicalists fell short. Although they did address themselves to the needs of the urban poor, both their membership figures and Solidaritet's readership overstate the actual degree of commitment to revolutionary syndicalism. But where they failed completely was in addressing the problems of the rural smallholder. There were no agricultural planks in FS's platform; it did not even mention the issue. This is all the more surprising because Christensen had once been employed as an agricultural worker himself and had written movingly of the experience. Why did FS not follow the IWW example of organizing outside of industry and attempting to reach agricultural workers? It would seem that FS was so locked into its image of itself as a trade union opposition group that it simply did not look elsewhere. Not until 1919 did it even begin to organize its own independent industrial unions, and it never attempted agricultural unions. FS's analysis did not fit agricultural Denmark, and so agricultural workers gave their allegiance elsewhere, to the Radical Liberals who were successfully working for agricultural interests.

The focus here has been on the needs and frustrations of the lower classes. Crane Brinton focuses on two other aspects—the collapse of the government and the needs of the middle classes. "Social antagonisms seem to be at their strongest when a class has attained to wealth, but is, or feels itself, shut out from the highest social distinction, and from positions of evident and open political power. . . . Where wealth, certainly the second or third generation of wealth, cannot buy everything—everything of this world, at any rate—you have a fairly reliable preliminary sign of revolution."[35]

Applied to the Danish situation in 1918, this also provides no evidence of imminent revolution. There was certainly no collapse of government, no bankruptcy, no military defeat, no perceived inefficiency. Nor were the new propertied classes shut out of political power. Everyone had equal and direct access to government participation. Independent farmers, organized in the Agrarian party, had pushed through responsible parliamentary government in 1901.

But perhaps the greatest deviation from Brinton's model is the absence of an ancien régime in Denmark in 1918. The overthrow of an ancien régime, associated with so many revolutions, was irrelevant in Denmark, as the ancien régime had quietly passed away during he course of the preceding century.

There is an epilogue to this story. There was a crisis in the smooth evolution of Danish democracy two years after the general strike when the ancien régime, in the person of the king, tried to reassert its power. This was the so-called Easter Crisis (Påskekrisen) in 1920. The story is a complicated one. According to the terms of the Treaty of Versailles, Denmark was to receive back portions of north Schleswig, the exact boundary to be determined by plebiscite. The ethnic-linguistic border had remained fairly constant during the period in which the area had belonged to Germany (1864–1920), and there was not much doubt as to the outcome. The first, most northerly, district voted overwhelmingly (75 percent) to return to Denmark. In the second, middle, district there was considerable Danish campaigning, but the results were equally conclusive for Germany (80 percent). Elections were never held in the last, most southerly, district as the outcome there was a foregone conclusion.

Danish conservatives were upset and felt that their government could—and should—have done more to influence the outcome, particularly in the city of Flensburg. The Danish Conservative party convinced itself that something ought to be done to regain Flensburg, despite the fact that 75 percent of the population within the city had voted for Germany. Perhaps an internationalization of the city could be arranged and elections held later, after the positive benefits of Danish citizenship became obvious. The Radical Liberal government insisted that the elections had been held and would be respected; the question was settled.

Not willing to give up, the Conservatives pressed for an immediate general election in Denmark, hoping to be swept into office on the issue. The Radical Liberals refused to call an election, saying that the reunification with south Jutland necessitated a new constitution, which in turn required two new elections to Parliament as well as a referendum on the new constitution. To schedule yet another set of elections would simply confuse the issue and be asking too much of voters. Additionally, a new election law which would lower the voting age to twenty-five was in the process of being written, and the Radical Liberals thought it only fair to wait until it went into effect. The Conservative party believed that it would do better under the old law.

There was a flurry of political activity at the end of March 1920, after Parliament had adjourned for its Easter recess. Although the coalition government of Radical Liberals and Social Democrats had only the slimmest of majorities (71 votes to 69), it never did actually fall. Yet someone managed to convince the king, Christian X, that the government no longer could command a majority in the lower house and that new elections should be held. When the prime minister, Carl Theodor Zahle, refused to call an election for the reasons given above, the king removed him from office and appointed a caretaker government led by Otto Liebe, a lawyer.

Technically, the king was within his legal and constitutional rights, but since the "change of system" in 1901, the monarch simply had not exercised these rights and had always chosen as prime minister a man who could claim the support of the majority of the Folketing. The king's action sent shock waves through the system. *Social-Demokraten* published a special edition on March 29 with a banner headline, "King carries out coup d'état." Even *Politiken* wrote of "the only coup in the history of our constitution."

The Social Democrats insisted on the immediate reinstatement of the

Zahle government and then issued a call for a general strike, to begin Tuesday, April 6, one week later. (Danes celebrate Easter from Thursday through Monday, so several of the intervening days were holidays.) In the meantime, the employers' organization had previously given notice of a general lockout, to begin on April 9. Unions were demanding paid vacations, cost-of-living increases, and collective bargaining negotiations that would be carried out on an industry-by-industry basis, rather than across the board as had been the case. Employers, on their side, had decided that the time had come to draw the line, that additional wage costs would damage the competitive nature of Danish goods on the world market.

It would seem that the Social Democratic call for a general strike was provoked by the combination of the political and the economic situation. In another week workers would be on the streets in any case, locked out. The Social Democrats feared the results of labor negotiations carried on under the eye of a bourgeois government appointed by the king, rather than with the support they could count on from their own government. Borgbjerg wrote in *Social-Demokraten* that "the general lockout hangs over the country and the people. The government is not one with parliamentary support and popular confidence and cannot ensure that the labor dispute is directed in a peaceful manner. The country is on the verge of political and social chaos."[36]

Some historians also feel that the Social Democrats were pushed into a more extreme position by the existence of a militant left-wing, syndicalist group in the labor movement. Tage Kaarsted speaks of "the revolutionary atmosphere" and Heinrich Larsen of the "mildly revolutionary atmosphere." What they maintain is that the Social Democratic leadership felt pressured into adopting the economic demands of the syndicalists in order to pacify and maintain control of the workers.[37]

But it is important to keep sight of the political situation as well. The Social Democrats would not have called a general strike solely for higher wages and to placate militants within their ranks. What distinguished this situation from others was the political involvement of the king. Social Democrats feared not only the results of a single set of labor negotiations but also the loss of democratic rights which had been previously guaranteed. The fight for responsible parliamentary government had been a long one, and if the king's action was not successfully challenged, it would turn the clock back almost fifty years. Here the reformist Social Democrats were prepared to make a stand.

As has been pointed out, the syndicalists initially refused to have anything to do with the general strike, contending that it was concerned with capitalist political issues. Whether the government was led by a Zahle or a Liebe was meaningless and irrelevant, they felt. But when Christian Christensen was released from jail he managed to convince FS that syndicalists, of all people, could not refuse to participate in a general strike. In addition, he made an agreement with the Social Democrats that they would not call off the strike until all demands had been met, both political and economic. The economic demands put forth by the syndicalists included the annulment of the September Compromise of 1899, which regulated employer-employee relations, and the establishment of negotiations by individual unions. This last demand had been initiated by DsF but was part of a long-standing FS call for decentralization.

That week saw frantic behind-the-scenes negotiations. The Social Democrats did not want to have to go on strike. There was apparently some fear among DsF leaders that it would be hard to get workers back to work once out, and that a compromise would be easier before a strike actually got started.[38] And the king expressed surprise at the depth of feeling aroused by his action. It would appear that he had not realized the degree to which democratic forms had taken hold during the previous nineteen years. At four o'clock on Easter morning, April 4, a compromise was reached. A new caretaker government, chosen by the politicians rather than the king, was established, and the bill for a new election law was to be passed, with elections held under its provisions on April 22, or as soon as possible thereafter. The general strike was called off; employers expressed a willingness to negotiate.

FS was furious. This was just what they had feared. They had been used by the Social Democrats to scare the king and the conservatives and then sold out for a political solution. What had happened to the economic demands? Some of the syndicalist unions went on strike anyway (or continued on strike, as some had walked off the job earlier). The seamen and longshoremen carried on a very bitter strike for two months. At times it almost seemed as though the strikers were fighting DsF and the Social Democrats as much as their own employers. The Social Democrats felt that the strikers were bent on splitting the working class and wrote angry denunciations in their newspaper. On June 15 the strike collapsed in complete defeat. Seamen's wages were reduced and their working day extended from eight to twelve hours, a retreat from the hard-fought concept of the eight-hour day. The strikers on their side felt that they had been abandoned by the rest of the working class. On the other hand, their failure severely damaged the credibility of the syndicalists.[39]

The following year, 1921, FS split apart. One group under the leader-

ship of Christian Christensen joined Denmark's Communist party to become Denmark's Communist Federation and accepted Moscow's Twenty-
one Theses. The rest of the membership evaporated, and the independent
syndicalist movement passed from the Danish scene for several years.
Although it did resurface later, syndicalists never again achieved the level
of their earlier membership or support.

The collapse of the Danish syndicalist movement came at the same time
as the strengthening of the Danish democratic system. The Easter Crisis
had shown the extent to which democratic forms had taken hold. This is
evident not only in the fact that parliamentary government was an issue
on which the Social Democrats felt strongly enough to threaten a general
strike but also, and perhaps even more, in the fact that the opposition
believed the Social Democratic threat. The king and the Conservative
party accepted the Social Democratic interpretation of the situation and
acceded to it, thereby, of course, strengthening the concept of responsible
democratic government and further reducing the possibility of revolution.

Notes

1. Erik Rasmussen, *Velfærdsstaten på Vej*, vol. 13: *Politikens Danmarks Historie* (Copenhagen, 1965), p. 184.
2. Crane Brinton, *Anatomy of Revolution* (New York, 1965), p. 4.
3. *Politiken*, Nov. 8, 1918, p. 6, and Nov. 10, 1918, p. 7.
4. See Dorrit Andersen, "Rådsbevægelsen: Nordslesvig 1918–20," *Sønder-
jyske Årbøger* 40 (1972): 147–85.
5. Marie Nielsen, "Revolution i Danmark," *Klassekampen*, Nov. 11, 1918,
reprinted in Morten Thing, ed., *Marie Nielsen* (Copenhagen, 1975), pp. 110–13.
6. Rasmussen, *Velfærdsstaten på Vej*, pp. 162–64.
7. Svend Aage Hansen, *Økonomisk vækst i Danmark* (2 vols., Copenhagen,
1972–74), 2:17–18.
8. Knud Knudsen, "Danske Påske efter 1. Verdenskrig," *Årbog for Arbejder-
bevægelsens Historie* 9 (1979): 30.
9. Carl Heinrich Petersen, *Den glemte Socialisme* (Copenhagen, 1981), p. 128;
Lisa Bang et al., *Fagoppositionens Sammenslutning, 1910–21* (Århus, 1975), p.
26; Carl Heinrich Petersen, "FS—Fagoppositionens Sammenslutning," *Verdens
Gang* 6–7 (1962): 196.
10. Therkel Stræde, "Fagbevægelse og Fagopposition: Lager- og Pakhusar-
bejdernes Fagforening og Forbund i København, 1890–1925" (Ph.D. diss., Ros-
kilde Universitet Center, 1977), pp. 439–40.
11. *Politiken*, Jan. 30, 1918. *Solidaritet*'s estimate of 35,000 to 40,000 participants is probably rather high. See Carl Heinrich Petersen, *Chr. Christensen og den
danske syndicalisme* (2 vols., Århus, 1979), 2:46–47.
12. Interview with Laurits Hansen in *Politiken*, Feb. 12, 1968, and tape of

Andreas Fritzner's memories, Nov. 12, 1963, as transcribed by Carl Heinrich Petersen, *Danske Revolutionære* (Copenhagen, 1973), 2:152–57.

13. *Social-Demokraten*, Feb. 12, 1918, p. 4.

14. *Berlingske Tidende*, Feb. 12, 1918, p. 5.

15. Viggo Sjøqvist, *Peter Munch* (Copenhagen, 1976), pp. 100–7.

16. Carl Heinrich Petersen, *Danske Revolutionære*, 2:158.

17. As quoted by Carl Heinrich Petersen, *Fra klassekampens slagmark i Norden*, 2d rev. ed. (Århus, 1975), p. 73; Ejnar Mellerup, *I festlige og farlige Tider* (Copenhagen, 1957), p. 86.

18. Ove Rode, *Dagbøger*, ed. Tage Kaarsted, as excerpted in Jørgen Olsen and Bjarne Schoubye, eds., *Reformpolitik eller revolution* (Copenhagen, 1973), p. 73.

19. Petersen, *Den glemte Socialisme*, p. 123.

20. FS program, 1910, printed as flysheets and reprinted several times in most FS publications; most recently reprinted in ibid., pp. 387–88; see also Chr. Christensen, "Hvem vi er og hvad vi vil!" *Solidaritet*, Jan. 6, 1917.

21. Petersen, *Chr. Christensen*, 1:67.

22. See Olsen and Schoubye, *Reformpolitik eller revolution*, pp. 34–42 for Christensen's and Hedebol's reports of the meetings.

23. An excellent collection of these articles can be found in Petersen, *Chr. Christensen*, 2:281–445, the section edited by Marianne Aarhus and Birgit Bruun.

24. See, for example, ibid., 1:66–67.

25. Rasmussen, *Velfærdsstaten på Vej*, p. 164.

26. *Aftenbladet*, Nov. 8, Nov. 12, 1918.

27. *Social-Demokraten*, Nov. 11, 1918.

28. See, for example, Jørgen Würtz Sørensen, *Bondeoprør i Danmark, 1438–1441* (Odense, 1983).

29. Hansen, *Økonomisk vækst i Danmark*, 2:231, 239, 243, 247.

30. *Statistiske Sammendrag 1913* (Copenhagen, 1913), p. 13; *Denmark: An Official Handbook* (Copenhagen, 1974), p. 535.

31. As quoted in Niels Finn Christiansen, "Revisionismens betydning for det danske socialdemokratis idéudvikling" (Gold Medal Ph.D. diss., Copenhagen University, 1965), pp. 105–6.

32. As quoted in ibid., p. 95.

33. Christiansen, "Reformism within Danish Social Democracy until the Nineteen Thirties," *Scandinavian Journal of History* 3 (1978): 322.

34. Olsen and Schoubye, *Reformpolitik eller revolution*, p. 97.

35. Brinton, *Anatomy of Revolution*, p. 64.

36. As quoted in Heinrich Schlebaum Larsen, "Træk af de faglige storkonflikter i 1920 og 1925," *Økonomi og politik* 29 (1955): 173.

37. Tage Kaarsted, *Påskekrisen 1920* (Århus, 1968), p. 261; Larsen, "Træk af de faglige storkonflikter," pp. 167, 175.

38. Larsen, "Træk af de faglige storkonflikter," p. 170.

39. See Knudsen, "Danske Påske efter 1. Verdenskrig," for a discussion of the effects of the strike on the syndicalists and in moving the social democrats further in the direction of reformism.

4

Sweden, 1917:

Between Reform and Revolution

STEVEN KOBLIK

During the winter of 1971–72, Swedish television showed a series of programs on the historical development of the labor movement in Sweden. These programs utilized a central theme: the leaders of the Social Democratic party and the trade union movement had failed to recognize the radical nature of the working class and under the guise of "reformism" had led the labor movement into complete cooperation with the extant capitalist system. Implicit to this interpretation was the idea that despite more than forty years of Social Democratic governance, contemporary Sweden was too "bourgeois" and that workers in particular had been turned into petty capitalists. The response to these television shows was considerable, especially from the established labor leaders who demanded equal time to defend the more traditional view that the history of the Swedish labor movement has been a series of small, progressive, but decisive steps taken within Swedish traditions that has over time led Sweden toward a fully democratic society.[1] This traditional view denies the possibility of, indeed the desirability of, a more revolutionary approach to the creation of a democratic socialistic state. One period where these two interpretations clashed forcefully was in 1917–18. The year 1917 has special significance for both groups. It appears, for those who believe in the possibility of radical change, as a golden and missed opportunity. In contrast, the labor establishment views 1917 as a major triumph of their reform policies. Was a revolution possible in 1917? Were the Social Democrats as successful in their reform politics of that year as the traditional view would have us believe?[2] Evidence exists to support each view as well as a number of alternative interpretations.

Table 4.1. Growth of total population and number of industrial workers, Sweden, 1864–1912

Period	Total population		Urban		Rural		Workers in manufacturing and mining	
	No. (in 1,000s)	% change	No. (in 1,000s)	% change	No. (in 1,000s)	% change	No. (in 1,000s)	% change
1864–1873	4,179		532		3,648		81	
1869–1878	4,325	3.5	595	11.9	3,731	2.3	104	27.5
1874–1883	4,507	4.2	684	15.0	3,833	2.8	118	14.2
1879–1888	4,643	3.1	768	11.2	3,875	1.1	130	9.9
1884–1893	4,752	2.3	866	11.3	3,886	0.3	162	25.1
1889–1898	4,882	3.0	958	11.1	3,924	1.0	212	30.4
1894–1903	5,066	3.8	1,064	11.1	4,001	1.0	268	26.4
1899–1908	5,253	3.7	1,190	11.8	4,063	1.0	310	16.0
1904–1912	5,429	3.4	1,318	10.9	4,111	1.1	329	5.9

Sources: population: Historisk statistik for Sverige, part I, table A4; number of workers: Bagg, Lundberg, and Sven-nilsson, Wages of Sweden, 1860–1930, part II, table 187.

Several spectacular events occurred in 1917: the split of the Social Democratic party in February; the Russian Revolution in March; increasing food shortages; a number of food riots and military mutinies; the collapse of two Conservative governments; the elections of the second chamber; and the creation of a Liberal–Social Democratic coalition government in October that eventually established parliamentary democracy in Sweden. The first five factors are often cited as clear proof of the revolutionary nature of 1917, while the latter three are believed to demonstrate the strength and correctness of the reformist tradition. How then are we to interpret 1917? This chapter questions both interpretations and seeks to raise interest in further research on the period. Three key areas will be examined: the nature and timing of the split in the socialist ranks; the significance of the popular upheavals of the spring; and the election results. One initial observation must, however, be made: Sweden in 1917 remained a society controlled by "the forces of order."

Indeed the conservative nature of Sweden should be underscored. Sweden's industrialization came late by western European standards—the first sustained growth period occurring after 1890.[3] Resulting social changes also developed slowly. Rural and small town components of Swedish society remained larger than industrial and city sectors (see Tables 4.1 and 4.2). Sweden all but skipped the period of classical mid-nineteenth century

Table 4.2. Shares of agriculture, industry, and other services in the gross domestic product, Sweden, 1869–1912

Period	Agriculture, horticulture, and fishing	Manufacturing, mining, and handicrafts	Other services
1869–78	29.3%	15.9%	54.8%
1874–83	27.5	16.7	55.8
1879–88	26.3	17.2	56.5
1884–93	24.9	18.7	56.4
1889–98	23.2	21.9	54.9
1894–1903	20.7	25.8	53.5
1899–1908	19.6	28.6	51.8
1904–12	19.2	30.3	50.5

Source: O. Lindahl, *The Gross Domestic Product of Sweden, 1861–1951*, table 1 (Medelanden fran Konjunkturinstitutet, series B:20).

liberalism.[4] When late in the century pressure for change came, it was the so-called popular movements that supplied the impetus.

The popular movements included the prohibitionists, the womens' rights and free church groups, the cooperative movement, and the various labor organizations. The sociological base and political ideology of these groups varied greatly, yet the very strength of the traditional forces encouraged them to cooperate. This cooperation took its most important form in the political arena where the two new "parties of movement," the Liberals (1899) and the Social Democrats (1889), worked closely for the enlargement of the franchise and the establishment of parliamentary democracy.

The long-term ramifications of this common struggle were significant. The sharp distinction between liberal and socialist normal in Europe was avoided in Sweden—at least until the 1920s. Their election alliances probably led the Liberals to support more progressive social reforms than they might have otherwise, while the Social Democrats found encouragement to be reformists from the outset. By the turn of the century, leaders of both parties agreed to work together to establish democracy in Sweden. Their struggles did not, however, produce the rapid, sweeping changes they had expected.[5]

The established groups in Sweden proved through a series of crises between 1902 and 1914 to be formidable opponents of significant political change. Their flexibility and willingness to exercise their authority slowed the march of reform. Their sources of power spanned a broad economic, social, and political spectrum. Their institutional power was particularly important. The bureaucracy, a remnant of Sweden's great-power period in the seventeenth and eighteenth centuries, increased its authority after the constitutional reform of 1866 when a bicameral legislature superseded the estates. The officials who controlled the legal system, ran the various levels of government, and formed the heart of the last non-parliamentary government—the Hammarskjöld ministry, 1914–17—were not disposed to give up their influence without a struggle.

Under these circumstances the crisis within the conservative ranks should be an area for research as important as studies of "the forces of movement."[6] The type of conservatism represented by the king and queen, like their counterparts in Germany and Russia, lived lives removed from daily reality and were no longer capable of responding to the demands of modern Sweden. A new conservatism was in the making—a conservatism that in time would be more flexible and responsive to change. The symbol of this type of conservative evolution was Arvid Lindman.

Lindman was a businessman. Although acceptable to the court, he certainly did not have either the social standing or influence with traditional monarchial elements of some other conservative parliamentarians. Unsympathetic to the demands for parliamentary democracy, Lindman nevertheless proved himself adept at leading conservatives in Parliament in parrying the thrust of the forces of movement for dramatic change before the war. Much in the manner of Disraeli, Lindman controlled the major prewar suffrage reform in 1907, which established universal adult male suffrage and proportional representation for the second chamber, and served as prime minister, 1905–11. Slowly he built an election alliance of conservative politicians that would become the base of the modern Conservative party. This party he would lead until the mid-thirties. In 1917 Lindman was the critical spokesman for "the forces of order." He watched the upheavals of 1917 with surprise, fear, and uncertainty. In the end it would be he, not some liberal or socialist rival, who made the final decision that led to the establishment of the left government in October 1917.[7]

The events of 1917 unfolded in the midst of a general European war. The war affected Sweden in two different but related ways: through an ongoing debate about the nature of neutrality and through direct ramifications of the war itself, including the collapse of traditional international trading patterns and divisions within the international socialist movement. In the autumn of 1914, there existed near unanimity that Sweden should maintain a policy of neutrality. The only significant exception to this consensus was a small group of conservatives, including Queen Victoria, a granddaughter of Emperor Wilhelm I, who advocated an alliance with Germany. The German government, however, gave no support to this courtiers' minority, and Sweden's foreign policy debate contested the nature, not the fundamental soundness of neutrality.

In this context it must be remembered that the government and King Gustav V, not Parliament, controlled the formulation and execution of Swedish foreign policy. Hjalmar Hammarskjöld, the prime minister, used his power to fashion a neutrality tilted toward Germany. At the same time he insisted that the corpus of international law and practice be applied to preserve the freedom of neutrals to continue their prewar trading associations. But as the hardships of war squeezed the near-totally mobilized societies of the belligerents, their respect for the rights of neutrals diminished. Hammarskjöld found the defense of his country's interests against mounting pressure from both belligerent camps increasingly daunting.

Initially Hammarskjöld held a strong position. Domestically there was a tendency to maintain a unified front to the outside world. Sweden's position as a major supplier of iron ore, steel, ball bearings, and munitions to all belligerents, as well as an important shipping power and transit country for trade between Russia and Great Britain, gave his government numerous bargaining tools. However, as the war progressed, the position of the neutrals weakened. Food supplies in northern and eastern Europe dwindled, and transatlantic trade was interrupted, especially through the efforts of Great Britain. Poor Swedish harvests made Sweden increasingly dependent upon agricultural imports from the Americas.

These developments made pro-German policies ever more difficult to implement. After the Battle of Jutland, followed by the return of Germany's fleet to port and inaction, Britain pressed Sweden into negotiations for a new trade treaty. The object was to force a shift in Swedish neutrality. Hammarskjöld resisted, but he also faced growing opposition at home. The Liberals and Social Democrats supported a more balanced neutrality, as did important elements of the Swedish business community. At the beginning of 1917, a full-fledged political crisis was at hand.

The chief issue was Hammarskjöld's refusal to accept the draft of a new trade treaty with Great Britain, particularly firm on using Sweden for transshipment of supplies to Russia. The premier's position was further undermined when the lower chamber rejected the government's annual defense budget. On March 4, 1917, Hammarskjöld decided to resign, distressing his king and catching Liberal and Social Democratic opposition by surprise. A three-week crisis ensued during which the embattled Conservative leader also faced increasing opposition in the ranks of his own party, where dissidents wanted him to give some small indication that he recognized the seriousness of the economic problems facing Sweden. Layoffs in the labor market and food shortages were growing. Arvid Lindman, the leader of this Conservative opposition, hoped, however, that the prime minister would compromise on the British treaty and remain in office. But Hammarskjöld believed that he was indispensable both to the king and to his party. He turned out to be mistaken. The moderate Conservatives in Parliament, led by Lindman and another businessman, C. J. G. Swartz, considered an accord with Britain more important than their chief's political future. King Gustav finally agreed on March 25, and a new government was formed with Swartz as premier and Lindman as foreign minister.[8]

This crisis occurred at a particularly tumultuous time in the war's history. Nicholas II had been overthrown ten days earlier, and the United States was about to become a belligerent. In Sweden the split in Conservative ranks occurred a month after the Social Democrats had suffered a serious and visible setback: secession of their left wing from the main body of the party. This split was no bolt out of the blue. Since its founding in 1889, a reformist tradition had dominated the party. Hjalmar Branting, the university-trained son of a professor, surfaced as the party leader, and his influence increased throughout the first quarter of the century. Socialist ranks grew rapidly in the period before the war. Recruits came not only from the working class but from other segments of society. Local political traditions made their impact on the fledgling party.[9] As the party moved toward organizational maturity, it was also plagued by serious ideological disputes. These disputes were similar to those experienced by socialist parties elsewhere.[10] The major issues were extraparliamentary actions, cooperation with left liberal parties, growing military expenditures, and the internal organization of the party. The reformist perspective as represented by Branting opposed extraparliamentary actions except in extreme circumstances, favored cooperation with the liberals, desired a party structure with considerable influence resting in the hands of the leadership groups, and generally opposed increased military expenditures. The radical perspective, as it developed in Sweden, opposed any cooperation with nonsocialist elements, desired either severe cutbacks in military expenditures or total abolition of military service, believed that the use of extraparliamentary tactics, particularly the general strike, would be necessary to establish a socialist state, and supported an institutional structure that permitted great differences of opinion within the party. After 1905 the visibility of the radical group grew perceptibly while the commitment to reformism among Branting and his supporters and the trade union leadership hardened.

The general strike in 1909, primarily a product of employer attempts to break the growing authority of the fledgling labor movement, strengthened both the reformist and radical perceptions.[11] The reformers thought that the failure of the general strike had demonstrated its futility, while the radicals remembered the behavior of the Liberals, erstwhile allies of the Social Democrats, in support of the suppression of the strikers. By 1912 the opposition organized into the Left Social Democratic Club, and the next four years witnessed an open struggle between the reformists and the Left Social Democrats for leadership of the labor movement. Although ideological issues were clearly involved, both factions tried to avoid a final confrontation. Instead each side referred to the other's tactical errors. The radicals complained: "It was the political tactics we didn't like. It meant that the very success of the Social Democrats [electorally] was the failure of socialism."[12] The reformers argued that the opposition's criticisms had exceeded the bounds of party loyalty, and they demanded a higher degree of party discipline, particularly with regard to the party's parliamentary representatives.[13]

By 1914 the radicals had made considerable inroads. They dominated the party locals in Stockholm and Göteborg, controlled the northern locals, and under Zeth Höglund commanded the Young Social Democrats at the expense of the second generation of reformists like Per Albin Hansson and Gustav Möller. Yet the radicals failed to penetrate the leadership of the trade union movement that provided the backbone of the party.[14] The contrast between the organized political opposition within the party leadership and the failure of the radicals to provide themselves with a countrywide grass-roots base can best be understood as a product of the particular character of the opposition group itself.

Throughout its existence the radical group was a diverse ideological lot. They shared a common hostility to the reformist tradition, but no common ideology. Carl Lindhagen, for example, the eldest member of the group and the only radical figure of stature comparable to Branting, had been a Liberal leader in the Riksdag for more than twelve years before he joined the Social Democrats in 1909. In reality he remained a radical Liberal.[15] The younger leaders Höglund, Fredrik Ström, and Karl Kilbom were influenced by, and in direct contact with, the revolutionary socialists on the Continent, particularly Rosa Luxemburg, Karl Liebknecht, and later Lenin. An interesting contrast to this ideological diversity was the apparent social cohesion of the radical leadership. An analysis of parliamentary representatives of the reformist and radical groups suggests some important differences in the two groups (see table 4.3).[16]

Even after qualifying the figures by pointing to the small number in the radical sample and the absence of family background data for members of both groups, table 4.3 seems to confirm the conclusions drawn by written sources: the radicals, at least initially, were primarily intellectual opponents of reformism. There is additional evidence that part of this antagonism was personal, perhaps based on an intergenerational conflict between would-be heirs to Branting's position.[17] Before the war, the great leader had shown considerable tolerance of young radicals and permitted them to hold prominent positions within the party. The party secretary, Fredrik Ström, was a radical. The war disturbed this coexistence as it pushed the left to a break with the reformers. What held them back was the fear that this would cost them their institutional base, the regular party apparatus. Their claims of representing working-class attitudes more ac-

Table 4.3. Age, occupation, and length of service of Social Democratic representatives to Riksdag

	Left Social Democrats	Reformist Social Democrats
Total sample	16	85
Average age	44	46
Average length of service:	4.3	5.8
	(without Lindhagen 3.4)	
Occupational distribution:		
Workers	2	33
Intellectuals*	7	20
White-collar workers	7	8
Small farmers	—	8
Businessmen	—	7
Upper-class professionals	—	5
Large farmers	—	4

Source: Official statistics.
*Intellectuals are defined here as newspaper editors, writers, and teachers.

curately, on the other hand, are hard to support at least in terms of occupational activities.

The war and its effect on international socialism certainly provided the impetus for the final split.[18] Both reformers and radicals had drawn their ideological inspiration from abroad. Branting himself felt closest to Jean Jaurès, and Jaurès's violent death in August 1914 symbolically represented the failure of the Second International to prevent the war. Throughout the conflict the Second International attempted to revitalize itself. Despite these efforts one failure followed another, the most spectacular of which was the abortive Stockholm Conference in 1917. Only peace could provide the possibilities for cooperation between the European reformers; they were too strongly committed to nationalism to work together during the war. Branting's efforts concentrated on the terms of the peace, and he quickly became a supporter of Woodrow Wilson. Wilson's peace program became the rallying cry of the Second International and the solution to the organization's immobility during the hostilities.[19]

In the fall of 1915, meanwhile, the European radicals met clandestinely in a small Swiss village, Zimmerwald, to discuss their options. The program adopted called for active steps to end the war, rejected nationalism and reaffirmed the international character of the socialist movement, and expressed opposition to cooperation with the Liberals. The Swedish representatives, Höglund and Ture Nerman, found themselves to the left of the adopted program and supported Lenin's faction.[20] Branting saw Zimmerwald as a direct threat to much that he held dear, domestically and internationally.[21] The struggle in Sweden clearly mirrored a larger split in European socialism. Fredrik Ström summarized the situation: "The struggle between left and right within socialism is not simply a Swedish occurrence but an international one. It comes driven by the world war, in nearly all the world's socialist parties."[22]

The conflict came to a head in Sweden in April and May 1916. Branting took the initiative. He used as an excuse a recent radical-dominated Young Social Democratic convention which the reformers had tried to prevent from being held. He insisted that the majority party newspaper, *Social Demokraten*, support the reformist program. The radical members of the editorial board, including Höglund, resigned in protest. In May the central committee of the party declared open war on the opposition. Ström quit his position as party secretary, and Möller replaced him. The radicals had lost their key organizational position and the columns of the most important socialist newspaper. They founded their own organ, *Politiken*, and soon afterwards began to campaign to gain a majority of delegates to the next party congress due to meet in February 1917. The congress would make the final decision.

The outcome was never in doubt. The reformists had the prestige of Branting, control of the party apparatus, and the complete support of the trade union leadership. The method used to induce the split was quite ingenious; rather than simply declaring the radicals outside the party and thereby taking the responsibility publicly for a division in labor's ranks, a series of "tactical" resolutions were presented—disciplinary questions, cooperation with the liberals, and the like—that would force the radicals either to leave the party voluntarily or swallow their principles. The advantage of this procedure for the reformers was that it gave the appearance that the radicals had split the party and refused to accept majority rule. The key votes were in the general range of 180 to 40, a comfortable margin of 140 votes for the reformist program.[23] Almost immediately discussions began among the radicals to form a new party. The Left Social Democratic party was created in mid-May.

The question of timing with regard to the party split is important. Branting took the initiative in the spring of 1916 to force a confrontation, which culminated in the spring of 1917 with the formation of a new party.

The evidence available does not permit the conclusion that there was a single determinant factor in Branting's decision. He could no longer avoid a conflict that had ceased to be "tactical" and was clearly ideological.[24] Although it was not entirely clear how much Branting was bothered by the clamor on the left that culminated in the anti-interventionist congress, other groups both within the party and outside of it needed some sign that he was willing to deal forcefully with his rebellious left. Liberal allies like Erik Palmstierna had been demanding a housecleaning for years.[25] Co-operation with the Liberals, which was after all a central thread in Branting's reformism, had to be reinforced for the trials of the election year. The direct attack on the radicals could leave no doubt as to Branting's commitment. There also was the bonus that a confrontation in 1916 clearly favored the reformers. Branting's prestige was extremely high, although the mood inside the socialist movement in general pointed leftward. It was better to root out the dissidents before they became too powerful; better, too, because the radicals would be forced to form their own institutions.

Still, Branting realized the risks of confrontation. Unemployment and inflation continued to climb throughout the spring. Food supplies declined. How could the left parties meet the needs of the suffering without playing into the hands of the Left Social Democrats? This question must have plagued Branting. The task was not made easier by the fact that it was the conservative elements that actually held power. They could hardly be relied upon to give up their positions voluntarily. Indeed, even if the left won the elections in 1917, progressives knew all too well that the Conservatives had consistently rejected parliamentary government. Why should Branting expect them to change in the midst of the war? The danger for the reformers was that they might discover that the opposition was correct, that only through revolutionary means or at least radical reform could a democratic, socialist state be born.[26] They had to maintain maximum pressure on the government and hope that when the crunch came the Conservatives would give way. Initial pressures concerned the economic issues: the trade negotiations with the Entente and a "cost of living" congress. The March revolution in Russia encouraged the reformers to press the Conservatives. It served as a warning to those who refused to bend to the demands for change.

The events of the spring of 1917 in Sweden, particularly the fall of the Hammarskjöld government and the demonstrations and hunger strikes in the military units, should be viewed with the Russian Revolution as a backdrop. Swedes were fascinated, thrilled, and terrified by stories from

Russia. The revolution began in the midst of the governmental crisis in Sweden. While Hammarskjöld was trying to isolate his critics by resigning, fresh winds from the east blew over Sweden. Although these events, as well as the maneuvers of the reformists, probably had no direct effect on the formation of the Swartz-Lindman government, the change at the top appeared to be a response to both. The new cabinet's self-proclaimed task was to solve the economic difficulties and to keep Sweden neutral. The left in turn called the shift in governments a step toward parliamentarism; a nonparty cabinet had been replaced by a partisan one.[27] Sometimes wishful thinking becomes reality—but often for very different reasons from those initially imagined. Change was in the air. Branting rushed off to Petrograd to welcome the revolution. Lenin stopped in Stockholm on his way to the Finland station. The Left Social Democrats were heartened by his encouragements. The world revolution was not far off. Each day brought new hope and new fears. Spontaneous rioting began in Sweden in mid-April; military mutinies soon followed. Was Sweden on the verge of its own revolution?

March had begun with food riots. A syndicalist-inspired "food demonstration" in Västervik on April 16 signaled the beginning of a series of leaderless demonstrations and riots that would last until June 6. In the two-week period between April 16 and April 28 relatively large-scale activities were reported at twenty-three different localities including Stockholm and Malmö. On April 20 the first hunger strikes in the military began. On the same day a soldiers and workers' council was formed in Stockholm by the Young Social Democrats. Our knowledge of the social origins of the participants is unfortunately weak. Their political demands were not revolutionary but rather directed at relieving immediate concerns such as food shortages and unemployment. The amount of social cleavage produced by the economic dislocations has not been measured and remains difficult to assess.[28] The September election returns suggest an increasing disaffection among the worse-off elements of Swedish society.

As this wave of unrest passed through Sweden, political leaders faced a difficult choice. Branting wanted to use the demonstrations to enact reformist programs while making sure that they did not lead toward a revolutionary situation. He stated his position to the party's central committee: "The immediate question is how the working class can best use to its advantage the world's reaction even within our country. We should try to use the discontent that exists to serve democracy."[29]

The government's response was not encouraging. It feared that the annual May 1 Labor Day festivities would be used to start a general revolution. Loyal military units were moved into Stockholm. A voluntary white guard formed with its headquarters at the officer training academy. These steps were premature; the reformists had no intention of letting the May 1 demonstrations get out of hand. They too feared that such a circumstance would benefit only the radicals.[30]

The last week in April offered a curious spectacle. Both the Conservative and Social Democratic leaders feared revolutionary developments. Shadows rather than substance seemed to spark their fears. Each group took what they felt to be appropriate measures. Repression marked the governmental response, while the Social Democrats tried to ensure that any serious discontent would be channeled toward a demand for democratic reform. Branting interpellated Swartz on the attitude of the Conservatives toward constitutional reform. It took six weeks for the Conservatives to respond; in the meantime the Left Social Democrats organized. How could the reformers block any potential radicalization of their supporters?

In order to shore up the reformist control of the labor movement, a "workers' committee" was formed on May 7. The committee itself turned out not to be of great significance, but its creation, the division within it, and its potential illustrated the temper of the times. Consisting of seven members—two members of the party central committee (Fredrik Thorsson and Värner Ryden), two delegates from the party secretariat (Möller and Hansson), two trade union leaders (Herman Lundqvist and Ernst Söderberg), and Branting as chairman—the committee held a few meetings that were marked by eagerness on the part of Möller and Hansson for overt action while the labor leaders remained opposed to any direct policies. They saw the committee as a potential to be used only in case the situation got unruly.[31] What possibilities were there for such a development?

The riots and demonstrations of April and May indicated how hard-pressed many Swedes were by the food shortages of 1916–17. This type of lawlessness was quite rare for twentieth-century Swedish history. Economic conditions and the lack of food put severe strains on a large part of the population. Rationing had been introduced in January but did not function evenly. People were hungry and frustrated, yet it is difficult to find evidence that would suggest that a revolution was near. Initially the discontent was undirected and apolitical. Sweden's tiny syndicalist faction furnished the most active political element in the initial demonstrations.[32] Could the Left Social Democrats capture the unrest and put it to a political purpose?

The Left Social Democrats failed to capture the full force of the food riots. Their attempts to form a "Swedish union opposition" collapsed.[33] The establishment of the party itself took too long for it to be able to take advantage of the situation. While the party represented a formidable section of the working-class movement—sixteen members of Parliament, the entire youth movement, and most of the effective ideologues—it proved difficult to accommodate all these diverse elements in a single party. Like the proverbial generals without privates, they floundered as they tried to develop a political program and organizational structure.[34] Unlike Russia, where the Bolsheviks maintained the strictest discipline among socialist factions, the radicals were less committed to a tight disciplined structure than the reformists. Without discipline, the possibility that the Left Social Democrats could utilize the unrest was minimal. The unrest of the lower classes remained by and large unguided, because reformists likewise failed to guide this discontent into regular political channels. The traditional historical view that the election results proved the success of the reformist position in capturing the disaffected therefore needs reexamination.

The unruly spring reached its climax on June 5 and 6. On June 5 the government responded negatively to Branting's interpellation on constitutional reform. Demonstrations held simultaneously with the Riksdag meeting were dispersed with excessive zeal by the police. The socialists were shocked by the police action, and many wanted to take immediate steps to end "police brutality." On June 6 working-class groups in Stockholm led by the Left Social Democrats held open meetings to discuss the possibility of an immediate general strike. Branting and the trade union leaders rejected the idea, and nothing happened. Already in April Lenin had concluded that the radicals would not lead a revolution, telling them: "Even you are bourgeois pacifists." More to the point was the radical sense of isolation and impotence. Höglund had just been released from prison after serving more than a year for his political activities in the spring of 1916. There could be little doubt about the result of some new adventure.[35]

June 6 marked the end of public demonstrations. Were the roots of the popular discontent so shallow that a show of force, the negative attitudes of trade union leaders, and the coming of summer could rip them out? Had the public accepted the cry of the Social Democrats and the Liberals to use the ballot box and become absorbed in the election campaign itself? Or was discontent unfilfilled or directed in other forms?

All political energy apparently was channeled into the September election to the second chamber. Traditionally the election has been seen as a defeat for the Conservatives and a victory for the Social Democrats that in turn produced a new government.[36] This conclusion was drawn from the change in the parties' strengths after the elections (see table 4.4). Certainly in terms of the change in the distribution of seats, the moderate left (Liberals and Social Democrats) achieved a stunning victory. Their opponents on both ends of the political spectrum lost more than 25 percent of their seats. But are these figures the only ones germane to an analysis of the election returns? How representative were the seats of the actual voting figures? Who was eligible to vote? What level of participation occurred? How did the proportional representation system affect the seat allocation? All these questions should be answered before interpreting the relationship between the election results and the relative standing of political parties in the fall of 1917.

Suffrage was quite restricted. Twenty-five percent of the population—males over twenty-five years old—theoretically had the right to vote. Actually only 80 percent of these citizens were declared eligible in 1917.[37] The right to vote could be lost for a variety of reasons—primarily the failure to pay taxes—and an indirect, multiple voting system was still extant for the first chamber, which had equal legislative power but was dominated by the forces of order. Of course, the lowest social classes were hardest pressed by these rules. Some 69 percent of social group III (consisting mainly of manual wage earners) were eligible in 1917; correspond-

Table 4.4. Distribution of parliamentary seats in the second chamber, fall 1914 and fall 1917

Party	1914	1917
Conservatives	86	59 (−27)
Liberals	57	62 (+5)
Social Democrats	71*	86 (+15)
Left Social Democrats	15*	11 (−4)
Farmers' parties	—	12 (+12)

Sources: Kungliga Statistika Centralbyrån, *Riksdagsmannavalen åren, 1911–1914* (Stockholm, 1915); *Riksdagsmannavalen åren, 1915–1917* (Stockholm, 1918).
*Figure after split 1917.

ing figures for social groups II and I (small and large property owners) were 92 and 83 percent. Social group II's high eligibility was due to the inclusion of the landholding farmers, who were nearly all eligible and who were the second largest voting group numerically after the "workers"— 251,238 and 295,323 respectively. By comparison only 61 percent of the "workers" and 49 percent of the sailors were eligible. Additionally the ineligibility of city voters had increased since the last election. Clearly the suffrage was not fully democratic, but most males could vote. Did they?

The election of 1917 was supposed to be of great significance. Participation by eligible voters was slightly lower than in the fall 1914 elections that occurred in the shadow of the outbreak of the Great War (65.8 percent in 1917 as compared to 66.2 percent in 1914). The difference was hardly significant, but the fall 1914 elections were not normally referred to as particularly volatile. Compared to earlier and later elections, voting figures were high. How were they dispersed?

The actual returns give a picture of the election quite different from the mandate distribution (see table 4.5). The Conservative defeat no longer appeared so overwhelming when it was clear that most Conservative voters had moved directly over to the two new conservative farmers' parties. The three conservative parties often listed the same candidates in electoral districts and together showed a loss of 23,133 votes from 1914 (a 9 percent decrease). Nor did the Social Democratic gains seem so large on closer inspection. The actual drop in votes was, of course, due to the existence of the Left Social Democrats; the socialists together had increased by 21,887 votes (8 percent). The important question must be in what proportion was the increased divided between the two groups? No definitive answer can be given, but some statistical approximations can be made.

Table 4.5. Election returns for regular elections to the second chamber, 1914 and 1917

Party	1914	1917
Conservatives	267,124	182,070 (−85,054)
Liberals	196,493	202,936 (+6,443)
Social Democrats	266,133	228,777 (−37,356)
Left Social Democrats	—	59,243 (+59,243)
Farmers' parties	—	61,921 (+61,921)

Source: See table 4.4.

If we make an assumption that each Social Democratic seat in 1914 represented approximately the same number of votes, we find that 3,094 votes were needed to elect a member from that party to the seat. Using this figure, an estimate of the relative strengths for the fall 1914 election can be made: Social Democrats, 219,674; Left Social Democrats, 46,410. Therefore the gains registered in 1917 would be 9,103 for the Social Democrats and 12,833 by the Left Social Democrats. The Social Democratic "landslide" in 1917 no longer appears so remarkable. What explained the difference between the large seat increase of the Social Democrats and the relatively meager vote increase?[38]

The particular nature of the proportional representation system played a major role in the victory of the moderate left in 1917 (see table 4.6). If a proportional representation system similar to the one that now exists in Sweden had been in place the total gain of the Social Democrats would have disappeared. The three new parties paid heavily for each seat while the Social Democrats utilized the system to their advantage. The average votes per seat were: Social Democrats, 2,660; Conservatives, 3,086; Liberals, 3,273; Left Social Democrats, 5,385; and the Farmers, 5,160. The contest cost the Left Social Democrats more than twice as many votes for each seat as it did the Social Democrats. Part of this variation rested with the way the vote was distributed by region. The new parties established large pluralities and tended to be regionally isolated. In many other areas they offered an established party's candidate as their own—for example, the Left Social Democrat had no independent office seekers in Scandia. Undoubtedly part of the difference was based on the effectiveness of the campaign organizations of the established parties. It is generally recognized that new parties do not utilize proportional representation systems

Table 4.6. Distribution of parliamentary seats, 1917

Party	By pure proportional representation	Actual	Difference
Conservatives	56	59	+3
Liberals	63	62	−1
Social Democrats	71	86	+15
Left Social Democrats	18	11	−7
Farmers' parties	19	12	−7

Source: See table 4.4.

as effectively as established ones. The Left Social Democrats also miscalculated badly, in Stockholm for example.

Before the election the Left Social Democrats held four seats from Stockholm, occupied by powerful figures within the movement. All four lost in 1917. Höglund, one of the defeated, conceded that his party had done much worse in Stockholm than they had expected. He blamed poor tactics and a hostility among "young workers" to parliamentary ideas for their abstention from voting. It should be noted, however, that the party's vote totals in the two Stockholm districts (1,619 and 1,939) were totals that in the more thinly populated northern districts produced elected seats.

Perhaps most interesting of all is the question of which groups voted for which parties, and in particular who were the swing voters and the nonvoters. Again no completely reliable data exist, but scholarly research, contemporary observations, and precinct returns suggest some common themes. None of the political parties, except of course the farmers' parties, was totally tied to a single class.[39] Jörgen Weibull concluded that in the elections of 1911 and 1914 the Social Democrats ran stronger among middle-class, white-collar workers than in the "workers" category. The Social Democrats were also weak among the agricultural workers.[40]

Contemporary observers believed that there had been a major swing of Conservative voters to the Social Democrats—a swing that Fredrik Ström ascribed to fear: "A large part of the bourgeoisie voted for Branting's party because of their fear that the revolutionary fire was on the march."[41] Leif Lewin's controversial book *The Swedish Electorate* also emphasized this swing.[42] Ludwig Widell's report in the official statistical survey of the election noted: the greatest decline of participation by eligible voters occurred in higher social groups (about 5 percent); participation was highest in larger city precincts, especially Stockholm, Malmö, Norrköping, and Linköping; the greatest growth for the Social Democrats occurred in the cities; the largest decline registered for the three conservative parties was also in urban areas; the Liberals grew almost exclusively in rural districts; and distinctive regional patterns of voting occurred.[43]

A summary of all of these data gives us a more sophisticated view of the election of 1917, although certainly not a complete one. A simple glance at the mandate division presents a highly inaccurate picture—that of a great Social Democratic victory. With the Swartz-Lindman government and the remaining conservative elements in Swedish society explicitly rejecting parliamentarism, it seems likely that they too would have taken a closer look at the election returns to judge the mood of the country.

Tension obviously was high among all elements of society, but it probably had been even higher in 1914. The election results indicated that the great, and critical, changes that occurred in 1917 were on the right, not the left. Here one finds great movement, confusion, and a certain degree of fear. The spectacular division of the socialists in February, the actual seat division after the election, the collapse of the Conservative government thereafter, the future domination of the reformists in Swedish politics, and scholarly interests that led naturally to studies of "progressive" changes have blinded us to this reality. Two new conservative parties established themselves during this year—larger together than the Left Social Democrats. The only significant increase of nonvoters came from social group I. There was a critical flow of conservative voters to the Social Democrats— voters who were probably upper-class, urban dwellers. Of the 28,330 votes gained by the three leftist parties only about half (13,378) can be explained as additional "workers" votes. The movement of social group I and II voters to both socialist parties should not seem so remarkable. Reformist social strategy sought precisely to legitimize the Social Democrats for these groups. The Left Social Democrats were regionally isolated and in all likelihood received support from rural elements in northern Sweden that previously had been liberal. The election showed the disarray of the conservative forces, not any fundamental change in Swedish politics. This confusion reached its height in the election postmortem that the Conservative leaders held.

The decision by the Conservatives to retire in early October was in many ways one of the most fascinating results of the unrest and the election. Again we know too little of these decisions. The Conservatives virtually to a man refused to recognize publicly the ideal of parliamentarianism. Their letters echo the same unwillingness.[44] Yet the crucial figures, Arvid Lindman, Carl Swartz, and Crown Prince Gustav Adolf, argued that some change had to occur as a result of recent events.[45] What they meant by recent events is debatable, but it did not mean solely the election results. More generally their feeling was directed toward the mood of the period, particularly the sense these men had that their world, "gamla Sverige," was gone and their desire to maintain unity on a commitment to neutrality during the remainder of the war. After the Luxburg affair in September (an international scandal that exposed covert Swedish diplomatic services provided to Germany), the Conservatives no longer claimed that they alone were credible as representatives for Swedish neutrality. A purely Conservative government was no longer acceptable even to the Conservative leadership. When attempts at an all-party coalition failed, the way was paved for the establishment of a Liberal-Socialist government headed by Nils Edén and Hjalmar Branting.

Was 1917 a revolutionary opportunity missed? Hardly: neither the disturbances of the spring nor the relative electoral successes of the Left Social Democrats indicated any real likelihood of a revolutionary upheaval. There was no organization both capable of and interested in leading a revolution. Lenin, more in sympathy with Branting's eventual insistence on party discipline than with radical calls for greater freedom to dissent, told the radicals in April 1917, "Branting is too smart for you."[46] Was 1917 the great triumph of reformism? Not in the sense that the moderate left controlled the pace of developments or deliberately manipulated developments for its own use. Despite the large parliamentary gains, the moderate left's total vote decreased by 4 percent in 1917. Conservatives held power in 1917 as they had in the past. Faced with a crisis of unknown yet broad proportions, should they have responded by rejecting as they had done in 1914 the demands for political reform? The causes and issues of 1917 repeated those of 1914. But Lindman could not bring himself to support another policy of confrontation. Forced to choose, he stepped aside. In that sense Branting had been right; gradual, progressive change proved possible.

Notes

1. The initial television programs were seen in the fall of 1971 under the title "From Socialism to Increased Equality." A widespread discussion of the programs occurred in the newspapers and academic journals; see *Historikeren og samfundet* (foredrag ved Nordisk fagkonferense for historisk metodelaere pa Kollekolle 6–10 Maj 1973) (Copenhagen, 1974), passim.

2. Gunnar Gerdner, *Det Svenska Regeringsproblemet* (Stockholm, 1946), pp. 9 ff.; Nils Andrén, *Fran Kungavalde till Folkstyre* (Stockholm, 1965), p. 111.

3. Lennart Jorberg, *Growth and Fluctuations of Swedish Industry, 1869–1912* (Lund, 1961).

4. For an insight into Swedish liberalism at mid-century, see the works of Goran B. Nilsson and Rolf Torstendahl, including the former's "Swedish Liberalism at Mid-Century" in Steven Koblik, ed., *Swedish Development from Poverty to Affluence, 1750–1970* (Minneapolis, 1975), pp. 141–63.

5. See Berndt Schiller, "Years of Crisis, 1906–1914," ibid., pp. 197–228; and Schiller, *Storstrejken 1909* (Göteborg, 1967).

6. At present we are limited to the highly suggestive works by Sven Anders Söderpalm, *Storgeföretagarna och het Demokratiska Genombrottet* (Lund, 1969), and *Direktors klubben* (Stockholm, 1976), and, on the development of Conservative elements, Rolf Torstendahl, *Mellan Nykonservatism och Liberalism* (Stockholm, 1969).

7. Queen Viktoria to Bishop Gottfrid Billing, Oct. 12, 1917, "Brev fran Viktoria," A. Gottfrid Billing Samling, University of Lund library.
8. Wilhelm M. Carlgren, Ministären Hammarskjöld-Tillkomst-Söndering-Fall. Studier i svensk Politik 1914–1917 (Stockholm Studies in History, vol. 11) (Stockholm, 1967); Steven Koblik, Sweden, the Neutral Victor: Sweden and the Western Powers, 1917–1918 (Lund, 1972), pp. 15–64.
9. The geographical component of Sweden's modern political development warrants more attention by historians than it has received. Distinctive geographical variations can be found in all the parties. The dependence of the Left Social Democrats on the area north of Uppland was such an example (Zeth Höglund, Fran Branting till Lenin [Stockholm, 1953], p. 137). Political scientists and other social scientists often focus on geographical components to political development, e.g., William M. Lafferty, Economic Development and the Response of Labor in Scandinavia (Oslo, 1971).
10. Ernst Sigforss, Ur mina Minnen (Stockholm, 1964), p. 100; Ragnar Edenman, Socialdemokratiska Riksdagsgruppen, 1903–1920 (Uppsala, 1946), p. 166.
11. See Schiller, Storstrejken 1909.
12. Höglund, Fran, p. 39, and Höglund, Revolutionernas år 1917–1921 (Stockholm, 1956), pp. 21–22.
13. Edenman, Riksdagsgruppen, pp. 129, 217 ff.
14. Knut Backström, Arbetarrörelsen i Sverige (Stockholm, 1971), 2:236, 244; Seppo Hentila, Den svenska Arbetarklassen och Reformismens Genombrott inom SAP fore 1914 (Helsinki, 1979).
15. Höglund, Revolutionernas, p. 29, and Höglund, Hjalmar Branting (Stockholm, 1928), 1:445–46.
16. Edenman, Riksdagsgruppen, p. 132.
17. Höglund, Fran, p. 81; Edenman, Riksdagsgruppen, p. 167.
18. Fredrik Ström, I stormig Tid (Stockholm, 1942), p. 212.
19. Arno Mayer, Political Origins of the New Diplomacy (New Haven, 1959), pp. 225–28; Martin Grass, Friedensaktivität und Neutralität (Bonn–Bad Godesberg, 1975), esp. pp. 181–224 and 262–71.
20. Höglund, Fran, pp. 178–79; Grass, Friedensaktivität, pp. 196–203.
21. Höglund, Branting, 2:80, and Revolutionernas, p. 23; Karl Kilbom, Ur mitt Livs Äventyr (Stockholm, 1953), p. 13.
22. Edenman, Riksdagsgruppen, p. 165.
23. Protokoll fran Sveriges Socialdemokratiska Arbeterpartis tionde Kongress, Feb. 12–20, 1917.
24. Höglund, Fran, p. 84; Agne Gustavson, "Mellan 'Hoger och Venster,' Branting och Palmstierna," in Jan Lindhagen, ed., Bilder av Branting (Stockholm, 1975), pp. 246–81.
25. Erik Palmstierna, Orostid, 1917–1919 (Stockholm, 1953), p. 9.
26. The dilemma of the Social Democrats can be seen clearly in their discussions during the late spring: Socialdemokratiska Riksdagsgruppen Protokoll, 1915–1917, April 27, 1917; Socialdemokratiska Partistyrelsens Protokoll, 1917–1919, May 20, 1917.
27. Carlgren, Ministären Hammarskjöld, and Koblik, Sweden, the Neutral Victor, have viewed Hammarskjöld's fall as a purely Conservative issue, related to the trade agreement with Great Britain. Gerdner's emphasis on the pivotal role of

the left (*Svenska Regeringsproblemet*, passim) is not supported by the extant evidence.

28. Carl-Göran Andrae, "Fran ord till handling," in Steven Koblik, ed., *Fran Fattigdöm till Överflöd* (Stockholm, 1973), and "Proletära Organisationsformer 1917: Militärdemonstrationerna och Arbétarkommittén," *Arkiv för Studier i Arbetarrörelsens Historia* 7/8 (1975): 88–108; Sigurd Klockare, *Svenska Revolutionen, 1917–1918* (Stockholm, 1967).

29. *Socialdemokratiska Partistyrelsens Protokoll, 1917–1919*, May 20, 1917, p. 21.

30. *Socialdemokratiska Riksdagsgruppen Protokoll, 1915–1917*, April 27, 1917; *Riksdagens Protokoll vid lagtima Riksmotet 1917: Andra Kammaren*, April 27 and 28, 1917, 4:21–23, 41–69.

31. Andrae, "Proletära Organisationsformer," p. 101; Jorgen Westerstahl, *Svensk Fackföreningsrörelse* (Stockholm, 1945), pp. 227–28.

32. Andrae, "Fran ord till Handling," pp. 216–18; Klockare, *Svenska Revolutionen*, pp. 18, 40 ff.

33. Backström, *Arbetarrörelsen*, p. 244.

34. Höglund, *Branting*, 2:148; Andrae, "Fran Ord till Handling," p. 94.

35. Ragnar Casparsson, *Vart Fattiga Liv* (Stockholm, 1961), pp. 304–6; Andrae, "Proletära Organisationsformer," p. 106; Ström, *I stormig Tid*, p. 199.

36. Ake Thulstrup, *När Demokratin Bröt Igenom* (Stockholm, 1937), pp. 180–81.

37. Kungliga Statistiska Centralbyrån, *Riksdagsmannavalen åren 1912–1913 samt Hösten 1914; Riksdagsmannavalen åren 1914; Riksdagsmannavalen åren 1915–1917*.

38. Höglund, *Revolutionernas*, p. 57.

39. See Jörgen Weibull's unpublished article "Yrke och Parti," for a more complete analysis of the problem. Using election statistics from the 1923 election, John Olsson, "De politiska Partifordelningar inom de olika sociala Klasserna i Sverige," *Statsvetenskaplig Tidskrift* 26 (1923): 82–93, came to the same conclusion.

40. Wilbull, "Yrke och Parti," p. 66; Gösta Carlsson, "Partiforskjutningar som Tillvaxtprocessor," *Statsvetenskaplig Tidskrift* 66 (1963): 172–213, concludes that the growth of the Social Democratic voters between 1911 and 1940 exceeded the pace of the growth of the working class.

41. Ström, *I stormig Tid*, p. 246.

42. Leif Lewin et al., *The Swedish Electorate* (Stockholm, 1972), p. 239.

43. *Riksdagsmannavalen åren 1915–1917*, p. 52.

44. Koblik, *Sweden, the Neutral Victor*, pp. 133–48.

45. Ibid., pp. 150–52, and Thede Palm, ed., "Joachim Akermans Anteckningar om Ministären Swartz," *Historisk Tidskrift* 88 (1968): 38–58.

46. Ström, *I stormig Tid*, p. 200.

5

A Labor Movement in the Communist International:

Norway, 1918–23

STEN SPARRE NILSON

Nineteenth-century Norway began as more of a name than a presence. The nation's position in the Middle Ages as an independent kingdom had long been lost, and it was reduced, in fact if not in name, to the status of a Danish province. Only the Napoleonic wars restored independence. When Frederick VI, king of Denmark and Norway, allied himself with the emperor of the French, a British blockade severed the close communication normally existing between the two kingdoms. Norway had to be administered separately, and the heir to the throne, Prince Christian Frederick, was sent across the sea to take up the position of viceroy. As a result of Napoleon's defeat, Frederick VI was forced to cede Norway to the king of Sweden, but his viceroy refused to accept this settlement. Instead he summoned a Norwegian assembly, hastily elected by male suffrage. This Storting drew up a constitution limiting the powers of the monarch and declaring Norway independent. It then chose Christian Frederick king.

The victorious Allies refused to accept the Storting's actions, however, and forced the first modern king of Norway to abdicate in favor of the king of Sweden. The monarch in Stockholm was to rule his second realm in a personal union, similar to the one between England and Scotland under the first Stuarts. This settlement failed to evolve into a complete union, because Sweden, too, was ruled by a foreign newcomer, the French marshal Charles Jean Bernadotte. This founder of a new dynasty agreed to rule Norway under the 1814 constitution because of the weakness of his own legitimist credentials. Uncertain of acceptance by the powers of the

Congress of Vienna, he wished to settle the problems of his dual governance as quickly as possible.

Thus Norway retained a considerable share of independence. Its foreign affairs were directed from Stockholm, but domestic affairs remained in Norwegian hands. Socially and economically the country was different from both Sweden and Denmark. More mountainous than either, it lacked great landed estates. Agriculture was dominated by independent farmers, mostly small landholders, commerce by merchants who exported fish, timber, and some mining products.

The Norwegian Constitution of 1814, still in force albeit greatly modified, remains Europe's oldest written constitution. Shaped by the democratic ideas of a society lacking a privileged estate, its franchise was wide, subject only to a low property qualification. The work of the legislators was subject to the king's suspensive veto, however, and his cabinet was not responsible to them. Since few of the farmers, merchants, and artisans who constituted the electorate in this large and thinly populated country were able to take an active part in politics, civil servants took the place of an aristocracy and controlled political life well into the second half of the nineteenth century.

With the advent of economic progress, the growing self-reliance of Norwegian citizens produced a growing insistence on greater participation in national governance. In the 1880s, the cabinet was made responsible to Parliament, and two large parties, Liberals and Conservatives, were organized on a national scale. Other important voluntary organizations, professional associations and temperance societies, grew in power and importance.

These transformations coincided with the harnessing of hydroelectric power, which created the base for manufacturing, and the emergence of labor unions. The Norwegian Labor party was founded in 1887 but did not gain any seats in Parliament until 1903.[1] National issues remained political: the fight against royal prerogatives, combined with the effort to loosen the bonds of Sweden, culminated in separation in 1905. During most of this period the Liberal party held the majority of Storting seats. As late as World War I, socialists as well as Conservatives were doomed to play the role of ineffectual opposition parties in Parliament. While Sweden introduced proportional representation in 1911 and Denmark in 1915, Norway continued majority elections in single-member constituencies until 1921. The particular form of the Norwegian electoral law favored the smaller towns and purely rural districts, strongholds of the Liberal party, at the expense of those parts of the country where the manufacturing industry expanded. In 1918 the extremes were represented by a section of Oslo with more than 32,000 voters but only one member of Parliament and Flekkefjord, an old trading town of 1,063 inhabitants who had the right to elect a representative to the Storting.

At the general elections of 1915 and 1918 the Norwegian Labor party obtained almost one-third of the total vote. But its share of the seats was little more than one-sixth in the 1915–18 Storting and dropped to one-seventh in 1918–21. No doubt this was one of the factors that increased the impatience of workers and union leaders with "bourgeois democracy," and toward the end of the war dramatic events took place in the Norwegian Labor party outside the parliamentary arena.

There has been a good deal of discussion about the contrast between the development of the labor movement in Norway and in the two other Scandinavian countries, a discussion briefly referred to both by Carol Gold and Steven Koblik in this volume. The radical wing took over all leading positions within the Norwegian movement in April 1918 and soon afterward declared its intention to join the Communist International. It did not attempt a revolution, however. Just as in the two neighboring countries, "the forces of order" remained in control of Norwegian society. This was so clearly the case that the leaders of the Comintern did not at first press for a reorganization of the Norwegian movement into a revolutionary vanguard. There can be no question of a missed revolutionary opportunity in Norway at the end of World War I.[2] But the very success of the radical wing was so striking, compared to what happened in Denmark and Sweden, that the fact seemed hard to explain.

Revolutionary tensions constitute a subject of interest to social science as well as history. According to a well-known sociological model, revolutions are most likely to occur when a period of economic and social improvement is followed by a sharp reversal. Sustained progress leads people to expect that the upward movement will continue, and when it turns out to be blocked, the result is anger and frustration.[3] This model can be used to illustrate the events during and immediately after World War I. From 1914 to 1918, all European countries went through roughly similar stages of social and economic change, neutrals as well as belligerents. During the first years of the war a substantial improvement in the lot of the poor actually occurred. Employment opportunities expanded dramatically as a result of the enormous increase in demand for all kinds of commodities. For many workers and their families the onset of war marked the first time in their memory when they could obtain steady work. But after the war had dragged on for years, its debilitating effect on the whole social fabric became more and more apparent. Governments no longer found themselves able to ensure vital necessities for their populations, and throughout Europe revolutionary tensions developed.

However, the strength of the revolutionary mood was by no means the same everywhere. In Sweden, and still more in Denmark, labor radicalism represented a very weak force. Although some riots did occur, moderate Social Democrats remained in firm control of the respective labor movements, and they had a large majority of the rank and file behind them. In both countries the outcome of the crisis of 1917–18 was the withdrawal of the Conservatives from the government in favor of a Liberal–Social Democratic coalition.

Events in Norway took quite a different turn. Here a Liberal majority government had been in office for years, so there could be no question of forming an alliance for the creation of a parliamentary majority against the conservatives. The Norwegian social democrats consequently found themselves in a less advantageous tactical position than their Danish and Swedish counterparts. But this could hardly explain the moderates' loss of control over the movement and their loss of control to radical forces, which received the backing of a majority at the National Congress of the Norwegian Labor party in the spring of 1918 on a program clearly envisaging the possibility of revolutionary action.

The historian Edvard Bull was the first to discuss the problem. Beside the possible influence of the parliamentary constellation, he was looking for a more fundamental difference to provide a better explanation. Bull argued "that the rapid, one-generation industrialization of Norway created workers who became radical,"[4] while the more gradual progress of economic change in Denmark, described by Carol Gold in chapter 3, allowed more time to acclimate, producing a more moderate working-class movement.[5] Sweden, on both counts, occupied an intermediate position.

This provides at best a partial explanation, however. Considerable complexity characterized the development in Norway, where the Labor party first joined the Communist International in 1920, next split into two factions in 1921, then left the Comintern again in 1923 with a further split as a result, before a process of reunification and deradicalization finally gained momentum in the second half of the 1920s.

It is not easy in a single chapter to present a satisfactory account of the dramatic development in Norway after World War I as well as its historical background. Focusing on the development of two strongholds, one radical, the other moderate, in the provinces of Tröndelag in the north, and Buskerud, southwest of the capital, provides a sense of the political and economic changes in Norway following the war. From the turn of the century, we can trace the main elements of the process of radicalization that made Tröndelag a stronghold and enabled its leaders to seize control of the Norwegian labor movement when the situation became ripe at the national level in 1918. The subsequent process of deradicalization can be studied at close quarters in Buskerud, the province that developed into a stronghold of the moderate faction.

Previous sociological attempts to explain labor radicalism in Norway in general terms should be noted as well as the limitations of their usefulness. Edvard Bull's thesis has been widely accepted by sociologists and political scientists. It touched on a classical theme in sociology and apparently corroborated Emile Durkheim's theory of mass society. Recently this approach has come under strong attack, but it retains its proponents and was argued with particular force in the 1950s and 1960s by a number of American social scientists, including Walter Galenson, William Kornhauser, Seymour Martin Lipset, and Mancur Olson.[6] In Kornhauser's words, "an uprooted industrial labor force, living in boom towns . . . came to constitute the mass base of the extremist Norwegian labor movement."[7] Lipset writes even more pointedly: "Norway was the only western European country which was still in its phase of rapid industrialization when the Comintern was founded, and its Labor party was the only one which went over almost intact to the Communists."[8] Nils Elvander identifies a " 'Bull-Galenson' hypothesis" about a connection between rapid industrialization, social anomie, and radicalization which "was commonly accepted in international political sociology."[9] In an ambitious attempt to reconfirm the theory, the American political scientist William M. Lafferty came forward with a modified version in the early 1970s. He indicated "that isolated economic processes were not the decisive element in explaining voter radicalism, but rather cultural and norm-related factors had the greatest effect."[10] This was a hypothesis of considerable interest. Lafferty took as his starting point the central sociological notion of a society's normative structure and the question of its maintenance or disruption. Moreover, he followed up his idea with detailed statistical analysis.

Norwegians have been more critical of Bull. Even his son and namesake, when studying aspects of the development in the Tröndelag area on the eve of World War II, found that industrialization had not proceeded more rapidly there than in many other parts of the country. It had merely been more protracted.[11]

The sociological approach of Bull's partisans does not always serve the study of politics. Normative patterns are sometimes reflected in political activity, but as a rule only in an indirect way. Moreover, in the case of Norway an entirely different and normative issue affected working-class politics during and after World War I, one which he and his followers overlooked: the controversy over the prohibition of alcoholic beverages. Its course offers an opportunity to study normative and political attitudes closely in different parts of the realm. It is possible to use quantitative data pertaining to general attitudes in the population as well as to internal politics of the labor movement. In both kinds of data, regional contrasts can be studied with the aid of statistical techniques.

The material used here consists on the one hand of referendum statistics dating from 1905, when the Norwegian electorate was asked to decide between a monarchical and a republican form of government, and returns from similar contests in 1919 and 1926, when the question of national prohibition of alcoholic beverages was on the ballot. On the other hand I also use data from roll calls at the Norwegian Labor party conventions of 1918 and 1919 in order to distinguish the makeup of radical delegations in 1918 and moderate delegations in 1919.

When the smallest administrative units—the communes—are classified on the basis of these criteria, five different regions appear, whose borders cut across most provincial boundaries. I have given them the following designations (see Fig. 5.1):

1. inner central area
2. outer central area
3. coast and outer fjords
4. valleys, mountains, and inner fjords
5. the northernmost part

Region 1, the "inner central area," comprises the capital city, Oslo, and its immediate environs, on the periphery of which lies a concentric area forming part of region 2, together with the next largest towns of Bergen and Trondheim. Despite its fragmented character the inhabitants of this second region had a common attitude as a result of their numerous commercial ties and easy communication with the "inner center." Coastal towns other than Bergen and Trondheim are included in region 3, together with the rural strip of land stretching along the coast from the Swedish border in the southeast toward the Arctic Circle. The interior of the country forms region 4, while region 5 consists roughly of all the territory (including towns) north of regions 3 and 4.

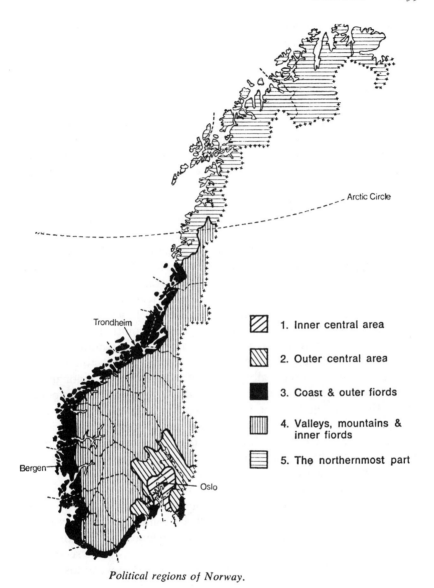

1. Inner central area

2. Outer central area

3. Coast & outer fiords

4. Valleys, mountains & inner fiords

5. The northernmost part

Political regions of Norway.

Figure 5.1. Political regions in Norway. (From S. S. Nilson, "Regional Differences in Norway: With Special References to Labor Radicalism and Cultural Norms," *Scandinavian Political Studies* 10 [1975]: 132.)

The five regions differed in political aspects. In the independence referendum of 1905, region 4 cast a larger proportion of republican votes than any of the other areas. Everywhere else, with the exception of a few localities in the extreme north, the vote was overwhelmingly monarchist in 1905, the inner central region taking the lead in this respect. Region 1 also cast the most votes against prohibition in 1919 and 1926. In both those years region 2 clearly differed from region 1, in which the temperance vote was lower, as well as from regions 3 and 4, where it was higher. Between regions 3 and 4, whose returns differed clearly in 1905, there was not much difference during the prohibition referenda. In the northernmost area, less homogenous than the other four, there appeared a very strong opposition to prohibition in 1926 along a great part of the coastline.

The latter phenomenon was a symptom of the importance of economic factors. Because of prohibition, the wine and liquor exporting countries of southern Europe retaliated against Norwegian exports of fish. Norwegian fishermen, especially in certain parts of the north, suffered great losses and turned against the temperance policy. Losses were also inflicted to some extent on the population of region 3, the western and southern coast; but here religious sentiment, expressed by the temperance movement, was very strong, which may explain why the prohibitionist stand was maintained so firmly. In region 4, an area of small-scale agriculture, forestry, and some mining, religion was a much less important factor. While the humble, pacific Christians along the coast had upheld the monarchy in 1905, more pugnacious elements among the farming and mining population of the valleys and mountains had supported the republic and the anti-Swedish stand. When they voted together with the coastal people against prohibition in 1919, it was less for religious reasons than as a protest against urban cultural norms as well as the big farmers and their "conspicuous consumption."

The percentages of the vote cast within the five regions against the monarchy in 1905 and against prohibition in 1919 and 1926, respectively, are shown in table 5.1. It comprises all the communes of the realm. In table 5.2, distributed among the same five regions, are the thirty-one localities that were designated by William Lafferty as those sending the most radical and most moderate delegations to the conventions of 1918 and 1919.

Table 5.2 tells us nothing about the relative weight of delegations from different localities at the crucial Labor congresses of 1918 and 1919. Lafferty's narrative fills that gap partially. Within the group of most effective radical localities, he tells us, delegations from region 4, with a

Table 5.1. Political regions in Norway, 1905–26

Region	Valid votes 1905*	% against monarchy 1905	Valid votes 1919	% against prohibition 1919	Valid votes 1926	% against prohibition 1926
1. Inner central area	71,945	15.3	180,601	69.5	256,360	82.1
2. Outer central area	62,255	17.9	151,074	50.5	188,065	70.2
3. Coast and outer fjords	90,163	18.4	220,293	20.1	241,434	32.1
4. Valleys, mountains, and inner fjords	76,132	33.4	177,393	22.5	191,745	38.6
5. The northernmost part	28,332	18.3	64,329	28.7	76,511	49.1
National total	328,827	21.1	793,690	38.4	954,115	55.7

Source: Official statistics.
* Male suffrage only.

Table 5.2. Political attitudes in localities by region, 1905 and 1919

	Radical			Moderate		
Region	No. of localities	% against monarchy 1905	% against prohibition 1919	No. of localities	% against monarchy 1905	% against prohibition 1919
1. Inner central area	6	11.1	58.2	4	12.2	59.8
2. Outer central area	5	23.9	52.3	3	12.0	40.7
3. Coast and outer fjords	3	19.0	34.3	2	17.7	24.1
4. Valleys, mountains, and inner fjords	4	37.0	29.4	3	26.8	8.7
5. The northernmost part	1	16.9	16.9	0	—	—
National average	19	21.2	45.0	12	17.1	35.6

Sources: William M. Lafferty, *Economic Development and the Response of Labor in Scandinavia* (Oslo, 1971), pp. 296–328, and official statistics.

great surplus of radical votes, played an important part. The situation was the reverse within the most moderate group. Here localities belonging to the same region were unimportant; they provided only a relatively small surplus of moderate votes. In other words, region 4 represented a radical stronghold within the Labor party. From table 5.2 it is apparent that localities in that region had the lowest antiprohibition vote in 1919. However, the radical faction of the party conventions of 1918–19 also received a substantial part of its strength from delegations representing the central regions, where a decidedly antiprohibitionist attitude prevailed, as shown in table 5.2.

We must conclude, therefore, that there existed in Norway at the end of World War I, two different types of labor radicalism in regard to the liquor question. The difference had to do with regional contrasts. Some localities combined radicalism not with a rejection of traditional norms, but on the contrary with an affirmation of old lower-class normative traditions. Thus even here, we cannot explain the political processes by focusing mainly on normative phenomena.

It seems appropriate to refer to what Charles Tilly says in a similar context: "Durkheimian arguments exaggerate the role played by deviance and individual disorder, while neglecting the analysis of organization and mobilization."[12] The latter should be studied at close quarters at the local level. In chapter 4, Steven Koblik has likewise emphasized the desirability of focusing on local aspects of political development in Sweden. A related argument has been put forward in general terms by Heinz Eulau. In the comparative analysis of "whole systems," notably nations and societies, the neglect of local variations leaves too much of national divergencies unexplained. Intervening between the individual and society are other units whose properties are relevant, Eulau says.[13] He argues that the units of political analysis are what he calls decision or action units in contrast to sociological units of common habits and values. At times such units are also units of common action, as for example when adherents of temperance in the national referendum of 1919 voted together in support of Norwegian prohibition, across provincial boundaries and despite party distinctions. But more often political units will cut across many sociological lines of distinction.

During the period under study, an important unit of common action was the county or province (*amt,* later called *fylke*), or more particularly the provincial party organization. Parties were organized on a provincial basis because the province in most cases represented a natural unit of communication with one town at its center, on which roads, railroads, and sea routes could converge. And of special political importance, in an age when the press had almost no competition from other mass media, a party-affiliated newspaper was published with a circulation that covered the whole of the surrounding province. This gets us back to two provinces that became headquarters of the radical and the moderate faction within the Norwegian labor movement: Tröndelag with the town of Trondheim and Buskerud to the west of the Oslo fjord.

In the course of the year 1917, as the food situation deterioriated rapidly, moderate leadership, which had been co-opted into the administration of wartime controls and rationing, lost control. A number of mass demonstrations occurred in the main cities of Norway. The iron and metal workers of Oslo initiated the movement. The insurgency's beginning in Oslo conforms to the picture drawn by James E. Cronin for the rest of Europe.[14] Since the turn of the century, working-class neighborhoods had become increasingly segregated from the middle and upper classes in the larger European cities, a sociological factor that provides part of the explanation why in one country after another the insurgency exploded there. For example, the connection between neighborhood ecology, separate subcultures, and politics was pointed out repeatedly (November 15, 1912; October 24, 1913) in the local Oslo socialist newspaper *Agitatoren* (*The Agitator*).

The movement soon spread from Oslo to other places in Norway but declined in later months. Then, at the end of the year, news arrived of the Bolshevik revolution in Russia. Soon afterward a renewed mood of militancy swept through the working class of one western European country after the other; but almost nowhere was there a radical faction sufficiently well organized to seize the fleeting opportunity and secure a leading position for itself. Norway was the exception.

Agitation in favor of a Bolshevik solution was started by leaders of the intellectual Norwegian Socialist Youth Organization and by some workers' councils of the capital demanding sequestration of all stores of food, workers' control over factories, and regulation of all production and exchange of commodities.

Although no concerted action was taken, the election of delegates to the annual congress of the Labor party, scheduled for the end of March 1918, reflected the mood of Norwegian workers. The congress defeated the moderate leadership by a margin of 159 to 126 votes and elected men of the radical wing. The delegates from Tröndelag, unanimous in supporting a revolutionary program, played a crucial role during the proceedings. Their leader, Martin Tranmael, was elected secretary general of the party.

The new Labor party leaders showed great skill during the years that followed, not least the new secretary general, who exhibited, among other qualities, remarkable flexibility. It appears that this may be ascribed to his heterodox background and experience: rural origins, commitment to temperance, and urban work experience as a housepainter.

The Tröndelag region is located in central Norway, two hundred to three hundred miles south of the Arctic Circle, covering an area of about seven thousand square miles from the Atlantic Ocean to the Swedish border. For administrative purposes it was designated the province of South Trondheim and comprised the town of Trondheim as well as five nonurban constituencies: the two coastal constituencies of Fosen to the west of the town, on either side of the entrance of the Trondheim fjord, and the three inland constituencies of Orkedalen, Guldalen, and Strinden (see fig. 5.2). The parliamentary constituency of Guldalen was divided into eleven communes for purposes of local administration and local elections.

As mentioned above, the Liberal and Conservative parties dominated Norwegian politics completely in the second half of the nineteenth century. A socialist party, the Norwegian Labor party, was founded at the end of the 1880s, but its initial growth was very slow. The industrial laboring class was small. Norway was still predominantly an agricultural country, with the Liberal party representing the majority of the farming population. Much of the activity of Labor leaders, nationally and locally, was directed at putting pressure on the Liberals to take a positive stand on issues of particular interest to industrial workers. But after the introduction of universal male suffrage in the 1890s, the socialists could begin to think of competing with the established parties.

Starting with the early years of the present century, statistics are available at the communal level from both parliamentary and local elections. In Tröndelag the socialists participated in these local contests in the town and in a steadily growing number of rural communes, with their share of the vote increasing steadily. By 1918 the Labor party obtained 40 percent of the total vote in the town and an average of 35 percent in the rural constituencies. This political development was paralleled by economic change, with manufacturing industry growing in the town as well as the surrounding areas.

Since socialism is an ideology appealing to the industrial working class, the growth in Labor party votes would be expected to reflect the growing number of workers in manufacturing industry, and it could be presumed that a process of radicalization occurred as the importance of old, small-

Figure 5.2. Map of Tröndelag. (Reprinted with permission from S. S. Nilson, "Labor Insurgency in Norway," *Social Science History* 5 [1981]: 397.)

scale, craftlike industries decreased, while a new labor force developed, consisting of uprooted individuals from the primary sector of the economy. The latter could be expected to support a radical socialist policy. However, the statistics throw doubt on such a thesis. It can provide only a partial explanation. Socialist votes were not concentrated merely in and around the industrial town of Trondheim; they were also located in great numbers in the Guldalen constituency, both in an old mining village at the outskirts of the province and in a series of predominantly agricultural communes.

The phenomenon of rural socialism is not unknown in certain other countries, particularly in the Mediterranean area. In a study of southern France, Tony Judt has shown how small-property-owning peasants, many of whom had been formerly employed as part-time workers in local workshops, turned socialist when hard economic times hit the countryside. They regarded state intervention in favor of agriculture, which was advocated only by the Socialist party, as offering a possibility of relief. In Judt's study, communes with a high socialist percentage of the vote were communes whose population was on the decline.[15]

But Tröndelag does not conform to this model either. No part of the province was marked by declining population, although there were considerable demographic and economic differences from one area to another. Table 5.3 shows the demographic development during the first two decades of the present century. In Trondheim, and still more in the Strinden constituency near the town, there was a rapid growth of population. There was also some increase in Orkedalen. In the other constituencies, few changes occurred, and their populations were almost stagnant.

Table 5.3. Population of Tröndelag, 1900–20

Commune	Number of inhabitants			Percent increase	
	1900	1910	1920	1900–10	1910–20
Fosen	39,935	40,802	41,770	2.2	2.4
Orkedalen*	18,713	19,913	21,852	6.4	9.7
Guldalen*	19,780	20,857	21,754	5.4	4.3
Strinden*	18,774	21,399	26,391	14.0	23.3
Trondheim	38,180	45,335	55,030	18.7	21.4

Source: Official statistics.
*The designations are now Orkdal, Gauldal, and Strinda.

During the same period, as shown in tables 5.4 and 5.5, the socialist share of the vote increased in every constituency. It is hardly surprising to find socialism spreading at a rapid pace in dynamic Strinden and rather slowly in Orkedalen, the constituency exhibiting a measured pace of economic growth, while making no headway in the stationary North and South Fosen constituencies. But the pattern is quite different in the case of Guldalen. Its demographic features indicate an economy as stationary as that of Fosen, yet its electorate proved highly susceptible to socialism. Very soon the Labor party had a greater share of the vote in Guldalen than

Table 5.4. Political attitudes in Tröndelag, 1905–12

| | Referendum | | Parliamentary elections | | | | Referendum |
| | % favoring republic | | % favoring Labor party | | | | % for prohibition |
Commune	1905	1906	1909	1912	1915	1918	1919
Fosen	16.8	2.6	2.0	4.1	13.9	21.6	80.2
Orkedalen	24.7	5.8	12.6	13.8	26.5	31.5	86.4
Guldalen	41.2	32.0	40.5	41.9	50.0	44.8	85.7
Strinden	20.1	22.6	30.1	37.6	45.2	41.1	74.1
Trondheim	28.7	36.8	38.3	40.7	44.6	39.5	48.2

Source: Official statistics.

Table 5.5. Electoral participation in Tröndelag, 1906–18

| | % of registered voters casting votes | | | | | |
| | Referendum 1905 | Parliamentary elections 1906 | Local elections 1916 | | Parliamentary elections 1918 | |
Commune	Males	Males	Males	Females	Males	Females
Fosen	61.9	49.3	48.5	17.9	63.0	19.5
Orkedalen	68.5	52.3	52.6	22.8	52.9	43.7
Guldalen	75.3	64.6	74.2	45.9	81.4	60.5
Strinden	72.7	57.4	56.6	33.1	66.1	40.4
Trondheim	77.8	71.6	63.1	50.9	71.5	64.2

Source: Official statistics.

even in and near the town of Trondheim. In other words, looking more closely we find not one but two strongholds of socialism in the area: first, the town of Trondheim and its nearest surroundings where a steadily increasing socialist vote parallels a rapid, though not explosive, process of industrialization, and second, the constituency of Guldalen, where no industrial expansion took place, but a similar growth in the electorate's response to socialism is reflected in the political data. The tables illustrate the development from 1906, the first year of detailed election statistics, through 1918. From the beginning, both the turnout and the socialist share of the vote were much higher in Guldalen than in the other rural constituencies; they were actually as high as or higher than the turnout and socialist vote in the town of Trondheim.

Tables 5.6 and 5.7 give data from the different communes within the Guldalen constituency. The first column of table 5.6 shows the number of registered voters in the different communes for the 1906 election; the

Table 5.6. Political attitudes in Guldalen, 1906–18

Communes	Number of registered voters 1906*	% of votes in parliamentary elections favoring Labor party				
		1906	1909	1912	1915	1918
Röros	1,068	45.2	49.3	47.5	56.7	45.7
Aalen	474	62.8	65.4	65.1	72.4	67.8
Holtaalen	192	33.1	35.7	34.2	53.3	50.6
Singsaas	332	15.6	31.0	29.8	42.1	37.0
Budalen	135	0.0	31.0	38.1	51.4	42.4
Stören	423	42.4	45.7	52.3	63.6	60.6
Soknedalen	461	3.6	18.3	27.0	35.4	31.8
Horg	513	19.7	27.0	33.8	46.9	47.9
Hölandet	245	1.7	16.3	9.9	17.6	16.3
Flaa	171	18.6	19.1	27.4	27.5	25.6
Melhus	562	22.7	25.5	32.5	36.1	37.2
Total Guldalen constituency	4,576	32.1	40.5	41.9	50.0	44.8

Sources: Norwegian newspaper reports and official statistics.
* Only men had the right to vote in 1906. There was very little change in these figures during the period in question, the population of every Guldalen commune being almost stationary; but with the introduction of female suffrage (restricted in 1909, universal in 1915), the size of the electorate was correspondingly increased.

Table 5.7. Political participation in Guldalen, 1906–18

Communes	Parliamentary elections 1906	Parliamentary elections 1909		Local elections 1916		Parliamentary elections 1918	
	Males	Males	Females	Males	Females	Males	Females
Röros	72.5	80.1	60.4	76.5	53.1	78.5	58.9
Aalen	76.4	90.4	80.3	83.5	55.8	90.0	75.3
Holtaalen	75.7	86.0	63.7	81.1	59.1	89.9	73.8
Singsaas	69.8	89.1	53.2	89.2	60.6	93.7	69.7
Budalen	68.2	72.1	39.0	89.0	76.2	94.9	82.9
Stören	64.1	72.2	53.2	76.8	56.2	79.3	61.6
Soknedalen	45.9	63.7	4.8	71.7	28.3	86.3	64.2
Horg	48.2	64.9	37.5	62.9	24.6	74.0	40.7
Hölandet	53.0	54.5	12.2	73.1	52.2	78.6	61.5
Flaa	72.5	83.8	67.1	51.7	31.6	80.7	60.4
Melhus	64.2	63.1	27.3	62.1	31.5	74.6	50.9
Total Guldalen constituency	64.6	74.7	51.9	74.2	45.9	81.4	60.5

% of registered voters casting votes

Source: Official statistics.

following columns show the evolution of the socialist vote in each commune. These are ranged in geographical order from southest to northwest,
down the valley of the river Gaula toward the town of Trondheim. The
figures seem to indicate a diffusion of political attitudes, not so much from
the expanding commercial and industrial town as from the mountain
district at the other end of the province. The lead was taken not by the
communes close to the town but by those that were located farthest away
from it. Similarly, the level of participation, which increased only gradually in most other parts of the constituency, was high from the very
beginning in the mountain district, as can be seen in table 5.7. This was the
district of century-old copper mining, with mines spread widely over the
mountain plateau that comprised the two communes of Röros and Aalen.
The activities were administered from the mining village in Röros commune, a stronghold of radicalism and incipient socialism at the turn of the
century. When Norway seceded from the Union with Sweden in 1905, the
socialists and the left wing of the Liberal party proposed the abolition of
the monarchy and the introduction of a republican form of government. A
referendum was conducted. Nationally, the republicans were defeated by
a majority of almost four to one, and in Tröndelag as a whole the score did
not deviate much from the national average (see table 5.4); but in the
Röros and Aalen communes some 60 to 70 percent of the votes were cast
in favor of the republic.

Other data confirm the special position of the mining district at the
beginning of the century. When the Labor party first participated elec-
torally on its own in Tröndelag, at the local elections of 1901, it presented
itself in the town of Trondheim, in the nearby partly industrialized commune of Malvik, Strinden constituency, and in Röros and Aalen. The
Labor list in Trondheim obtained a little more than 10 percent of the total
vote cast in the town in 1901 and more than 25 percent at the next
election, the parliamentary contest of 1903. In the rural areas, the party
division of the vote is not known at the communal level for either of these
two early elections. However, in a report dated September 4, 1903, the
leader of the provincial party organization, declaring himself relatively
satisfied with the result of the recent parliamentary election, pointed out
that the Röros-Aalen district was the only one in the whole province,
outside the town of Trondheim, in which the party had been organized
locally for any length of time. Thanks to the organizational base, delegates
from Guldalen had been in a large majority at the preparatory as well as
the constituent meeting when the rural Labor party branch of Tröndelag
was founded in the spring of 1903. Guldalen as a whole also soon became

the best-organized constituency within that branch, better organized than either Strinden (near Trondheim) or Orkedalen, and far better than the two Fosen constituencies, which together were termed "the dark continent" in one of the early annual reports to national party headquarters. In 1907 the number of inscribed party members was 99 in Fosen, 207 in Orkedalen, 285 in Strinden, and 808 in Guldalen.

These early events are easily explained in terms of the economic structure of Tröndelag at the beginning of the century. According to the 1900 census, Guldalen was the rural constituency that had the largest share of population in mining and manufacturing industry, 30 to 40 percent in mining alone. With the Norwegian Labor party still representing little more than the political branch of the labor unions, it was perhaps natural that the Röros-Aalen miners should cast the bulk of the socialist votes and also provide the initial impetus when the rural branch of the provincial party was launched.

It comes as more of a surprise to learn that Guldalen was still the leading socialist constituency a couple of decades later, in spite of the fact that its demographic and economic mix persisted while other parts of the province had undergone quite considerable changes. By 1920 both Orkedalen and Strinden had larger shares of their population engaged in mining and manufacturing industries than Guldalen. Only the two Fosen constituencies still remained much less industrialized (between 2 and 3 percent) than Guldalen in 1920 (see table 5.8).

In spite of the static conditions in Guldalen, however, the labor leaders of the old mining district had proved capable of utilizing the possibilities opened up by the introduction of male suffrage at the end of the last century and the establishment of single-member parliamentary constituencies shortly thereafter. The latter reform might have been presumed to work rather to their disadvantage, and so it certainly would have if the miners had formed an isolated group. But it turned out that a large part of the remaining population was attracted by their leadership and was willing to vote for their candidates.

Not even the miners located in the village of Röros itself were cut off from the rest of the Röros commune of the countryside in general. *Bergstaden* Röros had a population of somewhat less than 2,000 persons, living in 350 to 400 houses along the two half-mile-long village streets. Most of these dwellings were small, unpainted log cabins. Though the climate was too severe for the cultivation of grain, the surrounding plateau offered good grazing land. Some of it was in the possession of cattle farmers who lived in the mining town, but to a large extent it was subdivided into small

Table 5.8. Percentage of men, 15 years and over, employed in 1920

Commune	Farmers	Other independents in agriculture	Sons working on homestead	Workers in agriculture and forestry	Fishermen and sailors	Artisans	Factory workers	Miners	Construction workers	Employment in commune, teaching, etc.	Total
Fosen	23.2	2.6	15.3	7.5	38.6	4.9	2.4	0.2	1.5	3.7	100
Orkedalen	26.3	3.3	17.1	17.3	0.6	11.7	6.6	6.8	7.4	2.7	100
Guldalen	26.4	5.2	20.0	13.9	0.1	10.2	3.4	8.9	9.2	2.8	100
Strinden	16.6	4.3	15.4	16.9	2.4	12.1	18.7	0.4	4.6	8.7	100

Source: Official statistics.

individual plots owned by miners. Each one included a tiny barn for the storage of fodder. On such a plot enough grass could be grown, provided diligent use was made of manure, to sustain two or three cows through the long winter. In addition to the hay, however, it was necessary for the miner and his family to gather a certain amount of supplementary fodder in the form of reindeer moss, leaves or twigs of bushes, and grass growing around bogs on the more distant mountain plateau.

For centuries this way of life had been maintained with the aid of specific regulations, which mine owners could not change. A characteristic resolution, passed by the communal assembly in 1902 and submitted to the Liberal government emphasized "the crucial importance of upholding the right of miners to have one free day per week" at certain times of the year, so that they would be able to combine some agricultural work with their occupation in the mines.

Guldalen as a whole was an area of small-scale agriculture, where children helped work the farms of their parents. Many farms were very small, and the vast majority just supported the owner and his family. A few were larger, employing a certain number of hired hands the year round. As one moved from the mountain plateau down the valley one found an increasing number of the larger farms, although nowhere in Guldalen were they predominant.

Occupational information for the year 1916 shows the distribution of the Labor party communal assembly members in Guldalen constituency: farm owners, 24; miners, 11; other workers, 13; artisans, 11; others, 8. The 11 miners held their seats in the Röros and Aalen communal assemblies, while the other occupations were rather evenly represented throughout all the communes. Farmers were as strongly represented as workers. The assembly members' names and occupations are given in the Labor party's annual report. Among the farm owners were a few who were designated as "tenants," "sons of farmers," or "smallholders." Most artisans owned little plots of land, and many farmers as well as smallholders found some part-time work outside agriculture, such as roadbuilding. Classifications therefore tell only part of the story. Terms like *gaardbruker* (farm owner) and *smaabruker* (smallholder) were often used interchangeably. Sometimes the word *arbeiderbonde* (worker-farmer) was employed, not inappropriately.

At the electoral level, the Labor party obtained substantial support from smallholders and family farmers. Much of its propaganda was specifically directed at the agricultural population and was very similar to that of the Liberals' radical agrarian wing. Labor party spokesmen were at pains to point out that its program did not call for any collectivization of agriculture. Their "anticapitalist" land policy largely consisted of a denunciation of high rates of interest, which rendered the property rights of the debt-ridden peasant "illusory."

The miners of the mountain district were attracted by socialist ideas about workers collectively taking over the means of production in industrial society, but at the same time they felt that some kind of private property should exist in agriculture. The success of socialist propaganda in an area as predominantly agricultural as Guldalen is not surprising when seen against this background.

When the Labor party gained power at the local level it demonstrated an ability to cater to the interests of the rural population: to provide, for example, free textbooks in schools and free medical aid in cases of sickness and childbirth, financed out of taxation borne largely by the more prosperous farmers. Such practical, down-to-earth policies produced a noticeable effect on Labor party votes at the elections.

The man who started proselytizing activity outside the mining district, Svend Skaardal, was himself the owner of a farm; but before he took it over from his father, he had worked for many years in the mines and had taken part in the strikes that occurred around the turn of the century. While remaining definitely the miners' man, he had no difficulty in establishing contact with the agrarian community and gaining followers there. In 1907 Aalen elected him the first socialist mayor in a Guldalen commune.

The party soon got another forceful leader in young Martin Tranmael. Almost twenty years younger than Skaardal, he began to display his outstanding gifts as an agitator around the turn of the century. He too was the son of a farmer, and he never abandoned some of the values instilled by his rural upbringing, such as his commitment to strict temperance. Prohibitionism directed against the consumption habits of well-to-do townspeople and prosperous farmers was very strong among the rural population of Tröndelag, particularly in the mountains, where it gave expression to deeply imbedded traditional views. Tranmael was by no means alone in taking this stand. In the 1919 referendum 82 percent of the valid votes favored prohibition in the commune of Röros and no less than 95 percent in the commune of Aalen. The inhabitants of these areas held fast to the norms of their forefathers. Stern and frugal, they eked out a precarious living on the barren mountain plateau or in the snow-covered valley, whether as miners, cotters, or a combination of both. Most of them were fully convinced that temperance was the only proper course. They did not all possess the strength of character of Martin Tranmael, who seems to have hardly touched a glass of beer, wine, or liquor in his life. But they all upheld the principle as such, even if some considered it permissible occasionally to produce spirits for home consumption in their basements. They still rejected the life-style of modern city people, the merchants, shipowners, and factory owners, and of the prosperous farmers—drinking imported wine and liquor and tempting poor people to ruin their economy by doing likewise. To a man like Tranmael the consumption of alcohol was an expression of "corrupt capitalist society." He met the same attitude when he was active in organizing first the inhabitants of the mountain district and then the more purely agricultural population of Guldalen for political action through the Labor party.

The different parts of Tröndelag belonged to more than one of Norway's politicocultural regions, however. It was a circumstance to which Tranmael had to adapt. His own birthplace was in the northern part of Guldalen, not far from Trondheim, and at an early age he worked as a housepainter's apprentice in town. He learned how to organize among both urban and rural people. And temperance, for instance, was not very popular in the cities (see table 5.4).

If we are to understand not only Transmael's personal career but also the whole development of the Norwegian labor movement during the 1920s, we must keep in mind the complex character of that movement and the interaction of its different elements. The situation was highly fluid before World War I and during the early war years. This applies to Tröndelag as well as other areas. Its mountain community of miners was and remained a center of radicalism, but in other parts of the province the balance of forces within the labor movement kept shifting, particularly in the town of Trondheim. There a moderate faction possessed considerable strength for a long period. There was also a more radical faction represented in the labor unions, but although Tranmael and his friends helped organize the activity of militants in the town, they were often on the defensive within the local urban movement.

A third element consisted of the itinerant construction workers. Around World War I a number of them came to the Tröndelag area, engaged in building the new railway line southward from Stören through Soknedal and parts of Orkedalen (see fig. 5.2). These men were radicals, "uprooted" individuals of the type described by Edvard Bull. Through them Martin Tranmael came into contact with similar groups of men in other parts of Norway. There was considerable building and construction activity going on in northern as well as southern Norway, and when groups of laborers had finished their work in one place and were looking for new jobs elsewhere on roads, railways, or new hydroelectrical power stations, they often passed through the centrally located town of Trondheim. Many of them were impatient with the trade union leadership in Oslo. At this time its main policy consisted of securing long-term collective agreements with management, a strategy better suited for people in stable factory employment than for itinerants. If the latter were to have some influence on their wages and working conditions, they felt that more aggressive tactics were needed.

A Trade Union Opposition Group was formally constituted by delegates from various parts of Norway meeting in Trondheim in 1911, largely representing construction workers. Very soon they were joined by other radical elements, particularly miners and factory workers from new industries. The group criticized not only the central trade union leadership but also the established leaders of the Labor party, whose patient endeavors to influence Parliament and municipal bodies were assailed as being slow and ineffectual. Tranmael had a leading position within the group and engaged in several speaking tours throughout the country in the years before World War I. He attacked tendencies toward tactical collaboration with bourgeois parties in representative political bodies, and he advocated more violent methods of sabotage and obstruction. The Trade Union Opposition Group was supported by the more intellectual Socialist Youth Organization, but they remained in the minority within the Norwegian labor movement as a whole.

All this changed in the course of 1917, and as we have seen, the radical opposition, led by Tranmael, gained control of the March 1918 Labor party congress. Several factors must be considered in an evaluation of this development. The existence of an organized trade union opposition, around which the insurgency could crystallize, was certainly important. But concentrating as it did on special forms of industrial militancy, this group had hitherto been rather isolated. As late as 1917, it was able to muster only 71 out of a total of 279 delegates at the national congress of trade unions. However, some of its leaders, and Tranmael in particular, had succeeded in establishing close contact with other and quite different labor elements.

During the early part of the decade, socialists were still in the minority in most of the local representative assemblies of Tröndelag, urban as well as rural. They could achieve no practical results except by voting for measures with which they were only in partial agreement. Tranmael and his friends opposed all such forms of compromise with nonsocialists, and they warned strongly against socialists agreeing to stand as mayors unless they also had a majority in the local assembly in question. But the spirit of collaboration that developed during the first years of the war prompted them to become more flexible. After the local election of 1916, the Trond-heim Labor party agreed to fill the post of mayor, although the bourgeois parties between them still held a majority of the seats in the municipal assembly. Tranmael bowed to the decision and even accepted the position of deputy mayor himself. It was done, his local paper explained shortly afterward, "with great reluctance," but with the goal of showing that the party "did not shirk responsibility in view of the important tasks that awaited solution."[16] Growing food shortages occasioned an increase in the activity of municipal bodies, and throughout 1917 Tranmael as dep-uty mayor worked on the town's board of provisions, an administrative job that was important under the prevailing circumstances.

He had given an example of his flexibility, which some called opportun-ism. Not without reason was he once likened to a barometer, and indeed, he never failed to reflect accurately the mood of the working class. During the last year of the war that mood shifted rapidly, and in 1918, to the consternation of conservatives, the diligent deputy mayor was trans-formed once more into a fiery agitator. Tranmael made no attempt to exercise a restraining influence when news reached Trondheim of the revolution in Russia and the demands raised by Oslo's metalworkers. On the contrary, he seems to have utilized in an unexpected way the confi-dence he had gained with formerly moderate groups, such as housewives, through his patient work to secure the ever more precarious provisioning of the city. Even these groups were now in an almost insurrectionary mood, to which Tranmael responded without delay. The moderate leader-ship, recently in a strong position both nationally and locally, was at this moment overwhelmed by the insurgency.

Meeting in the middle of March, the urban and rural branches of the Labor party in Tröndelag unanimously endorsed the demands of Oslo's workers' councils for the requisitioning of stores of food and workers' control of industry. The latter idea corresponded to the wishes of con-struction workers as well as the old radical miners in the countryside and factory workers in town. In addition, the Tröndelag resolutions included a demand for workers' councils in the rural districts to carry out confisca-tion of farmland and its distribution to smallholders in cases where the owner did not cultivate his fields. There was a streak of peasant radicalism in the Norwegian movement. In this respect it resembled parallel develop-ments in Italy and Hungary.

Unlike Italy and Hungary, however, the radical victory was peaceful and undramatic. It remained confined to the labor movement. No actual attempt was made to overthrow Norwegian bourgeois society, despite a good deal of revolutionary rhetoric.

The identification of the main factors preceding the radical takeover of the Norwegian labor movement in 1918 leads to a similar analysis of the process of deradicalization. This process was aided by powerful general forces. In the atmosphere of international economic depression after the war, the hopes engendered by peace soon evaporated. The spokesmen of cautious and moderate policies could take the offensive within the Norwegian labor movement. But it is not easy to point out their power bases. At first sight it might seem as if there would be little difficulty in making a preliminary sociological study to lay the groundwork of a specifically political analysis. Quantitative material is available that appears to indicate with unusual clarity the ecological background of Norway's working-class radicals and moderates. However, on closer inspection it turns out that the evidence is not wholly convincing. While in some places it is possible to measure precisely the numerical strength of moderate and radical groups, similar attempts prove futile elsewhere.

Norwegian parliamentary elections were held at regular three-year intervals in the fall of 1918, 1921, and 1924. At the 1918 election the Norwegian Labor party presented an ostensibly unified front despite the moderate group's strong opposition to the radical leadership that had taken over in the spring. Somewhat later, however, the minority formally seceded. It presented its own lists of candidates at the next election, in fall 1921, under the label Social Democratic party. The majority remained formally united on a revolutionary program and presented itself as the "Norwegian Labor Party (Section of the Communist International)." Two years later, however, disagreement on the conditions of continued Comintern membership led to a second split when another group broke away, this time to found the Communist party of Norway. Thus at the 1924 general election three distinct socialist parties presented themselves, two of which adopted a radical program.

Table 5.9 shows the results of the 1921 and 1924 elections. It is possible to ascertain the relative strength of radicalism and moderation within the labor movement from these figures. There are places where an analysis of statistical data is sufficient to explain the appeal of different socialist programs. In the valley of Romsdal, a rural district in western Norway, for example, in addition to some cottage industry, there was a certain amount of construction work. The results of the 1921 and 1924 parliamentary

Table 5.9. Norwegian parliamentary elections, 1921 and 1924

Party	1921	1924
Norwegian Labor party	192,616	179,567
Social Democratic party	83,619	85,743
Communist party of Norway	—	59,401
Nonsocialist parties	628,464	649,230
Total votes	904,699	973,941

Source: Official statistics.

elections there are shown in table 5.10. Among the fifteen Romsdal communes, Grytten stands out. The large majority of radical votes was concentrated in that one commune, and the explanation is not hard to find. Grytten differed from the rest of Romsdal in being the site of construction work on the new railway which was to have its terminus there. The workers did not find the cautiously gradualist policies of the Social Democrats attractive, as did the sedentary men and women who were employed in the light industry of the valley. Construction workers in Romsdal voted for the Labor party in 1921 and divided their votes between Labor and the new Communist party in 1924.

There are other parts of Norway where social background seems to have determined the distribution of votes among the socialist parties of the 1920s. But such was by no means the case everywhere. In particular, two provinces on either side of the Oslo fjord should be mentioned. Although they had practically the same ecological background, characterized largely by wood-processing and consumer goods industries, they

Table 5.10. Party votes in Romsdal, 1921 and 1924

Party	1921	1924
Norwegian Labor party	324	249
Social Democratic party	1,262	1,272
Communist party of Norway	—	146
Nonsocialist parties	8,101	8,573
Total votes	9,687	10,240

Source: Official statistics.

presented a strong political contrast. Östfold on the eastern side was dominated by the moderate Social Democratic party. The manufacturing industries of the province had been established gradually over a number of years; its labor leaders were prominent in the moderate wing of the movement and exerted a large measure of control over the socialist press in the area. It was not very surprising, therefore, that Östfold should emerge as a stronghold of the Social Democratic party. What was surprising, however, was the contrast between Östfold and the province on the other side of the fjord, Buskerud. In the years up to and including the war the political coloring had been similar in the two provinces. But after the war the scene changed. In the 1921 and 1924 elections the overwhelming majority of Buskerud's socialist votes were cast in favor of the Norwegian Labor party (see table 5.11). The Labor party was now often called the "Tranmaelite" or "Tranmael-Communist" party after the new radical secretary of its national organization. From 1918 on, Martin Tranmael lived in the capital and had the Oslo branch of the Labor party as his local power base. Besides, he exerted considerable influence through the nationwide contacts he had established during his years of work in the Trade Union Opposition Group. But the group had never been of any importance in Buskerud, in either its urban or its rural areas.[17] Tranmael was without any particular personal influence in Buskerud, but what was commonly regarded as "his" party had a strong position there.

The contrast is striking between Östfold, where the Social Democratic party polled 74 and 79 percent of the socialist vote in 1921 and 1924, and Buskerud, where the Norwegian Labor party obtained 77 and 81 percent. Yet the political complexion of Buskerud had been rather similar to that of Östfold, and the core areas of these two provinces, which straddle the

Table 5.11. Party votes in Buskerud and Östfold, 1921 and 1924

Party	Buskerud		Östfold	
	1921	1924	1921	1924
Norwegian Labor party	16,686	18,417	5,426	4,807
Social Democratic party	4,979	4,447	15,765	18,305
Communist party of Norway	—	1,863	—	607
Nonsocialist parties	30,126	30,517	30,757	33,622
Total votes	51,791	55,244	51,948	57,341

Source: Official statistics.

outlets of the two major river basins in Norway, had a similar ecological setting. Socioeconomic factors cannot explain why, in the words of William Lafferty, Buskerud should be the province with the second highest percentage of Tranmaelite votes in the country.[18]

We must look behind the "Tranmaelite" label in order to understand what went on there during 1918–24, and consequently why the province came to play a key role in the eventual reunification of the Norwegian labor movement during the second half of the 1920s.

The outcome depended largely on the sense of timing displayed by those who took part in the organizational struggle, fought for many years before a decisive result was achieved. Certain general principles seem to be characteristic of such a process of interaction, in which each of the contending parties attempts to take advantage of the element of time. Their behavior is characterized by the alternate use of delay and equivocation, then of quick and clear action. When politicians are faced with a situation of uncertainty, they tend to resort to dilatory tactics, seeking refuge in ambiguity. And the period after 1918 was one of extreme uncertainty. Events were confusing. There seemed as much reason for great optimism as for extreme pessimism. At one moment the Bolsheviks were triumphant in Russia; a few months later they seemed about to be exterminated; then they were triumphant again. Wartime hardship and shortages in Norway, strongly felt during the winter of 1917–18, gave way to a short postwar boom, which again was followed by depression and unemployment from the autumn of 1920 onward.

Labor leaders tried to cope with uncertainty by postponing definite commitments. This was the reaction of moderates as well as radicals, on a national and a local level. The very basis of Norwegian socialist policy, including membership of the Communist International, contained an element of uncertainty and equivocation. Ostensibly the Labor party went over to the Communists, but if we look more closely, we shall see that it went only halfway.

Early on, Tranmael and other radicals who took over the leadership of the Norwegian Labor party in 1918 declared their intention to join the new Communist International, but only in September 1920 did the conditions of admittance become known. In twenty-one so-called theses the Russians demanded absolute obedience to Moscow. Many of the radical Norwegian leaders were anything but happy with the terms, but they found themselves in an awkward position. After their enthusiastic endorsement of the Russian Revolution and their many expressions of sympathy with the Russians during the months of Allied military intervention in 1919 and 1920, it would have been extremely difficult for them to advocate a sudden rupture with Moscow. So a temporary solution was found by means of further postponement. In October 1920 the Norwegians asked for admission to the new Communist International on modified terms. What they obtained was an assurance from the Comintern that in their case certain clauses would be suspended temporarily. No more than a temporary suspension was conceded, however. In principle, the Moscow theses had to be accepted, and sooner or later a complete reorganization of their party would have to be carried out in order to ensure the Russian goal, unquestioning obedience to the Comintern.

This was too much for a number of moderate Norwegian leaders to accept. They broke openly with the Labor party, launched their own Social Democratic party in March 1921, and ran their own candidates in the October parliamentary election. It would seem, perhaps, that now at last the national strength of the radical and moderate factions could be ascertained with precision. However, the situation remained ambiguous in a number of places, the most important being the province of Buskerud.

One of the earliest strongholds of the labor movement, Buskerud was the home and power base of Christopher Hornsrud, born in 1859, who until 1918 had been one of the party's moderate national leaders, and who in 1928 was to become the first Norwegian Labor prime minister. An important labor newspaper, *Fremtiden* (*The Future*), was published in Buskerud's largest town, Drammen. Its editor, Torgeir Vraa, a lifelong colleague of Hornsrud, had, like him, been among the first Laborites to be elected to Parliament.

By 1920 these elderly men found that they had a serious problem on their hands. Everywhere enthusiasm for the Russian Revolution was greatest among the younger generation, and during the period in question working-class youth in Buskerud had been roused and organized by a team of men dedicated to the cause of the Communist International. The leader of the Norwegian Socialist Youth Organization, fiery, thirty-year-old Eugene Olaussen, had made Buskerud his base of operations since 1917. An eloquent speaker, he attracted a considerable following, especially in the industrial areas in Buskerud communes outside the administrative limits of the towns. This was of importance not least in connection with the daily newspaper *Fremtiden*. According to the provincial party statutes, representatives chosen by the local Labor party branches in communes designated as rural had a strong position on the paper's editorial board.

In 1918, during the early period of enthusiasm for the Russian Revolution, possibly even men like Vraa and Hornsrud had believed for a moment that a practically bloodless revolution in Norway was imminent, that the "rotten structure" of Western bourgeois society could be made to collapse by means of a general strike. But if so, they were quickly disillusioned. Their strong faith in slow and gradual evolution soon reasserted itself. There was no doubt about their aversion to bloodshed and violence.

Vraa was, in fact, the first in the country to sound the alarm when the Moscow theses became known in Norway. In an editorial dated September 10, 1920, he denounced communist militancy and the incitement to civil war. "We are willing to accept the good things that come from the east . . . but not the barbarism," he concluded. However, although he maintained this point of view during the months that followed, he may have slowly come to feel that he had ventured into the open too recklessly. When other moderate leaders launched the Social Democratic party at the beginning of the new year, they seem to have expected Vraa and Hornsrud to support it. The disappointment was great among Social Democrats when at the last moment both the Buskerud veterans, and their closest associates, decided to stay in the Labor party after all and accept the compromise reached with the Comintern. Apparently they were convinced at the beginning of the new year that their province was not yet ripe for determined action. They would have to bide their time.

Apprehension with regard to the future of the provincial party and its daily newspaper was probably a powerful motive. Vraa in particular seems to have feared, perhaps not without reason, that if he broke with his old party he would be dismissed as editor of the paper which he had founded at the beginning of the century and built up through years of hard work until it was now a political force of considerable importance. He decided to stay on.

The sequence of events that ensued in Buskerud followed the pattern of what is called a "mixed-motive game."[19] The relation between the two provincial factions was that of a most uneasy alliance, a mixture of mutual dependence and conflict, of enforced partnership and merciless competition. The moderates, hoping that the radical success would only be temporary, were biding their time, waiting for more normal conditions to return, and avoiding direct confrontation with their opponents. The radicals for their part wanted time to consolidate the organizational position they had won. Both factions adhered formally to the line laid down by the central leadership in Oslo. Thus Buskerud appeared to be a strictly subordinate local organization directed by Tranmael and his friends in Oslo.

But the appearance of "Tranmaelite" centralization in the 1920s was largely deceptive. In Buskerud particularly, the Oslo leaders were without influence, while inside the province the opposing factions continually jockeyed for position. In 1921, when a man like Vraa decided to stay in the party, the radicals of Buskerud probably took note of his decision with mixed feelings. They had by no means forgotten his "barbarism from Russia" article of the previous autumn and had no intention of forgiving him. But it seems that they were content to let him have a free hand for a few months until the parliamentary election was held in October. The outcome in Buskerud appeared uncertain. Some local moderate leaders, foremost among them C. S. Bentzen, member of Parliament and chairman of the Labor party in the small town of Hönefoss, decided to join the new Social Democratic party. At a meeting held on March 5, 1921, the Hönefoss Labor party formally seceded and applied for membership in the new party. Similar proceedings took place in a few nearby communes. Here— but only in this one locality—the Social Democratic party did succeed in establishing itself as the party of the working class. While it obtained 70 percent of the socialist vote in Hönefoss in the October election, it was in the minority in the two other towns of the province and in nearly all of its twenty-four rural communes.

In most of Buskerud the Social Democratic vote was wholly insignificant. The new party had at its disposal only one daily newspaper with a rather restricted circulation, which could in no way be compared to that of *Fremtiden.* Vraa in his paper conducted a vigorous electoral campaign in his traditional style. According to *Fremtiden,* practical reform was what the elections were all about; day-to-day problems were the main concern. There was hardly any reference to international affairs. Vraa declared explicitly that the election of Labor party representatives to Parliament had nothing to do with the question of whether the Moscow theses should be applied or amended; he pointed out that the practical legislative program of the Labor party was the same as before. Also, as before, its foremost candiate was Christopher Hornsrud, the old Buskerud veteran who had now decided to call himself a communist. He defined communism, however, in a way which must have been anything but satisfactory to the men in Moscow. In an article written for rural voters and published on August 4, 1921 in the journal *Arbeiderbonden (The Worker-Farmer),* Hornsrud posed the question whether the Norwegian Labor party was now to be regarded as a social democratic or a communist party. The question made no sense, he declared; there was no difference between communism and social democracy, nor between communism and Christianity for that matter. "The social ABC of Christianity reads as follows: Do unto others as you would be done by! He who will not work, shall not eat!" That is also the social doctrine of communism, Hornsrud continued, asking, why then has a split occurred within the Socialist party in Norway? The reason, he answered, was to be found in the failure of the Socialist International at the outbreak of the Great War, when it betrayed its pacifist program. Because of what happened in 1914, a new international had to be founded after the war, and the Norwegian Labor party had joined it. In other words, Hornsrud asked his readers not to vote for violent revolution but for pacificism and Christian love.

After the election, the Social Democratic party attributed its defeat in Buskerud to the "dishonest campaign" of the provincial Labor party, which had by no means followed the official line laid down by Oslo; on the contrary, it had "concealed its true nature and succeeded in hiding its real face behind a mask of moderation." These remarks seemed to refer in particular to the influence wielded by the newspaper *Fremtiden*. In this respect the radicals of Buskerud had reason to be well satisfied with Torgeir Vraa. But he had now served his purpose and could be dispensed with. It appears that they prepared to get rid of him, intending to force his replacement as editor, by means of their representation on the board of *Fremtiden*, at the annual meeting which was to take place in the spring of 1922. Vraa, nervous, overworked, and uncertain of his backing, decided to temporize. He asked to be given five or six months' leave of absence on account of failing health. It was granted, and the radicals on the board profited from the occasion by putting one of their number in his place while he was away.

When he reported back in the autumn, they resorted to dilatory tactics, extending his leave of absence until the next board meeting in the spring of 1923—this time against his own wishes. It was now clear that they intended to have him dismissed and to take over the paper completely. Both sides prepared for the coming battle, and the moderates won. Starting early, they succeeded in remobilizing their adherents in the various local Labor party associations that were to nominate representatives to the newspaper's editorial board, marshaling sufficient numbers for a majority on the board to be secured. The radicals discovered too late that they were powerless to prevent the reinstatement of Vraa.

A final round remained, however, the outcome of which appeared most uncertain. Finally the moderate faction's control of the newspaper decided the issue. By the end of 1923, Moscow's patience with the Norwegian Labor party was exhausted. The Communist International asked for compliance with its rules, a demand that was heartily supported by the radicals of Buskerud. By quick and energetic action against "betraying the

International," they succeeded in having their point of view accepted in October 1923 at meetings of the rural Buskerud Labor party associations. The moderates for their part managed to achieve a slender majority in the towns for support of the national leadership of the Labor party, which, under Tranmael and his colleagues, was radical but against acceding to the Russian demands.

A few weeks later, at the National Congress of the Norwegian Labor party in the beginning of November, the rupture with Moscow became a fact. A substantial minority of delegates thereupon left the congress to launch a new party, the Communist party of Norway. The representatives from Buskerud had two alternatives open to them. Either they could join the new party at once, in which case they might well be able to bring the rural Labor party associations with them, but scarcely the urban ones. Or they could wait, maintain their Labor party membership, and ask for the final decision to be made at a meeting of the provincial Labor party as a whole. Encouraged by their quick initial success, they chose the latter line, hoping to secure a majority at the provincial meeting for continued membership of the International and thereby for secession and adherence to the new party.

To achieve this end, the radical Buskerud faction called for "unity" and warned against "premature steps," ostensibly upholding its Labor party membership while it declared that the new situation must now be discussed by the Labor party as such at the provincial level. This gave the moderates their chance. With *Fremtiden* in their hands, they proved able to outmaneuver the radical faction. They did publish its appeal in the party paper, but in such a way that its message appeared quite different from what had been intended. The emphasis was all on Labor party unity pure and simple. In a series of editorials and large headlines, the paper launched a full-scale campaign against the new communist party, the "party of secession," the "party of disunity," the activity of which could only lead, like that of the Social Democrats, to a weakening of the Norwegian working class.

The radicals, taken by surprise, found it necessary to change their tactics overnight. They suddenly abandoned their appeal for a provincial party meeting. A meeting of leaders of the rural Labor party associations alone was hastily convened on November 16. Here it was decided that these branches should join the Communist party. In *Fremtiden,* the editor attacked their "flagrant disloyalty," pointing to their contradictory statements and actions. In an optimistic mood, the moderate faction set out at once to start new rural Labor party associations. It worked energetically, while the radicals were in full disarray. They quarreled among themselves, putting the blame for their tactical failure on one another and thereby apparently destroying what may have remained of their credibility. In consequence, they suffered a crushing electoral defeat. In the parliamentary election of 1924 they received only between 3 and 4 percent of the total Buskerud vote—about one-tenth of the Labor party vote and less than half of the Social Democratic vote.

The Norwegian Labor party remained the one powerful pole of attraction for Buskerud's working-class voters, irrespective of their ecological characteristics and of the party's official stand as expressed by its central committee in Oslo. It had been a moderate, reformist stand in 1915, a revolutionary but noncommunist one in 1918 and again in 1924, while at the intervening election in 1921, the official standpoint had been expressed by the words "Section of the Communist International," which appeared in parentheses after the party's name. It looks as if none of this made much difference to the average voter—the whole factional tug-of-war probably appeared rather confusing, and above all tedious. Still, these struggles are not without interest to the historian.

While ordinary voters simply seemed to want a viable working-class party they could support, the more active elements had specific preferences. These were the people who could be counted on to come to party branch meetings in case of need, to support a certain group of leaders. But neither faction seems to have felt sure about its ability to mobilize a sufficient number of adherents for a takeover at the provincial level. There were dedicated radicals who would come out if they believed it necessary to prevent a betrayal of the revolutionary idea. But there were also quite strongly committed rank-and-file adherents of the old guard, the leaders who had carried through so many tangible reforms over the years.

The active adherents of the separate leadership groups may have differed in some cases with regard to their industrial background, but there are few signs of it. The mining town of Kongsberg was not a radical stronghold, despite the oft-quoted tendency of miners to favor radicalism. A special cause can be indicated: the Kongsberg silver mines had always been government property, and the security of state employment was a strong force making for moderation. Table 5.12 shows the developments in three towns of Buskerud and in its rural districts, compared to the national average. Though the political climate in Kongsberg was not so mild that the mining town became a moderate stronghold, the Social Democrats to begin with received almost as much support as the radicalized Labor party, and they succeeded in maintaining their position

Table 5.12. Percentage of total socialist vote in Buskerud elections

	Parliament 1921		Commune 1922		Parliament 1924			Commune 1925		
	SDP*	NLP†	SDP	NLP	SDP	NLP	CPN‡	SDP	NLP	CPN
Hönefoss	71.5	28.5	74.7	25.3	62.9	36.1	.4	72.7	27.3	—
Drammen	31.5	68.5	14.8	75.2	19.6	77.6	2.8	14.9	85.1	—
Kongsberg	44.5	55.5	19.2	80.8	23.1	69.0	7.9	33.0	60.4	6.6
Buskerud rural districts	15.0	85.0	16.1	83.9	15.2	75.5	9.3	8.5	86.1	5.4
National average	30.3	69.7	24.3	75.7	26.4	55.3	18.3	24.4	63.0	12.6

Source: Official statistics.
*SDP: Social Democratic party.
†NLP: Norwegian Labor party.
‡CPN: Communist party of Norway.

quite well. In the last contest that took place before the reunion with the Labor party, the local election of 1925, the Social Democrats received one-third of the total socialist vote in Kongsberg.

On the other hand, in the commune of Royken, which had some heavy industry, there was a concentration of radical votes. And Hönefoss, the small town that became the stronghold of the Social Democrats, had a good deal of small-scale light industry. But in general the factor of greatest importance seems to have been the generational cleavage. Young people had been much more strongly impressed by the Russian Revolution than their elders, and working-class youth was quite exceptionally well organized in Buskerud province. A young guard of activists seems to have formed the backbone of the radical faction.

However, perhaps the most important factor was the instability of the time, in which the opposing forces within the organization were so evenly balanced. This is what made it like a game, enhancing the importance of tactical moves and countermoves. The leaders of both factions sensed, apparently, that they risked losing everything if they showed their hand too openly. A false move, a single psychological mistake could upset the balance, discourage one faction while encouraging the other, and thus decide the outcome. For some time neither side dared to provoke a showdown. Nor did they call upon the central leadership in Oslo to resolve their disputes. Actually neither faction was "Tranmaelite." While the Buskerud moderates regarded Tranmael and his friends as much too radical, the radicals of Buskerud suspected them of being disloyal to Moscow. So the two factions continued their maneuverings within the confines of their province. There were circumstances under which it might have been possible to mobilize indignant party members in the different local branches in sufficient numbers to ensure control of the whole provincial party. But for this to happen they would have had to have felt threatened by the danger of the opposing faction's betraying either the revolution or the party of the Norwegian working class. Only when the latter outcome seemed imminent toward the end of 1923, as the radicals overplayed their hand, did the moderate leaders finally win. They knew how to strike while the iron was hot and in this way succeeded in giving the iron—the provincial party organization—its permanent shape.

With their position secured, they did not wait long before turning Buskerud into "the second headquarters" of the Norwegian Labor party, to use the words of the local Social Democratic paper. The expression seems justified. *Fremtiden* began to press for a "reunion of the working class," a fusion of the Norwegian Labor party and the Social Democratic party, a goal which was reached in the course of a few years. The result was a national electoral triumph in 1927. The following year, the first Norwegian Labor government was formed with Hornsrud as prime minister. It is true that it was short-lived, and radical elements within the party tried for a time to reassert themselves. However, after the exclusion of the Communists in 1923 and the return of the Social Democrats in 1927, the moderates were in reality in a strong position. Martin Tranmael and his friends eventually acknowledged the fact. He, who had built the radical alliance fifteen years earlier, was actively engaged during the 1930s in cementing the new alliance, which enabled men of moderation to play a decisive role within the party. Eventually they were called upon to play that role in Norwegian politics as a whole. After the Second World War, Labor became the very linchpin of the country's party system. And the end of that era is not yet in sight.

So much for a chapter in the history of the Norwegian labor movement during a crucial period and its difference from comparable events in the two neighboring countries. The point of departure was Edvard Bull's seminal essay in 1922, written at a time when the contrast was particularly striking. As noted, his perspective was readily accepted by American social scientists. This was hardly accidental. In fact Bull's line of thought fit very well with the Durkheimian tradition, which for years had been the strongest current in American sociology. As Lewis A. Coser noted, Emile Durkheim's influence extended beyond France and England. Perhaps his success was even greater on the other side of the Atlantic: "In the United States, his ideas, filtered through the work of Talcott Parsons and Robert K. Merton, have come to be the common fare in the social sciences. He is, if not the father, then the grandfather of us all."[20]

In a sense it is ironic that the radical historian Edvard Bull should have provided an argument strengthening the Durkheimian tradition. Himself one of the leaders of the revolutionary wing in the Norwegian Labor party, Bull rejoiced at the thought of traditional norms being eroded, while the deeply conservative Durkheim regarded such erosion as a most dangerous and deplorable phenomenon.[21] But in terms of logic they were in agreement, and no doubt there is truth in their contention. When common norms are shared by different classes of a society, they constitute a stabilizing political force. The stability will be more vulnerable if the norms are loosened. In the Norwegian case, young men who left their occupation in the primary economy to be wage earners in construction work or new industry would often become more open to revolutionary ideas. But their accessibility to such ideas does not mean that they would become rebels.

Critics of Durkheimian thinking argue that groups of anomic people, if left to themselves, will not initiate collective action. Charles Tilly denies that "unattached individuals and homogenized masses have any special propensity to form or join social movements."[22] His arguments appear convincing. Indeed, this chapter describes the process in the course of which the core of the Norwegian radical labor organization was created in the Tröndelag area, an area which later played a crucial role in mobilizing "uprooted" workers through the Trade Union Opposition and in engineering the takeover at the national level.

Another factor should also be mentioned in conclusion, which for years was overlooked. In a survey of recent Norwegian political history, written in 1967, Stein Rokkan referred to the remarks Bull had made about Norway's period of rapid economic growth, when new industrial plants were being built in isolated places in the rural periphery: "Increasing numbers of smallholders and fishermen took jobs on construction sites, in transportation and in manufacturing. This rapidly recruited labor force found it difficult to adapt to the rigors of industrial life." After nearly fifty years Bull's contention still represented, so Rokkan said, "the classic analysis."[23] But he was well aware that it was only a tentative hypothesis. Rokkan called for more painstaking research. And in two books William M. Lafferty undertook the task of testing Bull's thesis with the aid of statistical analysis. He finally came to the conclusion that the loosening of social norms hardly constituted a main explanatory factor.[24]

With great energy Lafferty searched for other possibilities, and one of his suggestions seems to offer an important clue. The radicalizing influence exerted by immigrants in the United States around the turn of the century through organizations such as the syndicalist International Workers of the World may have been at the back of his mind. He noted the presence, in certain areas, of foreign-born elements in the Norwegian population and undertook a statistical analysis to see whether any political influence emanating from these could be detected. However, the results came out negative. The proportion of votes cast for the Social Democrats proved to increase along with the percentage of foreign-born individuals in the total population. Lafferty's idea nevertheless deserves to be pursued further. The immigrants were mainly Swedes, and most of them settled in the border province of Östfold, where the Social Democratic wing of the Norwegian labor movement had such a strong position that the votes of newcomers would make very little difference even if they were all cast in favor of the radical wing.

Actually there is good reason to believe that many of the immigrant workers in Norway, as in the United States, were of a radical disposition. A large proportion among them was unmarried, independent, and unburdened by family obligations. We also know that Swedish immigrants were well represented among the workers on various Norwegian construction sites, where they came with more experience and training than the indigenous farmboys. For example, according to the report of the labor union in Rjukan, where Norway's first large hydroelectric plant was being constructed, between one-fourth and one-third of the union's 430 inscribed members were Swedes. Furthermore, after an unsuccessful large-scale Swedish strike in 1909, a substantial number of workers crossed the Norwegian border in search of employment. Not a few were radicals who took jobs in Norway because they had been blacklisted at home. Here was a direct causal link. Men from Sweden were active at the leadership level as well. There were influential agitators, and organizers like Albin Eines, who settled in Tröndelag after 1909 and had a crucial position as secretary in the Trondheim Federation of Labor, working hand in hand with Martin Tranmael.

Edvard Bull wrote that the concerns who founded and operated the large hydroelectric plants had "created a new working class" in Norway. This was an obvious exaggeration. The factories were so few in number that they could not possibly account for norms of class behavior. William Lafferty found that Edvard Bull's "uprooted" type of worker made up only about 15 percent of the total radical strength, as measured by the socialist results in the election of 1921. Although there is some uncertainty about the basis of his calculation, the type of worker in question undoubtedly did not constitute more than a small minority among those who voted in 1921 for the radical Labor party. But in itself this fact need not be regarded as decisive. It is clear that they were an important element in the radical vanguard, so their influence was in any case not insignificant. However it deserves to be emphasized that they were influential not because of their numbers but because they were effectively organized. And Sweden provided a good deal of the organizational skill and experience that was needed.

It must be said that Edvard Bull in a sense directed the discussion to a wrong track when he wrote that each Scandinavian labor movement had developed according to its own internal logic, determined by purely national conditions. In reality a large amount of interaction was inevitable in the case of three closely related neighboring countries with free movement across their borders and no language barrier at all. In the Norwegian movement Danish influence was most noticeable in the moderate wing, where one of the leaders in the period around World War I was the naturalized Dane Carl Jeppesen, for a number of years mayor of the Norwegian capital. But the Swedish impact on the radical wing was particularly important. It was felt not only in industrial organization but also in other ways. Thus the leaders of the Socialist Youth Organization were strongly impressed by the intellectual Swedish syndicalist Hinke Bergegren. In the last years before World War I, when there was little he could achieve at home, he made repeated visits to Norway. Here he found an outlet for his energies. Paradoxically, the contrast between the Swedish and Norwegian labor movements was partly caused by their close connection. The weakening of radicalism in Sweden as a result of its defeat in 1909 led to a strengthening of radicalism in Norway.

Nor should other foreign influences be forgotten. Some came from the west, others from the east. Martin Tranmael had made contact with the men behind the Industrial Workers of the World when he visited the United States for a short time in his youth. While nothing equaled the impact of the successful Bolshevik revolution in Russia at the end of 1917, one must not forget that the disastrous outcome of the civil war in neighboring Finland a few months later provided a strong impetus in the opposite direction. Norwegian labor leaders were reluctant to talk about this depressing event, but there is little doubt that it was a factor which influenced their thoughts and their behavior. In the end, they often spoke the language of utopianism, while acting like realists.

This blend of realism and utopianism remained the hallmark of the movement. That is perhaps the main reason why the experience of this small country became so distinctive, and of importance in a wider perspective.

Notes

1. Thomas K. Derry, *A History of Modern Norway, 1814–1972* (Oxford, 1973), passim.

2. See Paul Knutsen in *Historisk Tidsskrift* 66 (1985): 373.

3. James C. Davies, "Toward a Theory of Revolution," in James C. Davies, ed., *When Men Revolt and Why* (New York, 1971).

4. Edvard Bull, Sr., "Die Entwicklung der Arbeiterbewegung in den drei skandinavischen Ländern," *Archiv für die Geschichte des Sozialismus und der Arbeiterbewegung* 10 (1922): 329–34.

5. Chapter 3 in this volume, note 31.

6. Walter Galenson, ed., *Labor in Norway* (Cambridge, Mass., 1949), and Galenson, *Comparative Labor Movements* (Englewood Cliffs, N.J., 1952); Wil-

liam Kornhauser, *The Politics of Mass Society* (New York, 1959); Seymour M. Lipset, *Political Man* (London, 1960); and Mancur Olson, "Rapid Growth as a Destabilizing Force," *Journal of Economic History* 23 (1963): 529–52.

7. Kornhauser, *Politics of Mass Society*, p. 153.

8. Lipset, *Political Man*, pp. 69–70.

9. Nils Elvander, *Skandinavisk arbetarrörelse* (Stockholm, 1980), p. 48.

10. William M. Lafferty, *Economic Development and the Response of Labor in Scandinavia: A Multi-Level Analysis* (Oslo, 1971), p. 317.

11. Edvard Bull, Jr., *Trönderne i norsk arbeiderbevegelse* (Stockholm, 1980), p. 48.

12. Charles Tilly, *From Mobilization to Revolution* (Reading, Mass., 1978), p. 23.

13. Heinz Eulau, "Multilevel Methods in Comparative Politics," *American Behavioral Scientist* 21 (1977): 39–62.

14. James E. Cronin, "Labor Insurgency and Class Formation: Comparative Perspectives on the Crisis of 1917–1920 in Europe," *Social Science History* 4 (1980): 132.

15. Tony Judt, *Socialism in Provence 1871–1914* (Cambridge, 1979), pp. 109, 144–49.

16. *Ny Tid*, Trondheim, Dec. 29, 1916.

17. Jorunn Bjørgum, "Fagoppositionen av 1911," *Tidsskrift for arbeider-bevegelsens historie* 1 (1976).

18. William M. Lafferty, *Industrialization, Community Structure, and Socialism: An Ecological Analysis of Norway, 1875–1924* (Oslo, 1974), pp. 252, 258.

19. Thomas C. Schelling, *The Strategy of Conflict* (Cambridge, Mass., 1963).

20. Lewis Coser, *Masters of Sociological Thought* (New York, 1971), 174.

21. Lewis Coser, *Continuities in the Study of Social Conflict* (New York, 1967), 153–80.

22. Tilly, *Mobilization to Revolution*, p. 83.

23. Stein Rokkan, "Geography, Religion, and Social Class: Crosscutting Cleavages in Norwegian Politics," in Seymour Martin Lipset and Stein Rokkan, eds., *Party Systems and Voter Alignments* (New York, 1967), pp. 395, 441.

24. Lafferty, *Economic Development*, p. 37, and Lafferty, *Industrialization, Community Structure and Socialism*, p. 306.

6

Between Reform and Revolution:

Social Democracy and Dutch Society, 1917–21

ERIK HANSEN

The neutral Netherlands was spared the horrors of combat and its attendant casualties in the First World War. By general European standards the Dutch came through the war quite well. Population, housing, and equipment were intact and the basic institutions in place at the war's end. Despite this, wartime shortages had generated some riots, protest marches, and demonstrations. General unrest reached such a level in 1917 that the conservative parties were willing to concede a series of constitutional reforms, including universal male suffrage. Within this context, 1917 began an era of internal reform which ended four years later in 1921. During this half decade the Netherlands witnessed calls for revolution and a number of episodes that reflected revolutionary intent. But despite some heated rhetoric and a series of strikes, the existing social and political order remained intact. Dutch public life was dominated by reform, not revolution, during the turbulent years of 1917–21.

In the course of the nineteenth century the Netherlands evolved into a stable, capitalist, parliamentary monarchy.[1] By the end of the eighteenth century the Dutch nation was already urbanized and embraced an efficient, labor-intensive agriculture capable of supporting substantial urban populations.[2] Dutch agriculture had never embodied a powerful feudal social elite, and throughout the nineteenth century and into the twentieth century smallholders and tenants provided the nation with its internal food supply.

The European war did not change Dutch property relations. The area under cultivation increased steadily as a result of reclamation, draining, and diking, and the number of middle-sized farms declined sharply, as many apparently were broken up into smaller units. As a rule, the number of owners of all sizes of plots declined until 1910. By 1921 the number of owners had increased slightly across the board except for those who possessed 20–99 hectares. The war years had been kind to Dutch farmers. They stood to profit from food shortages in Germany and high German food prices. Meats, grains, cereals, dairy products, and the produce of some truck gardens along the German frontier were especially in demand. Meanwhile the number of agricultural workers increased slightly between 1910 and 1920, from 618,121 to 622,514, but their share of the total labor force declined during the same decade from 27 to 23 percent. More farms were being cultivated by relatively fewer people, and growing numbers were leaving the agrarian sector for other pursuits.

Unlike neighboring Belgium and Germany, the Netherlands did not respond quickly to the mid-nineteenth-century industrialization process.[3] For most of the Dutch economy, industrialization began well after 1870, and the economy as a whole did not become mechanized until the late 1880s and early 1890s. The application of machine power to the productive process accelerated rapidly in the 1890s and by 1914 the Netherlands was well on its way to becoming a relatively modern industrial society. Unlike Belgium, Germany, and Great Britain, the Netherlands did not contain extensive coalfields, and thus industrialization did not generate the mining communities and the allied metal and metallurgical sectors common to many industrializing societies. Industrialization in the Netherlands often entailed the mechanization of existing craft-trades and the light fabrication sectors, most of which were characterized by many small family-owned firms, where contact between owner and worker remained closer than in Belgian or German heavy industry. This meant, among other things, that the new working class tended to be scattered across the country. Apart from the Twente textile mills, the Netherlands did not contain a large number of concentrated blue-collar communities. Rotterdam and Amsterdam contained a substantial number of harbor workers. Neither city, however, was an industrial city. Rotterdam was a major transport center, while Amsterdam remained a commercial, financial, and administrative center.

The 1910 and 1920 census statistics confirm that the composition of the industrial labor force changed little more than its agricultural counterpart. Among the more important dynamic sectors were metalworking and metallurgy, growing from 5 to 7 percent of the labor force and adding more than 89,000 new jobs; food processing, which grew from 6 to 7 percent of the labor force and added almost 50,000 new jobs; and transport, which rose from 9 to 10 percent of the labor force and accounted for more than 62,000 new positions.

Dutch political institutions on the eve of the First World War were a distant legacy of the 1848 crisis.[4] The constitution that grew out of that watershed provided for a sharing of power between the central government, elected provincial governments, and municipal councils. The prime minister and his cabinet were responsible to an elected lower house, the Tweede Kamer, and a senate, the Eerste Kamer, which was elected by the provincial parliaments. National public life centered on the Tweede Kamer, which grew from 68 seats in 1850 to 100 in 1888. The 100 representatives were elected in single-member constituencies. If one candidate did not obtain an absolute majority on the first ballot, a runoff election took place a week later between the two highest candidates. The right to vote was restricted to adult males with property. In 1870 only 12 percent of the adult male population possessed the right to vote.[5] Modifications in the income and property requirements enlarged the electorate to 65 percent of the adult male population by 1913. Still, the lower socioeconomic strata were totally excluded from political life on the eve of the war.

Initially, the new parliamentary order embodied three powerful ideological blocs, the liberal, the Protestant, and the Roman Catholic.[6] The liberal elites dominated Dutch public life during the middle decades of the century. However, as the electorate grew, power gradually began to shift toward the two clerical blocs. Between 1891 and 1901 the liberal bloc divided into three groups, the Free Liberals who generally opposed universal suffrage and social programs, the centrist Liberal Union, and the mildly progressive Free Thinkers. The Roman Catholic bloc was never fractured in this way. Only once in the twenty-five years before the First World War did the Roman Catholic bloc slip below twenty-five seats in the Tweede Kamer. Until 1897, it was more of an association of local notables than a party. In that year a number of Roman Catholic electoral associations agreed to support a common Roman Catholic political program. Drafted by the dynamic writer, journalist, priest, and parliamentarian Hendrik J. A. M. Schaepman, the program laid the foundation for the Roman Catholic State party. Of the three blocs, the Protestant had been the first to organize. Led by the minister Abraham Kuyper, a number of Protestant leaders representing electoral associations endorsed a Protestant program in 1879. The program, drafted by Kuyper during the previous year, laid the foundations for the Anti-Revolutionary party that he led for over a quarter century. Like the liberals, the Anti-Revolutionary party suffered a number of serious internal splits. A strong and forceful person, Kuyper was a talented journalist, writer, theologian, public speaker, and a powerful leader within the Dutch Reformed Church. In 1887 Kuyper and a group of like-minded ministers withdrew from the Reformed Church, objecting to its centralized, grand bourgeois leadership, and established the more de-centralized and petit bourgeois Gereformeerde Kerk, which was also more fundamentalist than the Dutch Reformed Church. In the 1890s a number of Protestant deputies in the Tweede Kamer left the Anti-Revolutionary party, objecting to a number of practices, Kuyper's leadership and person-ality, the growing social concern of the Anti-Revolutionary movement and its increasingly petit bourgeois nature, and particularly Kuyper's sug-gestions that the suffrage be quickly extended. Led for almost a decade by the patrician lawyer A. F. de Savornin Lohman, the opposition factions formed the Christian Historical Union (CHU) in 1908. The CHU rapidly became a conservative alternative to the Anti-Revolutionary movement.[7]

By the turn of the century the liberal, Protestant, and Roman Catholic blocs were confronted by a new political challenge. In 1894 a group of parliamentary socialists withdrew from the Sociaal Democratische Bond (SDB), protesting the antiparliamentary and increasingly syndicalist course that the Bond was taking.[8] The group founded the Sociaal Demo-cratische Arbeiders Partij (SDAP), which quickly moved to replace the Bond as the Dutch section of the Second International. A few years later, the Bond was dissolved by the state, whose lawyers charged that the Bond was a threat to public safety. The Social Democratic Workers party thus emerged as the uncontested voice of the secular labor movement. From fewer than 1,000 members in 1894, the SDAP membership grew to more than 25,000 by the spring of 1914. In 1897 the new party elected its first two representatives to the Tweede Kamer; by the autumn of 1913, its Tweede Kamer delegation had risen to fifteen, and in the 1913 election the SDAP received a surprising 144,000 votes on the first ballot.

The party was led by Pieter Jelles Troelstra, an attorney and a persua-sive public speaker. While regarding himself as a Marxist, Troelstra was firmly wedded to parliamentarism and for years led the social democratic delegation in the Tweede Kamer. Commanding enormous respect within the party, Troelstra was able to shape and mold a following that usually controlled the SDAP. This centrist concentration, which sought to com-bine Marxist ideology with parliamentary practice, was flanked on its right by a reformist bloc and on the left by a Marxist opposition move-ment. The reformist bloc within the SDAP was best represented at the annual party congress by two Tweede Kamer deputies, the party's colonial expert, Henri van Kol, and Johan H. Schaper, and by Willem Vliegen, a journalist on the staff of *Het Volk,* the national daily newspaper of the SDAP. On most key issues the centrist and reformist groups tended to agree; the major split within the SDAP was between the left opposition and the balance of the party.

One of the original founders of the SDAP, Frank van der Goes, a patrician stockbroker turned political activist and writer, was also a Marxist social theorist. Van der Goes did as much as any one individual to spread Marxist doctrine in Holland.[9] In 1896 he founded the journal *Nieuwe Tijd* as the theoretical and scientific forum of the SDAP. Privately funded, *Nieuwe Tijd* became a forum for Marxist doctrine which was outside direct party control. Through contacts with Van der Goes, a number of gifted writers and intellectuals entered the movement, including Florentinus M. Wibaut, the poets Herman Gorter and Henriëtte Roland Holst, and Pieter Wiedijk, Amsterdam pharmacist and a gifted theoretician. After the turn of the century, the *Nieuwe Tijd* circle began to launch increasingly sharp attacks on Troelstra and the SDAP leadership, charging reformism and an excessive reliance upon parliamentary means. The issues covered a broad front ranging from educational and agrarian policy, political strategy in runoff elections, strike leadership and tactics, and relations with the trade union movement. These differences led to a series of heated party congresses. In 1907 the debate took an unexpected turn when J. C. Ceton, David Wijnkoop, and Willem van Ravesteijn began to publish a privately funded newspaper in Amsterdam, *De Tribune.* They used *De Tribune* to launch one attack after another on the SDAP leadership and were expelled from the party in 1909. They immediately founded a rival social democratic party, the Sociaal Democratische Partij (SDP). While hundreds of Marxists left the SDAP in 1909 to join the new movement, the rank and file remained faithful to Troelstra. On the eve of the war, the SDP held no seats in Parliament and was more like a political club, grouped around *De Tribune* and its three editors, than a mass movement. Even Marxists such as Wibaut, Van der Goes, and, for a couple of years, Roland Holst remained in the SDAP using *Het Volk's* weekly supplement, *De Weekblad,* as a platform for critical debate. On the eve of war, the Dutch Marxist community was thus split into two camps.

While the political left was led by the SDAP, the labor movement was seriously divided.[10] By 1914 there were six national trade union federations competing directly with each other. The Algemeen Nederlandsch Werklieden Verbond (General Dutch Employees Confederation [ANWV]) was the oldest of the group. Founded in 1871, the ANWV quickly rose to five thousand members. By the end of the century its membership fell to under twenty-five hundred, and it was no longer an important factor in the labor movement. The ANWV had a liberal orientation and was therefore sharply antisocialist. In 1877, Patrimonium, an association of Protestant workers and employers, was founded. Patrimonium, however, remained more an association than a trade union. Between 1894 and 1914, its membership remained stable at around thirteen thousand. In 1909 a number of independent Protestant trade unions formed the Christelijk Nationaal Vakverbond (Christian National Trade Confederation [CNV]), which had only eight thousand members by 1913. These two Protestant organizations were quite naturally flanked by a national Roman Catholic trade union federation. In 1909 church leadership allowed individual Roman Catholic trade unions to form the Rooms Katholiek Werklieden Vakbureau (Roman Catholic Employees Trade Bureau [RKWV]). From an initial membership of around eleven thousand, the RKWV quickly grew to thirty thousand by 1914. Like the CNV, the Roman Catholic Employees Trade Bureau experienced substantial growth between the world wars.

Back in 1892, the leadership of the increasingly revolutionary and syndicalist Sociaal Democratische Bond authorized the creation of a national federation of socialist trade unions.[11] It did this in response to a resolution from the Second International, of which the Bond was then a member. Known as the Nationaal Arbeids Secretariaat (National Labor Secretariat [NAS]), the new federation quickly attracted more than eighteen thousand members. NAS, however, was highly unstable. Some of its member federations were revolutionary, syndicalist, and antiparliamentary while others were social democratic and often led by men who were active in the SDAP. Within the next ten years, the social democratic trade unions withdrew from NAS. The organization virtually melted away after the 1903 general strike and regrouped by the eve of war. By 1914 NAS membership had risen to over nine thousand. The Secretariaat retained its initial syndicalist orientation and stood aloof from political parties and the election process.

In the meantime the major social democratic trade unions founded a national federation which, while totally independent from the SDAP, was generally viewed as a projection of the SDAP into the world of labor.[12] Known as the Nederlandse Verbond van Vakvereenigingen (Dutch Federation of Trade Unions [NVV]), the new federation rose from 18,000 members in 1906, the year after its creation, to 84,261 in 1914.[13] As the First World War began, the NVV was easily the largest and most powerful of the national trade union federations. In that year, Holland contained 265,985 organized workers, 137,893 of whom were in national federations. Some 128,092 were members of company associations or various types of nonaffiliated locals, regional federations, or national trade unions which chose not to affiliate with a national federation. The NVV alone accounted for almost one-third of all organized workers within the nation.

During the late nineteenth century a pillarization (*verzuiling*) process began to develop within Dutch society.[14] This process began to attract the attention of social critics, journalists, sociologists, and social theorists. The term referred to the tendency of groups within Dutch society to form their own civic organizations and media networks. There were four major *zuilen* on the eve of the war, the liberal, the Protestant, the Roman Catholic, and the social democratic. Two, the liberal and the social democratic, were clearly secular and were firmly rooted in social class. The Protestant and Roman Catholic *zuilen* obviously cut across such categories and drew their strength from the churches. All four had their own political parties, journals, newspapers, youth groups, sport clubs, and eventually radio and television programs. The process of pillarization was accompanied by political demands that Protestant and Roman Catholic school systems be subsidized on a parity with the state system, a demand which was realized in 1917. The *verzuiling* tendency within society rendered social democratic penetration of the working class difficult to the extent that the process itself created for many devout workers attractive confessional alternatives to social democracy.

Holland's last prewar elections took place in June 1913; the clerical parties won forty-six seats, the social democrats and the three liberal parties held fifty-four seats. Dr. Bos of the Free Thinkers proposed to form a progressive cabinet, pointing toward universal male suffrage and broader social reforms.[15] The proposed cabinet would have required the support of the Social Democratic Workers party's fifteen seats, the Free Liberals' ten seats, the Liberal Union's twenty-two seats, and the Free Thinkers' seven seats. Bos further proposed awarding two cabinet posts to social democratic leaders. On August 10 an extraordinary congress of the Social Democratic Workers party voted 376 to 317 to reject the Bos offer. Since the majority of the SDAP's parliamentary delegation favored participation, the intraparty debate that summer was particularly bitter. Nevertheless, the SDAP found itself supporting a liberal cabinet in preference to a clerical one. By August, the liberal Cort van der Linden proposed to form an extraparliamentary cabinet composed of liberals who endorsed the twin Free Thinkers' goals of movement toward universal suffrage and broadened social reform.

In August 1914, this liberal, extraparliamentary cabinet was confronted with the stark realities of an impending world war. Leaving aside for a moment the foreign and domestic measures forced upon the regime by wartime circumstances, a word or two about the initial goals of the Cort van der Linden cabinet is in order. It remained in power for virtually the entire war, from late summer 1913 until September 1918. In 1917 it wrote universal adult male suffrage into the constitution and opened the way for the inclusion of adult women into the electorate in 1921. At the same time, the liberals and social democrats agreed to accept governmental funding of private schools on a parity with the state system, thereby ending the confrontation over the schools that had frequently dominated Dutch public life during the last thirty years of the nineteenth century. In the meantime, a number of new and burning issues had arisen. The cabinet was quick to declare absolute neutrality and had to resist considerable pressure from both the Allies and the Central Powers to enter the war on one side or the other. Beyond this, the Cort van der Linden coalition had to regulate the flow of raw material in order to minimize dislocations and shortages generated by wartime circumstances.

These pressures continued throughout the war. From the British side there were constant fears that Dutch interests would purchase contraband materials, to which food and forage were quickly added in the autumn of 1914, ship them to Dutch ports, and then reship into the German Empire.[16] To prevent Holland from becoming a funnel through which these staples could enter Germany from distant neutral supplies, the British government reinforced its blockade policy with the doctrine of continuous voyage, arguing in this case that contraband could not be allowed to enter Holland preparatory to shipment into Germany. The Dutch, of course, were in a difficult position since their dependence upon foreign food and raw material supply virtually mandated an understanding with the one power that controlled the North Sea shipping lanes. At the same time they did not want to provoke a German occupation. In November 1914, a number of prominent bankers and import-export interests created the Netherlands Overseas Trust Company (NOT), a private firm, which acted as a purchasing agent for foreign materials.[17] NOT officials immediately signed agreements with the British promising not to allow reshipment of contraband into Germany. By 1917 NOT had over a thousand employees and dominated Dutch foreign trade. According to a number of Dutch historians, NOT had become a state within the state, despite its private status. Its leadership worked closely with government officials, negotiating trade agreements with foreign powers.

The first two and a half years of the war were not particularly difficult for the Dutch people. The Dutch economy was prosperous, serving, in part, as a supplier to the German Empire. Agriculture benefited immensely from food shortages and high food prices in Germany, generating a huge flow of black-market goods, especially meats and dairy products, into the empire. With time, the boom in meat and dairy markets created serious problems for the Dutch population, as farmers began an expansion of grasslands and herds, cutting back on vegetable, grain, and cereal production.

By 1917 the Netherlands began to face serious and dangerous economic problems. The German decision to unleash unrestricted submarine warfare seriously reduced neutral shipping. In June 1917 the United States, which had been somewhat of a champion of neutral shipping rights, placed export embargoes on materials bound for neutral neighbors of the German Empire. American exports to Holland fell from $97.5 million in the period of June 1915 to June 1916 to only $6.4 million in June 1917 to June 1918.[18] The intensification of economic warfare was clearly reflected in the level of activity in the Rotterdam harbor. In 1913 Rotterdam docked 10,527 ships, a number which fell to 7,547 in 1914, 3,760 in 1915, 3,152 in 1916, and only 946 during the first ten months of 1918.[19] In August 1916 the contraction of normal trade patterns reached such a point that Parliament authorized food rationing. By February 1917 rationing was intensified, and by July there was a series of food riots and demonstrations in Amsterdam protesting tight food supplies. Food remained in scarce supply until the end of the war. Holland was also confronted with a series of energy and fuel shortages during the last two years of the war. Before the war, Holland imported more than eleven million tons of coal, coke, and charcoal. By 1918 imports in this sector had collapsed to 1.44 million tons while domestic coal production had risen from 1.8 million tons to 3.16 million, hardly enough to cover the critical gap.[20] The nation experienced its first severe fuel shortage during the winter of 1916-17, the first of several cold and tightly rationed winters. The general deterioration in the quality of life is reflected in the death rate, which rose from 12.6 per 1,000 in 1914 to more than 17 per 1,000 by the end of the war.[21]

During the first three years of the war the social democratic left seemed to grow. While SDAP membership remained at around 25,000, NVV trade unions experienced rapid expansion, rising from a total membership of 84,261 in 1914 to 247,748 by 1920.[22] Beyond this, the number of collective bargaining contracts which NVV affiliates signed grew dramatically during the early war years. Improvements in the terms and conditions of labor were further reinforced by governmental agreements to transfer public monies into trade union unemployment funds as a means of protecting the labor force from the shocks of wartime unemployment.[23] Finally, the SDAP and NVV leaders anticipated a further strengthening of their position when Tweede Kamer elections were held. As noted, in 1917 universal male suffrage was introduced and the 100 single-member constituencies in the Tweede Kamer were replaced by a system of proportional representation. Pending the completion of constitutional reform, the political parties represented in the chamber agreed not to contest seats in the June 1917, election, allowing the chamber elected in 1913 to complete the revisions. New elections were held in July 1918, despite harsh wartime conditions. The results shocked the SDAP. While the party gained seven seats, its Tweede Kamer delegation rising to 22, the liberal parties suffered heavy losses and the clerical bloc emerged with 50 of the 100 seats in the Kamer. In September 1918 Ruys de Beerenbrouck formed a clerical cabinet with liberal participation. Table 6.1 shows the composition of the Tweede Kamer from 1913 to 1921.

Parliamentary isolation seems to have damaged SDAP prospects during the ensuing years. SDAP membership surged to 37,628 in 1918, peaked at 47,870 in 1919, and by 1922 had fallen back to 41,816. The NVV suffered the same type of losses, falling from a 1920 peak of 247,748 to

Table 6.1. Composition of the Tweede Kamer, 1913–21

Party	1913	1918	1922
Anti-revolutionary party	11	13	16
Christian Historical Union	10	7	11
Christian Democratic Union	—	1	—
Roman Catholic State party	25	30	32
Old Liberal party	10	4	1
Union Liberal party	21	6	10
Free Thinkers' party	7	5	5
Social Democratic Workers' party	16	22	20
Communist party	—	2	2

Sources: W. H. Vermeulen, *Schets eener Parlementaire Geschiedenis van Nederland* ('s-Gravenhage: Martinus Nijhoff, 1948–56), 3:237; Pieter J. Oud, *Het Jongste Verleden: Parlementaire Geschiedenis van Nederland, 1918–1940* (Assen: Van Gorcum, 1948–51), 1:394, 2:307; and Isaac Lipschits, *De protestants-christelijke stroming tot 1940* (Deventer: Kluwer, 1977), pp. 79–100.

217,467 in just one year.[24] This pattern of growth, stagnation, and sudden social democratic decline was reflected in the legislative and economic areas as well. While the clerical cabinet created a Ministry of Labor which was initially headed by the progressive Roman Catholic P. J. M. Aalberse and in 1919 initiated legislation shortening the workday and workweek and expanding pension and accident benefits, few major reforms were realized after 1921. In October 1919 the Hoge Raad van Arbeid (High Council of Labor) was established representing government, management, and labor. A sharp recession in 1920-22 signaled an end to reform and a powerful employers' counteroffensive. Tough bargaining, record levels of strikes and lockouts, a lengthening of the recently obtained forty-five-hour-week to forty-seven hours, and salary cuts prevailed between 1921 and 1922.[25] By 1922 a conservative stability developed which lasted until the depression.

SDAP problems were further compounded by an embarrassing episode which marked the end of the First World War.[26] On November 11, 1918, Pieter Jelles Troelstra predicted that the bourgeoisie was about to transfer power to the proletariat. Speaking in Rotterdam at the time, Troelstra repeated this proposition the following day in a parliamentary speech. This outburst of revolutionary rhetoric conceivably was triggered by a momentary vast overestimation of the German revolution, the example of scattered riots and demonstrations within both the Dutch military and civilian sectors during the previous weeks, and a statement on November 9 by Mayor Zimmerman of Rotterdam that he was prepared to play a positive role in the transfer of power to the proletariat. While Troelstra was immediately repudiated by NVV trade union leaders, members of his own parliamentary delegation, and fellow SDAP leaders, his statements resulted in a powerful antisocialist reaction and laid the partial foundations for the conservative course of Dutch politics in the 1920s.

When World War I began, the Dutch Social Democratic Workers party reacted the same way as the majority factions in the French and German movements. The German declaration of war on Russia came on Saturday, August 1. The Tweede Kamer was called into emergency session on Monday, August 3. Historically the SDAP parliamentary delegation had always voted against military appropriations and the party leadership had traditionally sanctioned antimilitary activity and pacifist agitation on the part of party activists.[27] Yet on August 3, every member of the Tweede Kamer delegation voted for military credits which the cabinet, while declaring strict neutrality, had requested in an effort to strengthen the army. On that day, Troelstra, speaking in Parliament, pledged social democratic support for the regime and seemed to be bringing the SDAP into a *union sacrée* with the bourgeois parties. "The moment of criticism has not arrived in my judgment because national sentiments over-shadow national differences in these difficult circumstances."[28] This sudden turn in a seemingly militarist and nationalist direction predictably led to a series of attacks upon Troelstra from pacifists and antimilitarists within the SDAP. Perhaps the most prominent of these was Rudolph Kuyper, a personal friend of Troelstra, a Marxist theorist, and one of the architects of the 1912 party program. Kuyper was quick to attack Troelstra's position and in September 1914 published a pamphlet, *No Man and Not a Cent,* which became a rallying point for social democratic pacifists and antimilitarists. Despite the criticism, the SDAP remained on the course laid down by Troelstra until the last year of the war.

During the first three years of war, the SDAP was deeply involved in the implementation of cabinet policy. The party supported the foreign policy of the cabinet and, after voting mobilization credits, a number of SDAP deputies emerged as parliamentary voices of the common soldier, often a social democratic draftee, with the conscious intent of making army life more attractive in terms of pay, material environment, and leave. As wartime regulations spread through the economy, these were usually supported by the social democrats, who, while often arguing that such controls did not go far enough or were designed to serve bourgeois interests, generally positioned themselves as loyal critics of the cabinet, serving a working-class perspective and mission. This orientation made it easy for Dutch social democrats to play an active role in the Zimmerwald movement and subsequent social democratic efforts to reach a negotiated peace at the international level. Internally, social democrats on the city and municipal councils were deeply involved in the formation, and particularly the implementation, of rationing policies. Trade unions were given subsidies through the municipal councils to strengthen their unemployment funds and thus social democratic trade union leaders had additional experience in working with nonsocialist, or antisocialist governmental authorities. When the National Support Committee was established in the autumn of 1914 to assist those in dire situations, the SDAP constituency shared in the benefits received and the party was given a distant and limited influence in policy formation. Even in the relatively harsh summer of 1917, the SDAP played the role of a loyal critic. When food riots broke out in Amsterdam in July, both SDAP and NVV leaders called on the population to remain calm and to halt illegal actions at once. While critical of the regime, both the official SDAP and NVV were firm advocates of law and order.

The general orientation of the SDAP was partially reflected in a pamphlet published by Troelstra in 1915. Entitled *The World War and Social Democracy*, the essay justified the position that Troelstra had taken within the SDAP and was aimed at radical, revolutionary social democrats in Germany and Holland as well as Dutch pacifist and antimilitary social democrats. In dealing with these groups, Troelstra argued that while modern imperialism was an outgrowth of the capitalist economy, it was not a necessary stage in the evolution of the capitalist social order. This struck directly at the left-radical currents within the German social democratic movement represented by Rosa Luxemburg, Karl Liebknecht, Karl Radek, and Anton Pannekoek, whose views received sympathetic coverage in the pages of *De Tribune*.

While attempting to contest the assumptions of the German radicals and their allies within the Dutch SDP, Troelstra also turned to critics within his own party. First, he argued at length that nationalism, national thought, and nationalist sentiments had penetrated the working-class culture far more deeply than many social democrats realized. While still regarding himself as a Marxist, Troelstra contended that the international social democratic movement would have to reconcile its traditional programmatic demands with the realities of working-class nationalism. Within this context, Troelstra defended SDAP support for mobilization credits on the grounds that it was responsive to the instincts of Dutch labor and that principled pacifism was bourgeois, or Tolstoyian, and was not necessarily social democratic in any case.[29] In defending the social democratic decision to support a strong defense posture, Troelstra was careful to distinguish between social democratic defense measures and bourgeois militarism. In so doing he pointed to previous resolutions of the Second International and to the thought of Jean Jaurès as expressed in his *L'Armée nouvelle*.[30] Concluding his defense, Troelstra turned to the issue of revolution. Would a major European war lead to a proletarian revolution? A resolution of the Second International adopted at the 1907 Stuttgart Congress certainly seemed to threaten such a development. More to the point for Troelstra was the recent publication by Herman Gorter of an essay calling for revolution and advancing the equation that capitalism leads to imperialism, which leads to war and then revolution. Here Troelstra ended on a strangely ambivalent note. While rejecting the radicalism of Gorter, Troelstra did point to the revolutionary implications of the Stuttgart resolution and seemed to raise the possibility of revolutionary action. "Summarized in this sense, the Stuttgart resolution constitutes a serious warning for the ruling class not to stretch the bow too far and for the proletariat an admonition, *if the time is ripe, to be prepared and ready for the deed.*"[31]

By 1918, however, Troelstra gradually lost faith in the bourgeois parliamentary order. Embittered by the failure of the Stockholm conference, he wrote in his memoirs that "my trust in the democratic-parliamentary method was shaken. I have never been especially taken by Parliament; I have worked hard in the chamber but I have never seen it as the only and all-solving force. During the war years it seemed all too clear how parliamentarianism can lead to the desire to work with the bourgeois parties at any price, at the expense of our international demands, for the national or nationalistic demands of the moment."[32] From the SDAP election congress in February 1918 until the autumn of 1918, Troelstra occasionally mentioned the possibility of revolution, particularly if the war lasted long enough. For example, on May 21 he argued: "Thus many materials for a revolution have accumulated in Europe. . . . Our task must be to direct the revolutionary spirit against the capitalist class. . . . If a revolution really comes, then I hope to be involved. But if a successful revolution comes, the SDAP must be its motive force."[33] In defending his subsequent actions, Troelstra also pointed to a statement by his colleague and later critic Johan H. Schaper, a reformist social democrat of the purest type. In the midst of parliamentary debate on October 15, 1918, Schaper warned: "Don't you make a mistake about us, we will not take part in reckless adventures, but if a storm of real revolutions sweeps out over Europe and also strikes Holland, have no illusions on which side we stand."[34] By midautumn, Troelstra was well aware of revolutionary stirrings within the German Empire. Already disillusioned, or so he tells us, Troelstra must have shared in the bitter disappointments generated by the July 1918 Tweede Kamer election.

In early November, Europe stood on the brink of the German revolution, a social action which Troelstra felt confident would cross the Dutch frontier. This confidence was further reinforced by a mutiny of Dutch soldiers at Karskamp on October 26.[35] The day before, soldiers at the camp began to protest insufficient support from the National Support Committee to their families, brief and infrequent leaves home, poor food, and poor relations with their officers. By the following day a few shots had been fired, a canteen and barracks burned, and officers ignored. Order was restored with relative ease, but the episode could be interpreted as a harbinger of things to come. By Saturday, November 2, Troelstra appeared at a meeting of the SDAP executive committee, arguing that the SDAP ought to prepare itself for revolutionary leadership. Troelstra was not planning anything at this point, however, nor was he suggesting that revolutionary plans be laid. He merely continued to assume that a revolution might break out spontaneously and that the SDAP ought to be ready for such an eventuality.[36] On Sunday, a meeting of NVV leaders and members of the SDAP executive committee was convened, in which Troelstra again pointed to revolutionary stirrings.[37] At both meetings, the majority of participants did not share Troelstra's views, and the two sessions resulted in little more than a manifesto calling for social reforms and an extraordinary NVV-SDAP congress. Troelstra later recalled that "the clever speeches of Vliegen made a greater impression as he advanced the largely correct contention, as it later turned out, that he saw nothing in the European situation which pointed to a coming general proletarian revolution."[38]

The subsequent week found Troelstra back in Parliament, criticizing conditons in the army and calling for military reforms and the dismissal of General Snijders, commander in chief of the Dutch army. On Saturday, November 9, Troelstra was contacted by SDAP activists in Rotterdam.[39] Mayor Zimmerman had spoken to several social democratic city councilors and inquired about social democratic intentions. Not knowing what to say or do, they turned to Troelstra in The Hague. Zimmerman, fearing an impending revolution, spoke in terms of an orderly transfer of power to yet unknown proletarian leaders. Zimmerman's perceptions were shaped by events in Russia and Central Europe, not developments in Rotterdam. He was convinced that the Russian and German revolutions signaled the beginning of a general European revolution which would strike Holland as well. Troelstra left immediately for Rotterdam, to confer with Rotterdam labor and social democratic leaders the next evening. On the night of November 11 he made his renowned speech predicting a transfer of political power to the proletariat. He was back in The Hague the next day and gave a similar speech to the Tweede Kamer that afternoon. The two harangues created the impression that the SDAP was ready to lead a revolution. But neither statement had been cleared with the SDAP executive committee, and both had caught most NVV and SDAP leaders off guard. One trade union leader and SDAP activist after another publicly repudiated Troelstra and openly denied revolutionary intentions. In the course of the next few weeks, the various arms of the social democratic movement rejected or denied revolutionary intentions in a way that could only discredit and humiliate the leader of their own party. Nevertheless, paramilitary volunteer units were quickly formed to prevent a proletarian coup. The Roman Catholic and Protestant trade unions both pledged loyalty to the crown and promised physical resistance should revolution occur. A powerful bourgeois and rural antisocialist reflex swept across Holland, and all because of the oratorical fantasies of the socialist leader, who was immediately disavowed by his party and its constituency.

The postwar era began with a dramatic surge in NVV and SDAP membership. During the war both clerical and social democratic unions grew rapidly. In both cases membership levels reach a peak in 1919–20 and then slumped. Despite the rapid growth of the NVV during the last years of the war and the first two years of peace, trade union officials and SDAP activists noted the rapid growth of the church-aligned trade unions with increasing concern. In 1912 more than 63 percent of workers belonging to major, national trade union federations were members of the NVV. By 1921 the NVV share in total national trade union federation membership had fallen below 45 percent. Table 6.2 shows the development of the trade union membership from 1912 to 1921. During the same period, the Protestant CNV trade unions increased their shares by 50 percent. Another point of concern to the NVV leadership was the enduring presence of the syndicalist NAS federations. At the turn of the century and throughout the subsequent decade, NVV leaders fondly predicted the total collapse of the syndicalist movement. Yet between 1912 and 1921 syndicalist membership increased sixfold.

The years immediately after the war were also characterized by an increase in strikes and labor violence. From their origins at the turn of the century until 1919, employer associations quickly evolved into sophisticated structures, often with highly professional staffs.[40] When the war ended management suddenly began tough bargaining and the relative generosity of the war years vanished. The new line led to a strike surge in 1919, which quickly fell off in 1920–21 as the economy slipped into a recession by 1921. Table 6.3 shows the patterns of strikes and unemployment.

The SDAP did not benefit from the recession, and the implementation of female suffrage did not improve its political base. The 1922 Tweede Kamer election, with Dutch women voting for the first time, saw the clerical bloc rise from fifty-one to sixty seats. The SDAP lost two seats.[41]

The SDAP leadership faced a number of interlocking problems as the war came to an end. First, some type of an understanding had to be reached about Troelstra's role in the movement. Could anything be done to recover from the humiliations of the November days? Second, since most party leaders repudiated revolution during the November disturbances, the time had clearly come to define exactly what the SDAP did represent. A number of major reforms that the SDAP had demanded for years had now been realized. Its favorite single goal before the war, universal suffrage, had been reached, and new objectives had been identified. Between 1919 and 1921 the SDAP leaders began to draft a new program which the movement pursued until 1939.[42]

Table 6.2. Membership of five major national trade union federations, 1912–21

	NVV		NAS		CNV		Patrimonium		Roman Catholic		Total
	No.	%	No.	%	No.	%	No.	%	No.	%	
1912	52,195	63.21	6,180	7.48	7,792	9.43	—	—	16,403	19.86	82,570
1913	61,447	54.84	8,097	7.22	7,944	7.09	13,614	12,15	21,096	18.82	112,046
1914	84,261	57.10	9,697	6.57	11,023	7.47	13,519	9.16	29,048	19.68	147,548
1915	87,598	55.71	9,242	5.88	12,327	7.84	12,800	8.14	35,257	22.42	157,224
1916	99,511	55.95	10,510	5.91	15,013	8.44	12,500	7.03	40,338	22.68	177,872
1917	128,918	55.95	14,309	6.21	20,506	8.90	11,800	5.12	54,855	23.81	230,388
1918	159,449	54.58	23,068	7.89	28,008	9.59	12,450	4.26	69,139	23.67	282,114
1919	190,942	50.67	33,626	8.92	46,338	12.30	14,150	3.75	91,807	24.36	376,860
1920	247,748	47.36	51,570	9.86	66,997	12.81	15,739	3.01	141,002	26.96	523,056
1921	217,467	44.50	37,125	7.60	73,819	15.11	14,226	2.91	146,030	29.88	488,667

Source: Ger Harmsen and Bob Reinalda, *Voor de bevrijding van de arbeid: Beknopte geschiendenis van de nederlandse vakbeweging* (Nijmegen: SUN, 1975), pp. 430–31. These figures exclude unaffiliated local unions and scattered minor federations. Precise figures for Patrimonium are not available until 1913.

Table 6.3. Strikes and unemployment patterns, 1912–21

	Strikes	Strikers	Duration	Unemployed	Rate of unemployment*
1912	265	19,620	4,281	—	—
1913	400	23,990	6,266	—	—
1914	250	13,953	3,923	—	—
1915	259	14,373	2,842	—	—
1916	356	17,146	6,089	—	—
1917	324	25,879	5,620	14,209	9.6%
1918	305	35,779	5,300	18,985	10.0%
1919	622	55,857	11,540	26,796	8.9%
1920	456	47,027	11,544	28,812	7.2%
1921	290	43,604	7,250	42,999	10.9%

Source: Centraal Bureau voor de Statistiek, *Jaarcijfers voor het Koninkrijk der Nederlanden: Rijk in Europa 1922* ('s-Gravenhage: CBS, 1924), pp. 86–88. These figures exclude lockout actions.
*Among union members covered by social insurance.

On November 16 and 17, 1918, an emergency congress of SDAP and NVV officials was convened, in Rotterdam, including delegates from the SDAP sections and the local NVV federations.[43] The congress, while broadly based and involving more than fourteen hundred people, adopted a series of immediate reform demands. The demands were immediate reform measures which strongly resembled the social democratic election program. None of them had revolutionary implications.[44]

In the aftermath of the congress, Troelstra, who was a member of the SDAP executive committee, drafted a resolution defining the SDAP's official position toward revolution and revolutionary change. The resolution approved the parliamentary course that the SDAP had followed without condemning revolutionary action or rhetoric. Known as the unity resolution, the draft was endorsed by the executive committee and was laid before the annual party congress, April 20–22, 1919, in Arnhem, which approved it overwhelmingly. This action was a striking personal triumph for the controversial leader and allowed him to continue as the titular head of the SDAP and to lead the party faction in the Tweede Kamer. In the course of the debate, he was, however, criticized by Vliegen, Schaper, and Professor W. A. Bonger, all of whom rejected revolution as a serious SDAP alternative.[45] In retrospect, it also appears that none of these critics, however reformist they might have been, really wanted to humiliate

Troelstra further or to force him out of his current role within the movement. The resolution provided an acceptable compromise. It embodied a measure of revolutionary rhetoric without compromising the reformist orientation of the movement.[46]

Like most late-nineteenth-century European social democratic parties, the SDAP had a party program which was really a general statement of largely philosophical principles. This was backed by a number of immediate reform demands which served as the electoral program. The movement, surprised by the European unrest of 1918, lacked blueprints. How would a socialist economy be organized? How would social democratic political institutions be structured? What type of society did the SDAP leaders propose to mold? In partial answer to these questions the executive committee of the SDAP appointed a blue-ribbon party commission to draft a report on socialization and nationalization policies. This report was the first of a number of programmatic studies commissioned and adopted by the SDAP.[47] It embodied a fairly detailed plan for the nationalization of key industries, natural monopolies, utility services, and elements in the transportation sector. The socialization report was followed in 1923 by a report on business organization and codetermination, another one on new political institutions in 1931, and finally a systematic model for a planned economy, *Het Plan van de Arbeid* (*Labor's Plan*), in 1935. It was generally assumed that all of the plans would be put into effect by acts of Parliament. None of them had revolutionary implications. The 1920 report thus foreshadowed the general SDAP style between the world wars.

There were no dramatic developments within the SDAP between the Arnhem congress and the July Tweede Kamer elections in 1922.[48] Activists were generally pleased with the socialization report. Pacifists and strongly antimilitarist members of the party were further encouraged by the relative ease with which the March 27–29, 1921, party congress endorsed disarmament, an action especially pleasing to party members who were outraged by the support the Tweede Kamer delegation had given to the regime on war credit requests during the First World War. Troelstra, for his part, resumed his role in Parliament and within the SDAP until he left public life in 1924. Immediately after the November crisis, he began to draft a series of articles which ran in *De Socialistische Gids* from March through August 1919. These were then published as a brief volume, *The Revolution and the SDAP*, at the end of the year.[49] Troelstra continued to defend his acts of November, arguing that social democrats should still prepare to lead a proletarian revolution.[50]

For the next two years, Troelstra and other SDAP leaders pointed to the religious sensibility of many Dutch workers and their resultant predisposition to vote for the appropriate clerical party as a major barrier to the SDAP's quest for power. Increasingly embittered by seemingly permanent opposition status, Troelstra began to press for the abolition of the Senate and the creation of a national socioeconomic council composed of representatives of the trade unions, management, employers' associations, retail associations, farmers' groupings, and professional associations.[51] This body, which represented the economic nation, would advise the unicameral legislature on matters of socioeconomic importance and would develop policy reports for the legislature. This reform proposal generated scant public support and the thorough and detailed election program drew few voters to the SDAP. A waning movement actually weakened further as the party lost two seats in the July 1922 elections.[52] It still remained, however, the second largest party in the nation, surpassed only by the Roman Catholic State party.

Meanwhile the discontent of the war years turned the SDP from a club into a major splinter party whose support was largely confined to Amsterdam. In the June 1917 elections 17,288 people voted for SDP candidates, and a year later the SDP received 31,043 votes, 2.3 percent of the national total, sufficient to elect Wijnkoop and Van Ravesteijn to the Tweede Kamer.[53] In autumn 1918 a congress of the SDP voted to transform the party into the Communist party of the Netherlands (CPN). Growth of the party was in part due to its collaboration with other organizations devoted to single-issue agitation. The most general and flexible of these was the Samenwerkende Arbeidersverenigingen (Cooperating Workers' Unions [SAV]). Created in August 1914, SAV included NAS, the SDP, independent syndicalist unions, and the International Anti-Militarist Union.[54] It was later broadened to include an anarchist group and Henriëtte Roland Holst's Revolutionair Socialistisch Verbond (Revolutionary Socialist League [RSV]). In April 1916 SDP leaders created the Agitation Committee for Demobilization, which included the Federation of Christian Socialists, strange allies indeed for the future leaders of the communist movement. The SAV was transformed into the Revolutionary Committee against the War and Its Consequences. The new group immediately adopted a resolution demanding demobilization, strike actions, and a ban on food export.[55] As these agitational actions were launched, the RSV was absorbed into the SDP and Roland Holst entered the circle of SDP leaders.[56] Despite the agitations, the SDP had just over a thousand members in the autumn of 1918, 20 percent of whom lived in Amsterdam. The

SDP electorate in the transition from war to peace ran far ahead of its membership. The party received more than fourteen thousand votes in Amsterdam alone during both the July 1918 parliamentary elections and the 1919 municipal elections.

Despite a number of sharp debates within the Dutch communist movement, the years between the end of the war and 1922 were not particularly dramatic.[57] Over these thirty-six months Ceton, Wijnkoop, and Van Ravesteijn had firm control of the movement, and as late as 1921 the CPN was for all practical purposes virtually indistinguishable from the old SDP.[58] With women voting for the first time in 1922, the CPN electorate jumped to 53,661 in the Tweede Kamer election. However, its relative position in Dutch politics remained the same. As was the case with other left-wing organizations, CPN membership grew rapidly just after the war, leaping from just over a thousand in autumn 1918 to eighteen hundred by April 1919. At this point, dramatic growth stopped. By the end of 1921, the CPN still had no more than two thousand members.

Like the SDAP and SDP, the Nationaal Arbeids Secretariaat experienced rapid growth during and after the First World War and by 1921 had begun to stagnate. The First World War resulted in a steady rise in NAS membership. From 9,697 members at one point in 1914, NAS membership first slumped to 9,200 in 1915 and then began a steady rise, exceeding ten thousand in 1916, fourteen thousand in 1917, and 23,000 by 1918.[59] In short, NAS had more than doubled during the war, due to several factors. First, harsh social conditions in the major cities drove some unorganized laborers into the arms of NAS organizers. Second, the leadership broadened its cooperation with the SDP and became even more deeply involved on agitational fronts, giving NAS a public image and tightly associating its federations with antiwar, pacifist, and antimobilization attitudes. This allowed NAS to contrast its antimilitarism with the social patriotism of the SDAP leaders and their NVV allies.

The broad strategy of the NAS leaders during the war was to continue their demands for a syndicalist socialist state, arguing that war and capitalism would ultimately lead to revolution. The war was presented to NAS workers as a capitalist war in which Dutch labor should not take sides, thus opening the door to extensive front cooperation with bourgeois pacifist groups. The ultimate goals of NAS were thus maintained while temporary front actions began which focused upon specific issues. The antimilitarism of NAS was quickly turned against the social democrats. The 1914 NAS report proudly noted that "the position of the social democratic and modern trade union press was completely different. The representatives and leaders of these groups have concluded a 'Gods peace' with the regime and the class which robs the people, oppresses and places in jail those who protest this policy and conditions of slavery."[60] By December 1914 NAS joined the SDP in leading the demobilization agitation. NAS maintained its peace actions throughout the war and from spring 1916 until well into 1918 was an active participant in the Revolutionary Socialist Committee against the War and Its Consequences. This activity led to extended cooperation with the SDP.[61]

While the actions had no effect upon the regime or national policy, they do seem to have drawn thousands of workers into the NAS orbit. However, one must note that the types of resolutions approved by a February 17 Congress of the Revolutionary Socialist Committee against the War and Its Consequences and the subsequent NAS congress of March 31–April 2 bore on familiar issues—demilitarization, higher wages, better food supply, and substantial social reform. When the November crisis broke, the NAS leaders were as surprised as the SDAP members, but while NAS played no role in the events of November 9–11, it was able to use the Troelstra episode as a club against the SDAP. There was one interesting development within NAS leadership circles as the war came to an end. NAS had no direct organizational ties with a political party. Rather than link NAS to the SDP in the July 3, 1918, Tweede Kamer elections, Harm Kolthek and a circle of friends founded the Socialistische Partij (SP).[62] The new party garnered more than 8,900 votes, enough to elect Kolthek to Parliament. While the SP was not a party per se, thousands of NAS supporters were eligible to vote for the first time, and thus the SP did provide a temporary syndicalist political body without compromising any NAS principles.

During the immediate postwar era a number of tensions began to assert themselves within NAS. By 1920 NAS membership had risen to 51,000. At this point a steep decline set in as membership fell to 37,125 in 1921; 31,391 in 1922; and down to 23,280 by 1923.[63] Between 1919 and 1923 a sharp debate erupted within the NAS leadership over the relation between NAS, the political parties, and Parliament. A substantial number of NAS supporters wanted to maintain total independence from political parties and to continue the further development of NAS as an independent force within the labor movement. The orientation was most effectively represented by the two Lansinks, father and son.[64] Between 1919 and 1921 B. Lansink, Jr., chaired NAS while his father served as NAS secretary. The Lansinks and their supporters were bitterly opposed to organizational ties with the CPN and were even more bitterly opposed to NAS membership in the Soviet Profintern. From 1919 until 1921 the faction was able to prevent a movement of NAS into the communist orbit. To the extent that the group favored international ties, it sought by 1921 to bring NAS into the International Federation of Revolutionary Trade Unions, a syndicalist concentration which was just then taking form in Berlin.

Between 1919 and 1923 the communist minority within NAS quietly evolved into a temporary majority. As noted, a number of NAS members had joined the CPN by 1919. Led by E. Bouwman and Henk Sneevliet, the communist group sought to bring NAS into the Profintern as quickly as possible.[65] They were not able to do this until 1923 for a number of reasons. First, there was strong opposition within NAS itself. Second, the CPN relations within NAS, while often entailing front actions, were underscored by deep suspicions. Were not the NAS men really anarchists and syndicalists in communist guise? Third, was there not a real danger that Sneevliet and his men might someday push Ceton, Wijnkoop, and Van Ravesteijn aside, should tens of thousands of NAS members suddenly move into the CPN? These issues remained unresolved in 1921. The Sneevliet faction eventually won, and in 1923 NAS entered the Profintern for four unhappy years. Having led NAS into the communist labor international, Sneevliet led them out again in 1927. Until its dissolution by German occupation authorities during the Second World War, NAS remained an independent force on the Dutch leftist labor front. The Lansinks and their supporters, outraged at the 1923 decision to join the Profintern, left NAS, taking 7,700 NAS members with them, and founded the Nederlands Syndikalistisch Vakverbond (NSV).[66] The NSV melted away over the years and by 1940 counted only 1,614 members. NAS membership dropped to less than 14,000 in 1923 and only once in the entire interwar era would it ever surpass 20,000 again.

Taken as a whole, the 1917-21 era did not have the dramatic effect on Dutch society that it did on other European nations. Wartime shortages did fan a measure of social unrest and thus gave temporary strength to both the reformist SDAP and NVV and the revolutionary SDP and NAS. At no time during this half decade was there any serious possibility of a working-class revolution; thus wartime hardships led more to agitation, demonstration, and often temporary membership within a left-wing group. With the coming of peace and the gradual normalization of economic activity, the left organizations either stagnated or began a sharp decline. At the same time, the 1917-21 era completed a process of political and limited social reform that had begun in 1848. Universal suffrage was finally realized. State responsibility for those in desperate or difficult socioeconomic circumstances was generally recognized by all parties, laying the foundations for the contemporary welfare state. The issue now turned on funding and the financial allocation made to social programs and welfare, rather than the principle itself. Finally, that great issue of nineteenth-century Dutch politics was laid to rest; parochial schools were now funded on a parity with the state system. The SDAP shed any revolutionary pretenses it might have had, and its SDP rival became the CPN. The NVV remained the strongest single trade union confederation in Holland but by 1921 was losing ground to the religiously oriented unions. NAS had its last burst of growth at the end of the war but by 1921 was slumping back toward its former membership. By 1921 its day had temporarily passed, as had that of all revolutionary forces on the Dutch left.

Notes

1. There are a number of good surveys of the Netherlands in the nineteenth century. The best in English is Ernst H. Kossman, *The Low Countries, 1780–1940* (Oxford, 1978). In Dutch, there are a number of multivolume works with a volume or two dealing with the contemporary periods, such as L. G. J. Verberne, *Nieuwste Geschiedenis*, vols. 7 and 8 in Hendrik Brugmans, *Geschiedenis van Nederland* (8 vols, Amsterdam, 1935–38), and vols. 11 and 12 in J. A. van Houtte et al., *Algemene Geschiedenis der Nederlanden* (12 vols., Utrecht, 1949–58). This distinguished series is now being replaced by a totally new edition. On Dutch parliamentary life, see the series *Schets eener Parlementaire Geschiedenis van Nederland* (5 vols., 's-Gravenhage, 1948–56), and on the interwar era, Pieter J. Oud, *Het Jongste Verleden* (6 vols., Assen, 1948–51). Oud also has a useful general survey, *Honderd jaren: Een eeuw van staatkundige vormgeving in Nederland, 1840–1940* (Assen, 1961). The author would like to thank Mies Campfens of the International Institute for Social History, Amsterdam, for her aid in providing materials for this essay. Dutch spelling has changed over the decades, and thus all titles are cited as they were originally published.

2. For excellent discussions of Dutch society on the eve of industrialization, see Jan de Vries, *The Dutch Rural Economy in the Golden Age* (New Haven, 1974), and Joel Mokyr, *Industrialization in the Low Countries, 1795–1850* (New Haven, 1976).

3. For a full discussion of late-nineteenth-century industrialization, see Jan A. de Jonge, *De industrialisatie in Nederland tussen 1850 en 1914* (Amsterdam, 1968).

4. For excellent discussions of Dutch politics in the nineteenth century, see Johan Goudsblom, *Dutch Society* (New York, 1967); Hans Daalder, "Parties and Politics in the Netherlands," *Political Studies* 1 (1955): 1–16; Robert Bone, "The Dynamics of Dutch Politics," *Journal of Politics* 1 (1962): 23–49; Hans Daalder, "The Netherlands: Oppositions in a Segmented Society," in Richard A. Dale, ed., *Political Opposition in Western Democracies* (New Haven, 1969), pp. 188–236;

and the articles by Th. van Tijn, "The Party Structure of Holland and the Outer Provinces in the Nineteenth Century," and "De wording der politieke partijorganisaties in Nederland," in G. A. Beekelar, ed., *Vaderlands verleden in veelvoud* (Den Haag, 1975), pp. 560–601.

5. Centraal Bureau voor de Statistiek, *Jaarcijfers voor het Koninkrijk der Nederlanden* ('s-Gravenhage: 1915), p. 315.

6. See Isaac Lipschits, *De protestants-christelijke stroming tot 1940* (Deventer, 1977), for a systematic discussion of Protestant politics in the nineteenth century. On the Catholic community see Ludovicus J. Rogier and N. de Rooy, *In vrijheid herboren: Katholiek Nederland, 1853–1953* (The Hague, 1953). For sketches of Abraham Kuyper and Herman Schaepman as political leaders, see Jan Romein and Annie Romein, *Erflaters van onze beschaving*, 9th ed. (Amsterdam, 1971), pp. 747–49.

7. Lipschits, *De protestants-christelijke stroming*, p. 80.

8. For a detailed account of the split within the Bond, see D. J. Wansink, *Het socialisme op de tweesprong: De geboorte van de S.D.A.P.* (Haarlem, 1939); and A. F. Mellink, "Het politiek debuut van Mr. P. J. Troelstra, 1891–1897," *Tijdschrift voor Geschiedenis* 1 (1970): 38–58.

9. A scholarly biography of Van der Goes has yet to be published. For an excellent contextual introduction to the Dutch Marxist community in the nineteenth century, see Fritz de Jong, ed., *J. Saks, Literator en marxist: Een bijdrage tot de geschiedenis van het Marxisme in Nederland* (Amsterdam, 1954). For a good general history of the SDAP see H. van Hulst, A. Pleysier, and A. Scheffer, *Het roode vaandel volgen wij: Geschiedenis van de S.D.A.P. van 1880–1940* ('s-Gravenhage, 1969), see also Harmen de Vos, *Geschiedenis van het socialisme in Nederland in het kader van zijn tijd* (2 vols., Baarn, 1976), and Ger Harmsen, *Historisch overzicht van socialisme en arbeidersbeweging in Nederland: Van de begintijd tot het uitbreken van de eerste wereldoorlog* (Nijmegen, n.d.). For memoirs of the era, see Pieter J. Troelstra, *Gedenkschriften* (4 vols., Amsterdam, 1927–31); Johan H. Schaper, *Een halve eeuw van strijd* (2 vols., Groningen, 1935); and Florentinus M. Wibaut, *Levensbouw* (Amsterdam, 1936). For the official SDAP history, see Willem H. Vliegen, *Die onze kracht ontwaken deed: Geschiedenis der sociaaldemocratische arbeiderspartij in Nederland gedurende de eerste 25 jaren van haar bestaan* (3 vols., Amsterdam, n.d.).

10. For excellent introductions to the late-nineteenth-century Dutch labor movement, see the initial chapter in John Windmuller's *Labor Relations in the Netherlands* (Ithaca, N.Y., 1969); and Izaak J. Brugmans, *De arbeidende klasse in Nederland in de 19e eeuw, 1813–1870*, 7th ed. (Utrecht, 1967); Louis G. J. Verberne, *De Nederlandsche Arbeidersbeweging in de negentiende eeuw* (Amsterdam, 1940); Ger Harmsen and Bob Reinalda, *Voor de bevrijding van de arbeid: Beknopte geschiedenis van de nederlandse vakbeweging* (Nijmegen, 1975); and Fritz de Jong, *Om de plaats van de arbeid* (Amsterdam, 1956). For Roman Catholic labor, see Cornelis J. Kuiper, *Uit het rijk van de arbeid: Onstaan groei en werk van de Roomsch Katholieke Vakbeweging in Nederland* (2 vols., Utrecht, 1924–27). On Protestant labor, see R. Hagoort, *Patrimonium (Vaderlijk Erfdeel): Gedenkboek bij het gouden jubileum* (Kampen, 1927); R. Hagoort, *De Christelijk Sociale Beweging* (Franeker, n.d. [1956]); H. Amelink, *Onder eigen banier*, 2d ed. (Utrecht, 1950); and Amelink, *Met ontplooide banieren* (Utrecht, 1950).

11. Harmsen and Reinalda, *Voor de bevrijding van de arbeid*, pp. 66–69.

12. See de Jong, *Om de plaats van de arbeid*, for a good survey of the NVV during the early twentieth century.

13. Harmsen and Reinalda, *Voor de bevrijding van de arbeid*, p. 430.

14. For a contemporary discussion of this process, see Arend Lijphart, *Verzuiling, pacificatie en kentering in de Nederlandse politiek* (Amsterdam, 1968).

15. For a thorough discussion of the 1913 cabinet formation, see G. B. van Dijk, "De Kabinets-crisis van 1913 in de Nederlanse Pers," *Bijdragen voor de Geschiedenis der Nederlanden* 1 (1966–67): 36–57.

16. See C. Smit, *Nederland in de Eerste Wereldoorlog 1899–1919* (3 vols., Groningen, 1971–73), for a systematic discussion of Dutch diplomacy within a broader European context.

17. For a quick introduction to the NOT and Dutch trade policy during the war, see Gerd Hardach, *The First World War, 1914–1918* (Berkeley and Los Angeles, 1977), pp. 15–17. For older and more detailed Dutch treatments, see Hendrik Brugmans, ed., *Nederland in den oorlogstijd* (Amsterdam, 1920); and Pierre H. Ritter, *De donkere poort* (2 vols., Den Haag, 1931).

18. Hardach, *First World War*, p. 30.

19. Carl W. de Vries, *Nederland, 1914–1918* ('s-Gravenhage, 1955), p. 257.

20. Ibid., p. 259.

21. H. J. Scheffer, *November 1918: Journaal van een revolutie die niet doorging* (Amsterdam, 1968), p. 19.

22. Harmsen and Reinalda, *Voor de bevrijding van de arbeid*, p. 430.

23. See Windmuller, *Labor Relations in the Netherlands*, pp. 41–45.

24. Harmsen and Reinalda, *Voor de bevrijding van de arbeid*, p. 430.

25. See Windmuller, *Labor Relations in the Netherlands*, pp. 41–45.

26. For an exhaustive treatment of this entire episode, see Scheffer, *November 1918*. Troelstra defends his actions in his *Gedenkschriften*, 4:162–248. His colleague Willem Vliegen gives a different perspective in *Die onze kracht ontwaken deed*, 3:416–42.

27. Van Hulst, Pleysier, Scheffer, *Het roode vaandel volgen wij*, pp. 53–54.

28. Cited in ibid., p. 53.

29. Pieter Jelles Troelstra, *De wereldoorlog en de sociaaldemokratie* (Amsterdam, 1915), p. 93.

30. Ibid., pp. 94–95.

31. Ibid., p. 131.

32. Troelstra, *Gedenkschriften*, 4:164–65.

33. Ibid., p. 167.

34. Ibid., p. 168.

35. For summary discussions of the Harskamp mutiny within the context of broader events, see Kossmann, *The Low Countries*, pp. 558–59, and Scheffer, *November 1918*, pp. 19–21.

36. Troelstra, *Gedenkschriften*, 4:185–86.

37. Ibid., pp. 184–85.

38. Ibid., p. 185. For a reformist interpretation of these events, see Vliegen, *Die onze kracht ontwaken deed*, 3:420–22.

39. Troelstra, *Gedenkschriften*, 4:191–92.

40. See Windmuller, *Labor Relations in the Netherlands*, pp. 46–50.

41. *Verslag over het jaar 1921*, p. 1, bound in *Verslag van het zeven en twintigste congres der S.D.A.P., gehouden op 13 en 14 Januari 1923, te Utrecht* (Amsterdam, 1923).

42. For an excellent discussion of the SDAP between two wars see H. F. Cohen, *Om de vernieuwing van het socialisme* (Leyden, 1974).

43. Vliegen, *Die onze kracht ontwaken deed*, 3:443–53.

44. Ibid., 3:445–46.

45. *Verslag van het drie-en-twintigste congres der S.D.A.P., gehouden op 20, 21 en 22 April 1919, te Arnhem* (Amsterdam, 1919), pp. 10–19.

46. Cohen, *Om de vernieuwing van het socialisme*, pp. 15–21.

47. *Het Socialisatievraagstuk: Rapport uitgebracht door de commissie aangewezen uit de S.D.A.P.*, 3d ed. (Amsterdam, 1920), pp. 187–93.

48. For a discussion of these years, see Cohen, *Om de vernieuwing van het socialisme*, pp. 21–29.

49. Pieter Jelles Troelstra, *De revolutie en de S.D.A.P.* (Amsterdam, 1919).

50. Ibid., pp. 124–25.

51. For a superior analysis of Troelstra's sociopolitical thought and its evolution, see Ernest Hueting, Frits de Jong, and Rob Neij, *Troelstra en het model van de nieuwe staat* (Assen, 1980).

52. Cohen, *Om de vernieuwing van het socialisme*, p. 39.

53. For a general introduction to the SDP as it evolved into the CPN, see A. A. de Jonge, *Het communisme in Nederland: De geschiedenis van een politieke partij* (Den Haag, 1972), pp. 9–43. There are a number of biographies dealing with figures on the Marxist left; see Frits de Jong, *J. Saks, Literator en Marxist*; A. J. Koejeman's popularized and admiring *David Wijnkoop: Een mens in de strijd voor het socialisme* (Amsterdam, 1967); and Cajo Brendel, *Anton Pannekoek: Theoretikus van het socialisme* (Nijmegen, 1970). Herman de Liagre Böhl has published a superior volume on Herman Gorter: *Herman Gorter: zijn politieke aktiviteiten van 1909 tot 1920 in de opkomende kommunistische beweging in Nederland* (Nijmegen, 1973). For an autobiographical account of the origins of the SDP and its evolution into the CPN, see Willem van Ravesteijn, *De wording van het Communisme in Nederland, 1907–1925* (Amsterdam, 1948).

54. De Jonge, *Het Communisme in Nederland*, pp. 26–27.

55. *Jaarverslagen 1916 en 1917 van het Nationaal Arbeids Secretariaat* (Amsterdam, 1917), pp. 34–35.

56. De Jonge, *Het Communisme in Nederland*, p. 28.

57. See ibid., pp. 34–41; and van Ravesteijn, *Wording*, pp. 182–224.

58. De Jonge, *Het Communisme in Nederland*, p. 31.

59. Harmsen and Reinalda, *Voor de bevrijding van de arbeid*, p. 430.

60. *Jaarverslag van het Nationaal Arbeids-Secretariaat in Nederland* (Amsterdam, 1915), p. 22.

61. *Jaarverslagen 1916 en 1917 van het Nationaal Arbeids-Secretariaat* (Amsterdam, 1917), p. 35.

62. De Jonge, *Het Communisme in Nederland*, p. 31.

63. Harmsen and Reinalda, *Voor de bevrijding van de arbeid*, p. 430.

64. See the brochure by B. Lansink, Sr., *De juistheid van doel en taktiek der onafhankelijke vakbeweging* (Amsterdam, n.d.), for a clear statement of the Lansink faction's syndicalist position.

65. For two thorough and fairly recent biographies of Henk Sneevliet, see Max Perthus (Piet van't Hart), *Henk Sneevliet: revolutionair-socialist in Europa en Azië* (Nijmegen, 1976); and Fritjof Tichelman, *Henk Sneevliet: Een politieke biografie* (Amsterdam, 1974).

66. For a summary description of NSV, see Harmsen and Reinalda, *Voor de bevrijding van de arbeid*, p. 156.

7

Violated Neutrals:

Belgium, the Dwarf States, and Luxemburg

HANS A. SCHMITT

The preceding chapters in this book have dealt with European countries whose responsible, representative governments used their mandates
to declare their neutrality in 1914 and to remain at peace throughout the
First World War. This approach has very properly excluded lapsed neutrals, such as Italy, Bulgaria, Romania, and Greece, that supported one
side or another between 1915 and 1917. Not yet explored is a small group
of nations that became belligerents or reluctant participants because of the
interference of more powerful neighbors in their domestic affairs. This
chapter examines these states.

The best-known case of violated neutrality was Belgium, recognized on
April 19, 1839, by the Concert of Europe as "independent and perpetually
neutral." Strategically important because of its position between Dutch
Zeeland and the French Channel coast, Belgium, the oldest industrial area
on the continent, was invaded by Germany on August 2.

Belgium was ruled by a German dynasty, the house of Saxe-Coburg-
Gotha, and by a king, Albert I, born of a Hohenzollern mother and
married to a Wittelsbach wife. For more than a decade before the invasion
Germany had been the best customer of its thriving industrial establishment. In Parliament, Belgium's Catholic majority felt little affection for
France's anticlerical Third Republic, while the country's Flemish population, especially in the commercial metropolis of Antwerp, represented the
secular side of growing Francophobia. Nevertheless, the government decided to defend Belgium's neutrality against all comers. The army was
mobilized on July 31, and while it was later forced to abandon every

stronghold except a small corner between the Yser River and the French border, the retreat to this line of resistance took three months and threw off the German invasion schedule.

While at war with Germany, Belgium also tried to keep its distance from the Allies. King Albert refused to put his army under either French or Allied command. His country did not subscribe to the Allied declaration of September 5, 1914, whose signatories pledged not to sign a separate peace with the Central Powers. As late as 1916 the Belgians attempted to negotiate with both sides a restoration of their prewar status, even though their government had found a refuge on French soil in Le Havre. They abandoned this evenhandedness only after the Allies declared on February 4, 1916, that the restoration of Belgian political and economic independence constituted one of their war aims, and especially after this objective became part of Woodrow Wilson's Fourteen Points. At this juncture divisions emerged in Belgian councils. A growing faction at Le Havre wanted to abandon neutrality altogether. Their postwar goals included reparations from Germany and a list of territorial demands: control of the mouth of the Scheldt River, as well as annexation of Dutch Limburg and the Grand Duchy of Luxemburg.

After the war Belgium did give up its neutrality. It joined the Allied occupation of the Rhineland and France's invasion of the Ruhr. On September 7, 1920, the kingdom signed a military pact with France, despite Flemish objections. Belgian expansionist ambitions were, however, rejected by the Paris Peace Conference where "brave little Belgium" received little more consideration than did other small powers. It obtained only the districts of Eupen and Malmedy from Germany; the border with Holland and Luxemburg remained unchanged.

On the domestic front, 1914 found Belgians bitterly divided on a number of issues familiar to students of modern European history. As in France and Italy, Liberals and Catholics fought for control of the schools as they had since the middle of the nineteenth century. An act to subsidize parochial schools at levels determined by local governments suspended the conflict without ending it.

Social changes provided another source of conflict. Between 1880 and 1914 the rural labor force decreased by 30 percent while the number of persons employed in industry nearly tripled. The urban population rose from 30 to 60 percent of the nation's population. Agricultural decline was hastened by free trade, which encouraged food imports. Industrial developments made up for these losses by creating fortunes and jobs, but many industrial workers suffered from submarginal working and living conditions. Unions sought to alleviate these privations by providing their constituencies with access to political power. A general strike in 1893 forced the enactment of universal male suffrage, tempered by multiple voting for men of property and education. The struggle for equality, therefore, continued, but the last great strike effort, launched in 1913, still failed to win equal suffrage for all men.

At the same time, Belgium's ethnic divisions became increasingly intractable. The boundary separating Germanic from Latin civilization bisected the country from east to west, separating Flemish Antwerp, West and East Flanders, and Limburg from French-speaking Luxemburg, Namur, Hainault, and Liege, and dividing Brabant, the ninth province, which included Brussels. Higher birth rates and universal suffrage increased Flemish numbers and political influence. On the eve of the war their movement had prominent spokesmen in all three major parties: Catholic, Liberal, and Socialist. The equality of both languages in the transaction of official business no longer satisfied these leaders. In the years before the war, bilingual, upper-class Flemings, notably the faculty and students at the University of Ghent, demanded that their alma mater become a Flemish institution. This agitation moved Francophone spokesmen to organize in defense of their culture and to advocate administrative separation of the two ethnic regions. The controversy cut across class and party lines and provincial boundaries. Even the members of each "nation" were far from unanimous in their pursuit of solutions.

Finally, Parliament's annual budget debates during the decade before the war were enlivened by spirited clashes between advocates of greater preparedness and their opponents who believed that neutrality constituted an adequate and obviously less expensive defense. When, on December 23, 1909, King Albert ascended the throne, he warned that "the army is not prepared to carry out its mission" of defending Belgium against attack.[1] The Catholic majority emerging from the election of 1912 increased draft quotas, in spite of opposition from a majority of Liberals and all Socialists. War came before the full effect of this increase could be felt, but the performance of Belgian forces more than justified both royal partisanship and its support by the parliamentary majority.

The German invasion put an end to most of these quarrels. Parliament and the citizenry supported resistance with enthusiastic unanimity. Liberals and Socialists entered the cabinet, the latter apparently in response to a royal promise that universal male suffrage would be enacted after the war. Educational and budgetary quarrels were likewise suspended. But the Germans kept alive the ethnic battle, hoping to cut the ground from under the Belgian war effort. Flemings were separated from Walloons in prisoner-of-war camps, a Flemish department was established in the occupation hierarchy, and in 1916 the occupation regime transformed Ghent into a Flemish university. The country was divided into linguistically separate administrative districts the following year. Consonant with this last step, the Germans allowed the convocation of a consultative Council of Flanders, a measure arousing violent counterdemonstrations both in Brussels and Antwerp.

The 1914 mobilization, proceeding in tandem with retreat, left Belgium-on-the-Yser with an army consisting of a majority of Flemish ranks, commanded by French-speaking officers. A movement known as the Flemish Front kept autonomism alive in the trenches, without diminishing the fighting spirit of its members. The equanimity with which these men carried their burdens—separation from their families in occupied Belgium coupled with more than three years of near-inactivity—indicates that allegiance to the common fatherland took precedence over ethnic grievances.

In the end, the unifying effect of the war and the collaboration with the enemy by some Flemings in occupied Belgium seriously retarded the Flemish movement's progress during the ensuing years. Although the king's message to Parliament on November 22, 1918, reflected extensive sympathy with Flemish aspirations, Parliament conceded very little. A law passed in 1921 required all government officials to speak the language of their jurisdictions. Only in 1923 did the lawmakers confront the question of the University of Ghent. The use of Flemish was permitted in its lecture halls, a concession far short of what the German occupiers had calculatingly volunteered seven years earlier.

Other proposals in the royal message received far speedier attention. The first postwar government, reconstituted to obliterate any potential division between exiles and inhabitants of occupied Belgium, included six Catholics, three Liberals, and three Socialists, the latter holding key portfolios in justice, public works, and labor. This coalition refused to entrust reform to the lengthy process of constitutional amendment. Their spokesmen declared that both veterans and a population which had suffered through four years of occupation should be granted the same political rights as affluent war profiteers. Accordingly, they presented Parliament with a bill granting the vote in the coming election to all men twenty-one years of age or over, as well as mothers and widows of men killed in action. Except for the opposition of a few Catholic conservatives, this measure expressed a national consensus and passed with little debate. Elections held in November 1919, accordingly, produced a chamber whose Catholic majority declined from 100 to 73, while the Liberal majority emerged with only 34 seats, a loss of 11. The big winner was the Socialist party, whose contingent increased from 40 to 70 seats. (In contrast to other developed countries on the Continent, the new Communist party played no important role, then or afterwards.)

The same Parliament next amended the constitution, including the proviso that the future enfranchisement of women, if and when enacted, would likewise proceed by legislation rather than constitutional amendment. In the social sphere it legislated the eight-hour workday and the forty-eight-hour workweek. Unions were given the right to strike, and individuals the untrammeled right to organize. The transition from war to peace passed without threat of violent upheaval. No assault on the political order took place. King and dynasty enjoyed unprecedented popularity, strengthened by Albert I's personal patriotism and commitment to reform. Neither future debates on neutrality and language rights, nor the financial disarray left by war and occupation, nor, in the end, the depression seriously challenged the Belgian constitutional system until the end of World War II.[2]

Meanwhile, the dwarf states of Europe (such as Monaco and San Marino) seem to have sat out both World World I and its problematic aftermath with the exception of Austria's satellite Liechtenstein, where the great conflict produced a radical reorientation in foreign relations and a new constitution. Together with Luxemburg, the principality was a remnant of Metternich's rather than Bismarck's Germany. Past associations with Germany—ending in 1867—had been uninterrupted since the beginning of the eighteenth century, when the Liechtensteins, a family of Austrian magnates with large estates in Bohemia, acquired the bankrupt seigneuries of Vaduz and Schellenberg on the east side of the upper Rhine River facing Swiss St. Gallen. A Habsburg emperor, grateful for the family's services, elevated this piece of scenic real estate to an imperial principality. Napoleon, impressed by Johann I Liechtenstein's sangfroid during the retreat from Austerlitz, included him among the sovereign ranks of the Confederation of the Rhine. From this ephemeral association Liechtenstein drifted just as automatically and passively into the Germanic Confederation.

Leaving the administration of this sixty-nine-square-mile property in the hands of a hired administrator, the princes in their Viennese palace behind the Burgtheater installed absolutism and Austrian law as well as a Ständeverfassung (corporate constitution) as decreed by the German Articles of Confederation. Until 1842 none of them visited the principality, and the rest of the world seems to have learned of its existence mainly from literary sources. Clemens Brentano loved "the little Land Vaduz . . . since childhood because of its curious name, without ever knowing where it [was] situated." Jean Paul's Siebenkäs, better informed, sought refuge in its borders from a shrewish wife. Alexandre Dumas, on the other hand, recorded in his *Impressions de voyage* a one-night stay at Vaduz "in a miserable, dirty inn, serving inedible food."[3]

Like other members of the German confederation, Liechtenstein observed 1848 with a new constitution, quickly abandoned during the sometimes reactionary decade of the 1850s. Because of its geographic distance from the rest of Germany, it never entered the Zollverein but concluded a customs union with Austria. During the 1860s it adopted a second constitution, joined Austria in the war against Prussia, and separated from Germany after the Germanic Confederation had been dissolved. During the ensuing decades it gradually turned over management of its transport, mails, and foreign affairs to Austria.

Though Liechtenstein remained at peace during World War I, having retired its company-sized army in 1867, it did not formally declare its neutrality for fear of offending Austria. The prince remained an Austrian subject, and members of the family continued to serve the house of Habsburg. But the application of Austrian censorship regulations, the decline of the Austrian krone, and the closing of a sizable textile enterprise, its only major industry, together with food shortages that required budget-breaking purchases from Switzerland financed by the prince's private purse, unleashed a movement for self-government and separation from Austria. In January 1918 direct elections of the fifteen-member Parliament were held for the first time, and in November the Landtag took the unprecedented step of dismissing the regent and insisting that his successor, though still appointed by the prince, be subject to legislative confirmation.

Not satisfied with these achievements, Liechtenstein patriots enacted a new constitution in 1921, which placed the election of two goverment councillors and their deputies, as well as control of the government, in the hands of Parliament. The ruler retained a veto over legislation, a prerogative not exercised until 1960. No one advocated abolition of the monarchy, however, and the reformers went out of their way to demonstrate respect for the Catholic church. The constitutional article stipulating state supervision of education guaranteed the inviolability of its teachings.[4]

It has been claimed that much of this democratization was designed to prepare a shift of associations from moribund Austria to the more prosperous neighbor to the west, Switzerland. The principality's old regime of the nineteenth century had viewed the republican "companions of the oath" at most a threat, at least a bad example for its own citizens. After 1918 standards and precepts changed, and Liechtenstein, both ruler and subjects, found it opportune to ride the democratic wave. On the other hand, the Swiss, who had kept their distance from the quasi-absolutist principality, agreed to negotiate with the emerging constitutional monarchy. The Helvetians assumed representation of Liechtenstein interests abroad and management of their postal system and after prolonged negotiations concluded a customs union on March 29, 1922. Still a rural backwater, the principality had survived its dubious wartime neutrality—the Treaty of St. Germain, without comment, identified Liechtenstein and Switzerland as the western neighbors of the Austrian republic—but had undergone significant political changes without challenge to its existence.

The survival of this tiny, defenseless state was never in jeopardy. Neither internal revolution nor external realignment threatened the sovereignty so capriciously bestowed by Napoleon in 1806. But the change of front was accompanied by some definite, if subtle, steps designed to put distance between Liechtenstein and past German associations. Between 1918 and 1923 an anonymous revisionist amended the national anthem. The two references to the "German Rhine" disappeared from the text while "the dear homeland Liechtenstein . . . in the German fatherland" became "the dear homeland Liechtenstein which is our fatherland."[5] This was only the beginning. Germany's annexation of Austria in 1938 produced what one observer has called "a negative national consciousness": "We knew that we were not Germans."[6] Henceforth confusing a Liechtensteiner with an Alemanic Swiss would cause a frown. Confusing a Liechtensteiner with an Austrian elicited merely a smile followed by a patient explanation of the difference.[7] No one seems to take Liechtensteiners for Germans anymore.[8]

Luxemburgers, another small German tribe separated from Germany by the outcome of the Austro-Prussian war, are still occasionally mistaken for Germans, at least by Americans. They resent this error even more than do Liechtensteiners when mistaken for Swiss. However, there is a great deal more to Luxemburg history than this small dissonance.[9]

By the beginning of the nineteenth century Luxemburg was more of a name than a presence. The name recalled a line of Holy Roman emperors among whom Charles IV, the promulgator of the Golden Bull of 1356, was the most famous.[10] The presence disappeared, certainly from German history, when one of Charles's heirs sold the duchy to Philip the Good of Burgundy. From the fifteenth to the nineteenth century, therefore, it shared the fate of the Burgundian patrimony. Divided between Bourbons and Spanish Habsburgs, the latter's low-country portion passed to the Austrian branch in 1713. Under Napoleon, Luxemburg became briefly a French department. The Congress of Vienna finally elevated the territory to a grand duchy and gave it membership in the Germanic Confederation under the rule of King William I of the United Netherlands. This increase in rank cost Luxemburg its districts east of the Moselle, Sûre, and Our rivers, which were ceded to Prussia.

Dutch control of Luxemburg was shared by a Prussian garrison, representing the German Confederation in one of central Europe's major bastions of defense. King William made up for this diminution of his authority by including the grand duchy among the provinces of the United Netherlands listed in the Dutch Constitution of 1815, a high-handed and illegal act which he had ample cause to regret and rescind when Belgium seceded in 1831. As a result of that event Luxemburg was partitioned once more. The Walloon section of 1,700 square miles became the Belgian province of Luxemburg. The house of Nassau-Orange retained the smaller German residue of 1,000 square miles. Now Luxemburg finally became self-governing, and in 1841 it received from the king–grand duke a separate constitution, modeled on the French Charter of 1814.[11]

The revolutionary year 1848 also shook Luxemburg's status quo. A new constitution, replicating the Belgian system, confined royal authority to the executive sphere. After eight years of incessant haggling between monarch and Parliament, however, William III followed the example of his German peers and restored the basic law of 1841.

Among the German confederate states Luxemburg alone remained neutral during the Austro-Prussian war. The subsequent dissolution of the Bund opened also a new chapter in its history. Luxemburg City's status as a federal fortress ended. The future of the fortifications, as well as the Prussian garrison, became a European problem.

Liquidation of the existing order began on the dynastic level. In Germany, the older line of the house of Nassau had been expropriated when Prussia annexed the duchy of Nassau.[12] In Holland the head of the younger line, William III, entered into negotiations with France to sell the remainder of the Nassaus' German patrimony to Napoleon III, contingent on a plebiscite and the consent of all other interested parties. This prospect caused an outcry throughout Germany, where the burgeoning national movement objected to any transfer of German subjects to French control.

Prussia made itself the spokesmen of these objections, and a conference of great powers was convened in London to work out a remarkably intelligent compromise. Luxemburg's fortress was razed, and Prussia agreed to withdraw its garrison. The grand duchy was neutralized as Belgium had been some thirty years earlier, but no one objected to its continued membership in the German Customs Union. The following year, 1868, a new constitution restored the reforms of 1848, including a Parliament with genuine legislative powers and control of the budget.[13]

More significant changes in the economic sphere followed. In the United Netherlands of 1815 the landlocked grand duchy between the gravelly hills of the Moselle Valley and the wooded mountain country of the Ardennes was easily the poorest of eighteen provinces. About thirty years later, in 1842, membership in the German Customs Union, combined with the preferential treatment that Belgium's free-trading industrial economy accorded the exports of its smallholder agriculture,[14] became the first stage of a spectacular economic takeoff. When increased grain shipments from overseas infringed on Luxemburg's grain markets, its farmers switched to animal husbandry to keep established trading lanes open. Between 1875 and 1913 the size of the dairy herds doubled, while butter production increased more than twentyfold. On the eve of the war, Germany had replaced Belgium as the dominant outlet for these rapidly increasing surpluses.

Compared to what came next, however, this agricultural boom was literally and figuratively small potatoes. It took the arrival of the industrial revolution to put Luxemburg on the economic map of Europe. Industrial development transformed the pauper of the Low Countries into a thriving community, whose per capita income in 1914 exceeded that of the United States and Great Britain.

This miracle began in the laboratory of two English chemists, Sidney Thomas and Percy Gilchrist, who discovered how to turn the highly phosphorous ore from Luxemburg and Lorraine mines into iron and steel of competitive quality. The first year of the modern industrial era began in Luxemburg in 1886 when the first Thomas foundry opened in Dudelange. Because of low surface-mining costs, blast furnaces quickly proliferated, turning the country's southern Minette region into a miniature Ruhr. By 1914 Luxemburg had become the world's sixth largest producer of iron, and it ranked eighth in the production of steel, ahead of Belgium, Italy, and Japan.[15]

To be sure, this spectacular growth brought neither political strength nor economic independence. Luxemburg's position within Germany's economic boundaries continued to be a major prerequisite, as was the proximity of the growing industrial complexes of Ruhr, Saar, and Lorraine. Since the grand duchy had no coal deposits, 91 percent of its annual consumption came from the Reich. German firms bought most of the Minette's iron and steel, as much as 60 percent of the latter. Having purchased the Luxemburg railways from the French Compagnie des Chemins de Fer de l'Est in 1872, Germany also controlled the transport that moved these commodities from factory to consumer.

Besides raw materials and markets, Germany was the major source of capital. Luxemburg's largest money trader, the Banque Internationale, was controlled by German banks. The largest portion of the industrial plant belonged to the Deutsch-Luxemburgische Bergwerks & Hütten A.G. (Deutsch-Lux), the Gelsenkirchener Bergwerks A.G., and Felten & Guillaume of Cologne. Even the production facilities of multinational or non-German owners, ARBED (Acieries Réunies de Burbach-Eich-Dudelange) and Ougré-Marihaye, decided in 1904 to join the Association of German Steel Producers (Deutscher Stahlwerksverband) in order to survive.[16] The board meeting of the Banque Internationale convened in Cologne; Deutsch-Lux shareholders held their annual meetings in Berlin.

In a time of peace and plenty, no one minded the German control, not even the competing French and Belgian interests. Even Luxemburg farmers were able to put new land into production and harvest larger crops with the new supply of cheap fertilizer, an important by-product of iron and steel making.

Increased production and income from field and factory produced a demographic reversal. In the 1880s emigration had brought population growth to a virtual standstill. After the beginning of the industrial boom the population grew within twenty-five years from 211,000 to 265,000. Luxemburgers stayed home, and in some years immigration exceeded emigration. Even minor industries such as leather refinement (employing 2,000 people, including 1,400 women), quarry mining, masonry, and construction, experienced new growth and rising incomes.[17]

As in prewar Belgium, Luxemburg's towns grew rapidly while its rural cantons lost population. During the second half of the nineteenth century Luxemburg City nearly doubled its number of inhabitants; the city of Esch more than tripled in size. But percentages can be misleading. In this case they signified that Luxemburg City by 1910 reached 45,000 inhabitants, Esch 16,000, the other two major industrial towns, Differdange and Dudelange, 14,000 and 10,000. Large villages grew into small towns.[18]

Luxemburgers still claim that in their country everyone knows each other, undoubtedly an exaggeration, even in 1913, but reflecting a sense of unity lacking in larger, more assertive nations. In fact, this local myth may tell us something about life in the industrial cantons of the Minette, and how it differed from their urban counterparts in Germany, France, and Belgium. Luxemburg and the steel towns changed in size, even character, but still remained manageable, coherent communities.

But industrial Luxemburg developed other, more problematic characteristics. By 1913 the total work force in mines and mills stood at 32,000, only half of whom were native Luxemburgers. Of the other half, roughly a third were French or Belgian, one-sixth preponderantly German, with a few Dutch and Swiss rounding out the figures. These foreigners caused few problems, for they spoke languages the indigenous population understood, and many of them commuted across the border. The largest of the alien contingents, close to 6,000 Italians, however, constituted a breed apart. Their language isolated them, even though many of them lived in the grand duchy an average of three years. They performed the dirtiest and most poorly paid work and were blamed for the fact that wage levels in Luxemburg were 20 percent lower than in adjacent Lorraine. They were considered unruly and temperamental, although police records in Esch reveal them to have been less prone to crime than other foreign or indigenous groups in the Minette. Italians presented an abused minority and stood outside whatever working-class solidarity may have drawn together the inhabitants of Luxemburg's southwest.

In the long run, however, these very inequities, combined with ground rules imported from neighboring countries, strengthened social peace. The adoption of the Belgian law code in 1879 prohibited collective action for the purpose of raising wages and improving working conditions. At the turn of the century the changing social structure was reinforced by German social legislation, providentially introduced at the time of maximal industrial growth.[19] Finally, Luxemburg workers seem to have been remarkably docile. Before 1900 labor organization was confined to trades, including small associations of printers, brewers, and glove workers. Only the printers ever struck for higher wages, in 1897, but their endeavors failed. In the capital a few hundred metalworkers organized but split immediately over affiliation with the powerful German metalworkers' union. Neither faction carried enough weight to become effective. The largest workers' organizations were the Catholic workers' societies, whose first chapter was founded in Rumelange in 1906. Their activities centered on the local cells, reflecting established patterns of small-town club life rather than class war militancy. They do not seem to have catered to

Italians, even in towns like Esch and Differdange, where these strangers made up 20 to 25 percent of the work force. On the contrary, they applauded the government's policy of using this minority to insulate local labor against recession. At the first sign of a downturn, foreign workers were sent home, protecting the locals from unemployment. Foreigners in the steel mills were the crucial safety valve preventing economic distress and unrest. The only violent work stoppage in the iron and steel industry before the war occurred in the last week of January 1912 in Differdange and involved only Italians protesting low wages. These hapless aliens lost their battle to a combination of police, German strikebreakers, and the hostility or indifference of their Luxemburg comrades.[20]

The political sphere likewise remained tranquil until the last decade before the war. Under the Constitution of 1868 some 5,000 voters, or 3 percent of the population, paying a minimum property tax of thirty francs, elected a chamber of forty-nine legislators whose work was subject to the suspensive veto of a Council of State appointed by the monarch. The cabinet was responsible to Parliament. From 1867 to 1915 chamber and government were dominated by the Liberal party, rechristened Parti Démocratique in 1896. Its leader since 1888 had been Paul Eyschen, the deputy and former director general of Justice and Public Works. The longevity of ministries and the lack of a clear-cut separation between political and civil service careers reflected the small supply of ministerial candidates, which had a similar effect on government in other small German states.

But Luxemburg's geographic and ethnic borderland status also produced marked deviations from the German norm. In the absence of an indigenous aristocracy, a propertied and professional upper class speaking both German and French dominated politics as well as cultural life. This elite recognized and benefited from the country's economic dependence on Germany, and the Liberal majority among them had applauded Bismarck's Kulturkampf and his hostility to socialism. Since the passing of the Iron Chancellor their allegiance had shifted, however. They preferred Belgium's constitution to Germany's, as their own system reflected, and France's separation struggle between church and state prompted them to look westward for inspiration. Jurists, who used French in their courts, as well as educators and men of letters, became preponderantly francophile. Most of them had attended French rather than German universities. They belonged to the local chapter of the Alliance Française, which, in the absence of a German counterpart, dominated the cultural life of the placid capital. Nor was French cultural penetration confined to the precincts of higher education. Many urban artisans—cabinetmakers, tailors, and hair-dressers—had served their apprenticeship in France.

Yet, this Latinization of a small Catholic nation on Germany's western border did not invariably benefit political liberalism. One example was the religious conversion of Luxemburg's monarchs to the Roman Catholic faith. The rules of the Nassau family compact of 1783 required that a male member of the Weilburg branch succeed in Luxemburg when Wilhelmina became queen of the Netherlands in 1890. He turned out to be Duke Adolf of Nassau, whom the Prussians had sent into exile after their war with Austria. The seventy-three-year-old grand seigneur became the first grand duke to reside in Luxemburg. In 1905 he was succeeded by his son William IV. This last direct male descendant of the house of Nassau had married the infanta of Portugal, who bore him only daughters, six of them, all raised in their mother's Catholic faith. Wilhelm's death in 1912 therefore, brought a woman to the throne, Grand Duchess Marie Adelaide, extremely devout and, as it turned out, celibate in her inclinations. At first the beautiful and pious ruler increased the rapport between the dynasty and the rural, church-going population in particular. In an entirely unpremeditated and accidental way her presence encouraged an increasingly well-organized opposition to urban Gallophile liberals, culminating in the organization of the Catholic "Party of the Right" in 1914. Over the long term, however, the religious predispositions of the grand duchess provoked conflicts that later generations can but see as a prelude to the deeper divisions generated by the First World War.[21] The traditional harmony between the two branches of government was put to the first severe test when the liberal regime won a last major victory with the passage of the Loi Scolaire of 1912. This measure decreed that clergy should be removed from all supervisory school positions and restricted to the teaching of religion. Grand Duchess Marie Adelaide signed it reluctantly, but after extensive soul-searching she may have decided then to oppose future measures of secularization. In the years that followed, goverment and Parliament found her unwilling to sanction liberal appointments to major educational posts.

Clerical resurgence also coincided with the appearance of a major political presence on the left after property qualification for voters had been reduced by two-thirds. In 1902 the new Social Democratic party elected five members to the chamber. Led by the party's founder, the Esch physician Michael Welter, all gained seats at the expense of liberal incumbents. In 1905 their number rose to seven. On religious and educational questions they sided with the government party, but, as in Belgium, their demands for suffrage reform elicited more support among Catholics than liberals. In contrast to Belgium, however, their presence did not bring Catholics to power at once. It was only the German occupation and its discontents that would end liberal hegemony in Luxemburg.[22]

The First World War embroiled Luxemburg before Belgium. Two days after Austria's declaration of war on Serbia, the Germans blockaded bridges over the Moselle and Sure rivers. On August 1, Prime Minister Eyschen requested French and German promises to respect his country's neutrality, a demarche soon rendered academic by German acts. In the evening of the same day a platoon of German infantry occupied the Ulflingen railway station on the border between Luxemburg and Belgium and tore up the tracks into Belgium. At 5 A.M. on August 2 large invasion forces crossed the Moselle at Wasserbillig. A brave Luxemburg gendarme protested the wholesale tresspass but was quickly disarmed. This ritual challenge was twice repeated, but in the end Luxemburg's 315-man militia was ordered back to the barracks, and the occupation continued on schedule. Shortly thereafter, the aggressors crossed into France and invested Longwy, after whose fall on August 26, Luxemburg became a rear area until the German retreat in 1918.

Ruler and government in turn addressed formal but unspecific protests to their German counterparts. They invoked neither the Treaty of London of 1867 nor the railway accord of 1872, which prohibited Germany's use of Luxemburg tracks and rolling stock for military purposes. After Marie Adelaide had confirmed the grand duchy's neutrality in a speech before Parliament on August 13, there remained no choice but to live with a situation which no one could remedy. Piecemeal efforts to preserve vestiges of sovereign independence continued, however. Although German laws punishing treason and espionage were unilaterally introduced, Eyschen's government successfully opposed the establishment of German military courts on Luxemburg territory. It also gained the exemption from military service of Luxemburgers residing in Germany.[23]

Officially, neither side challenged the contention that Luxemburg was neutral; no one declared war on the tiny victim. At the same time neither side committed itself to respecting the country's independence. No one doubts that a German victory would have transformed the grand duchy into a member state of Germany's monarchic federation. The consequences of an Allied victory were less predictable. On August 8, 1914, President Poincaré reportedly told the Belgian ambassador that Luxemburg had "not done its duty." But who would punish that dereliction, and how? Would France annex it, or would Belgium? France had coveted the redoubt on the Alzette since the days of Louis XIV; Belgium had never become reconciled to the partition of 1839. The war years produced no commitment to either claimant, and it is significant that a French statement of war aims issued early in 1917 did not even mention Luxemburg.[24]

For the time being, Luxemburg became a cog in the war machine of the Central Powers. Cut off from the rest of the world, farms and factories supplied only Germany; their owners, workers, and consumers profited or suffered on a scale which reflected the invader's fortunes of war. On August 4, 1914, German currency became legal tender, importing German inflation. Prices of staples doubled during the ensuing year and continued to rise, despite local price controls. Foreign sources of food supply dried up immediately. Efforts by the United States to add Luxemburg to its Belgian relief operation were halted by the Allies, who contended that the grand duchy's welfare was a German responsibility. The occupiers had supply problems of their own and felt no obligation to preserve Luxemburg's unique standard of living. When the Eyschen administration bought grain from Romania in 1915, Germany denied transit and shipping facilities. Pushed against the wall, Luxemburg concluded a secret agreement with the Reich, in which it surrendered the right to make separate purchase agreements with neutral suppliers in return for a share of German imports proportionate to its population. This formula did not count German troops living off the land in the grand duchy and disregarded the growing black-market traffic across the Moselle border into Prussia's Trier presidency.[25]

In 1915 Parliament gave the cabinet summary powers to safeguard the country's economic interests for the duration. The occupier reduced these powers to the vanishing point. Many Luxemburgers would have liked an embargo on all food exports. But as long as heavy industry ran on German coal and sold its entire output to German industry, no one could prevent German purchases of agricultural products.[26]

Significant changes in the labor market added to Luxemburg's economic vulnerability. The most serious immediate consequence of the war was not invasion but unemployment. Between July and September 1914 military operations halted production, and almost 22,000 of 32,000 industrial workers were thrown out of work. By 1915 heavy industry returned to 50 to 70 percent of prewar work levels; other manufacturers were less fortunate. The shock of massive, if temporary, unemployment was at this juncture only partially mitigated by the hasty departure of foreign workers, who sometimes left without paying their bills or picking up their last paychecks.

At the end of this volatile first year of the war, the percentage of Luxemburgers in mining and in the steel industry had therefore risen from 55 to 82 percent, and concern for their welfare forced the government to do whatever it could to keep Luxemburg supplying whatever market it could reach. This meant, of course, "working for the king of Prussia," though not under the austere conditions usually associated with that idiomatic expression. Between 1914 and 1918 Luxemburg ore prices increased 50 percent, while those of iron and steel more than tripled.[27] As consumer industries shriveled, dependence on iron and steel production and its only customer, the German government, became total. This one-sided relationship determined the levels of Luxemburg survival, at least for the 40 percent living in the capital and the towns and villages of the Minette.

The result was hard times, at least by Luxemburg standards. Even during the best of the war years, 1916, ore mines and iron and steel mills attained only 92, 80, and 95 percent of 1913 production. During 1917 and 1918 iron and steel production fell by 50 percent not as a result of fluctuating demand but of the faltering German coal supply.[28] All other industries—textiles, leather, stone and cement, and breweries—suffered catastrophically from a continuation of raw material shortages and price increases. In February 1916 the last cotton mill closed its doors. In March the government confiscated all woolen cloth and sold it at regulated prices.

One wonders to what extent the unemployment of artisans and workers in these depressed sectors was cushioned by increased employment in iron and steel. By 1917 when the mills once again employed almost as many people as in 1913, Luxemburgers constituted 70 percent of the labor force. But the rise in their number had not been steady. Between 1913 and 1915, 1,860 Luxemburgers lost jobs in heavy industry, which at the same time employed 6,751 fewer foreigners. Then came an upturn. In 1916 the foreign labor force shrank by another 488 while the native contingent almost doubled to 5,804. The year 1917 witnessed both an increase in foreign workers (1,354) and indigenous employment (1,706), while the figures for 1918 include some 1,200 layoffs involving this time a surprising two Luxemburgers for every alien dismissal.[29] The departure of thousands of foreign workers reduced their significance as a safety valve against unemployment, though not to the extent of explaining why the 1918 layoffs hit primarily Luxemburgers. For these there may be a political explanation.

All available statistics indicate, therefore, that except for the first months of the war, unemployment was not a serious problem. But steady work did not protect the quality of life. For the most fortunate among the working populations, the steelworkers, wages doubled between 1913 and 1918. By 1917, however, the price of bread had quadrupled and potatoes cost five times more than in 1913 and were rationed. Similar increases affected the price of coal and firewood, a particularly cruel burden during the unusually severe winter of 1916–17. These were controlled prices; on the black market these staples fetched much more, so that the maximum prices set by the government became in fact minimum prices.[30]

As in belligerent countries, the war deepened socioeconomic divisions through the maldistribution of profit and loss. In Luxemburg, as everywhere else, bank records document this development. During the first two years of the war, personal savings accounts grew by 250 percent. Somewhere between 85 to 90 percent of their owners were either entrepreneurs or farmers. Few workers put anything away.

These figures leave out a number of social categories and require extensive refinement, but certainly buttress the contention that the emergency distributed its attendant burdens far from equally. Apart from rationing, the government accentuated inequities by a rather haphazard policy of subsidies. Bread did not rise as much as other staples because of such subventions. Beginning in 1916, civil servants received cost-of-living supplements; in 1918 railway workers as well as indigent households could apply for a dole which amounted to one-fourth the cost of bread, sugar, butter, and other staple rations.[31]

Social divisions accentuated political rivalries. The war did not reduce policy differences between throne and cabinet. In 1915 the grand duchess refused to sanction the government's candidate for the directorship of the Ecole Normale. Eyschen offered his resignation but died of a heart seizure before the monarch had responded. A short time later the president of the chamber died just as suddenly. Marie Adelaide refused to attend the civil funeral that he had requested in his will.

These clashes created an image of the monarch as chief of the Catholic party rather than the nation. Without a leader who stood above parties, traditional political stability died with Paul Eyschen. He was followed by a short-lived caretaker government which called elections. These resulted in a virtual deadlock between right and left and were followed in quick succession by two national union coalitions (Catholic-Liberal-Socialist) whose members were unable to reconcile their differences.[32] The most dramatic event during this fluid situation was the steelworkers' strike of 1917. This crisis demonstrated the government's helplessness and the society's deepening divisions.

It took a war to produce Luxemburg's first massive demonstration of worker militancy. At the bottom of it was hunger, although political arguments played their part. This particular confrontation began with an organization of a consumers' protective league whose members convened in Esch on August 27, 1916, to protest high prices and rationing. Leaders of the overwhelmingly working-class audience decided that more than protests were needed and initiated a departure from the clubby tradition of past Luxemburg unionism with the founding of a Union of Miners and Steelworkers. The leaders of this effort were two locksmiths, Bernard Herschbach and Pierre Kappweiler, who had not previously been active in any union or party. They insisted, in fact, that their organization stand above parties as well as church and state quarrels. Within a short time they claimed 1,000 members, recruited from Catholics as well as anticlerical working-class families, and in some instances from white- as well as blue-collar occupations. It was clear that this new movement was at least in part fueled by workers' resentment against the socialists' parliamentary coalition with liberals over what appeared to them totally irrelevant issues.

Only days later, metalworkers organized in Luxemburg City, in this case under socialist leadership. In parliamentary elections the following spring Herschbach and Kappweiler successfully contested liberal seats in Esch, once again with Catholic as well as socialist support, and entered the Chamber under the banner of a new Free People's party. Their victory was the product of a surging protest vote following a hard winter. It was followed by a demand for a 50 percent wage increase which the mill and mine owners refused even to discuss. They pointed to wage increases since 1914, without acknowledging either the rise in their own returns (ARBED's dividend per share was thirty francs in 1914, ninety francs in 1917) or explaining why they had just increased the price of meals served in factory canteens. Appeals to the government to intervene went unheeded. At this point events began to move rapidly. On May 31, 4,000 workers voted to strike, despite pleas from Herschbach, Kappweiler, and their socialist colleagues in the chamber to stay on the job. By June 1 the strike spread throughout the Minette, though not as thoroughly as in Esch, where 90 percent of all industrial workers stayed home.[33]

The work stoppage was peaceful, and its leaders made no political demands. It produced two consequences. The short-term effect was immediate German intervention. A state of emergency was proclaimed, infantry and cavalry poured into Esch, and machine-gun emplacements were set up at factory entrances. Forced labor from France and Belgium replaced some of the strikers. On June 5 the local German commander met with some of the union leaders. He explained to them that his government would not tolerate striking a war industry close to the front, threatened to put strikers before military courts—and to intern the foreigners among them—but offered to discuss their demands with the owners. (There is no evidence that he ever did this.)[34]

Luxemburg's government, whose refusal to enter the controversy triggered the strike, protested the German action and ordered police to take no orders from the occupiers. More important, by June 10 the workers were back at work. Nothing seemed to have been gained except the bankruptcy of the young union's treasury and the firing of strike leaders. Both Germans and factory management had compiled blacklists of union activists, and this source may account for the disproportionate number of Luxemburgers fired in 1918. But in long-range terms the steel strike began a new era in Luxemburg politics. Though a losing cause, it had been supported by all parties in Parliament. For a short time union membership declined, but by the end of the war these losses had been recovered, new leaders elected, and ties with socialist and Catholic organizations strengthened. A new left wing among the chamber's Catholics, led by Pierre Dupong (Luxemburg's premier during World War II), began to attack industrialists for collaborating with the occupier. Socialists had learned to place workers' emancipation before priest-baiting.[35]

These shifts and realignments led to another government crisis. The parties sought to pacify the population by embracing a program of electoral reform. In the summer of 1918 elections were called, the second during the occupation, for an assembly with powers to amend the constitution. This contest turned into a liberal disaster without changing the parliamentary deadlock. In the canton of Esch the Parti Démocratique lost ten seats to the Social Democrats, who emerged as the second strongest party, while the clericals held their own. The new chamber contained twenty-five members of the Catholic party, ten liberals (as compared to twenty-one), and seventeen deputies of the socialist and People's parties. A new coalition headed by the Catholic Emile Reuter promised universal suffrage, a solution of the food problem, and defense of Luxemburg's independence. On October 8 it sent a letter to Woodrow Wilson demanding the evacuation of foreign troops. With a great deal less unanimity, by a vote of 28 to 20 (Liberals and Socialists), it also decided to put the future of the dynasty to a referendum. That parliamentary vote took place on November 13, 1918. The war had just ended, but its conclusion raised the levels of domestic discontent without ending all threats to Luxemburg's independence.[36]

Germany's defeat brought another occupation and changes in the country's international status, as well as a reorganization of Luxemburg's heavy industry. These circumstances combined to preserve the political status quo and initiate a new era of prosperity. It is, therefore, necessary to describe them before concluding with an account of the grand duchy's near-revolution of 1918–19 and the last wave of labor militancy in 1921.

In the last weeks of the war German discipline disintegrated. Rifle fire from passing troop trains struck Luxemburg farmers and livestock in the fields. In Bettembourg, German soldiers threw hand grenades into the railway station. After the armistice, these tormentors departed as unceremoniously as they had arrived, to be followed by a passage of American troops, who staged a review before the embattled grand duchess and General Pershing. On November 22 Marshal Foch led a French contingent into the capital, where he established temporary headquarters.

During the French occupation the Paris peace conference convened, to which Luxemburg was not invited. The grand duchy's fate was one of many issues that divided its major participants. In December a cabinet delegation traveled to Paris where it was left cooling its heels. The French were not yet ready to negotiate with the leaders of what Clemenceau in an unguarded moment called "Luxemburg's 300,000 *boches*." On April 29, 1919, however, a second contingent was allowed to appear before the Big Four and was assured that France and its partners supported their country's right to self-determination.

Meanwhile Luxemburg had terminated its membership in the German Customs Union, effective December 31, 1918, and had begun to seek a similar arrangement with France, if possible, and with Belgium, if necessary. Belgium, in turn, had rejected Clemenceau's proposal of an economic union involving all three countries. The issue was therefore unresolved when the Treaty of Versailles officially liquidated Germany's special position in Luxemburg. Article 40 confirmed the grand duchy's withdrawal from the Zollverein and removed Germany from the list of guarantors of Luxemburg's neutrality. The peace treaty also attempted to secure for Luxemburg industry an uninterrupted supply of German coke as "before the war" (art. 244), a stipulation the unsettled conditions in Germany turned into a dead letter.[37]

France's railway treaty of February 7, 1920, recovering the prerogatives lost in 1872, finally ended the drift. This accord became a serious impediment to a more significant French objective, a military alliance with Belgium. King Albert's government, whose efforts to revive his country's 1839 claim had failed, grew uneasy over the prospect of French encirclement as threatened by the presence of French forces in the Rhineland and the grand duchy. When Belgium nevertheless agreed to join the Allied occupation in Germany, it exacted a price, and accordingly, France told Luxemburg that it must negotiate a joint customs arrangement in Brussels. Despite popular preference for the French solution, these pourparlers began at once; after a full year they produced an agreement on July 25, 1921. The Belgian Parliament ratified the treaty with overwhelming majorities, while in Luxemburg's chamber the vote was only twenty-seven to twenty-one in favor, with both opposition parties voting against or abstaining.[38]

Throughout this time Luxemburg had also waged a stubborn struggle for continued recognition of its neutrality. The Treaty of Versailles reflected one measure of that effort's success. The question of whether or not Luxemburg had "done its duty" during the war was put *ad acta*. Unlike Belgium, however, the small cattle and steel country decided to remain neutral and demanded recognition of that intent when applying for admission to the League of Nations in 1920. The request was granted on December 16, but with the explicit assumption that the treaty of 1867 was no longer in force. Each side drew its own conclusion: Luxemburg that its status remained unchanged; the League that Luxemburg would amend local laws to conform to the obligations of membership.[39]

A shift in the control of heavy industry paralleled these political changes. The termination of Luxemburg's membership in the Zollverein separated the grand duchy from Ruhr coal, and even after special negotiations with Germany in 1920 coal receipts still amounted to only 40 percent of the prewar record. Luxemburg iron and steel lost free access to the finishing facilities of Ruhr, Saar, and Lorraine. Outright ore and metal exports to Germany were still possible under the peace treaty but were rendered unattractive by the collapsing Germany currency, whose decline also made German steel more competitive on third markets. High tariffs kept Luxemburg products out of France while Belgium supplied its own needs.[40]

The enterprises that confronted and overcame these handicaps had changed since the war and in ways clearly designed to leap over these new barriers. In 1920 a consortium of French and Belgian interests, including the owner of the Rodange mills, Ougrè-Marihaye, founded Hautes Fourneaux et Acieries de Differdange–St. Ingbert–Rumelange (HADIR). This firm acquired Deutsch-Luxemburg's holdings in Luxemburg, the Saar, and Lorraine. Luxemburg's multinational ARBED, acting as agents for a combine including Schneider-Creusot and the Banque de Bruxelles, bought out Gelsenkirchen in Esch and Belval. The German share of Steinfort went to a Belgian purchaser.[41]

These new industrial constellations also sought to overcome their raw material supply problems in part by buying into non-German coal mines: ARBED in the Belgian Campine and in Dutch Limburg for instance, HADIR in Lorraine. They also met head-on another consequence of the separation from Germany, the need to finish their own steel. From the start HADIR enjoyed the best of both worlds—its acquisitions included a large finishing plant at St. Ingbert in the Saar—while ARBED built facilities in Esch and bought a 50 percent interest in Felten-Guillaume. In 1921 it acquired additional plants in Belgium as well as South America. These efforts, matched by a gradual recovery of German coal exports, effected a return to prewar levels of production. The organization of a worldwide sales network accompanied the shift to increased steel production and opened new markets. Here, ARBED showed the greatest initiative, founding in 1920 its own subsidiary, Comptoir Métallurgique Luxembourgeois (COLUMETA), an eventual chain of more than fifty offices ranging from Stockholm to Tokyo and from Sydney to New York and Buenos Aires. Eight years after the market stabilized in 1921, ARBED became the largest European steel concern after Germany's Vereinigte Stahlwerke. HADIR marketed through the multinational and worldwide Société Générale pour le Commerce de Produits Industriels (SOGECO), and Rodange used the facilities of Belgium's Société Commerciale. The extent of their joint success can be gauged from the Belgo-Luxemburg Economic Union's status during the interwar period as the largest exporter of steel in the world.[42]

Yet when turning from multinational boardrooms to the narrow corners and scenic cobblestoned lanes of downtown Luxemburg City, we confront political and economic unrest more in tune with the German past than the Belgian future, climaxed by another wave of strikes which occurred after many of their causes had been removed. At the outset, the country was being treated like an enemy. It was still occupied, Belgium sought to annex it, and nobody seemed willing to give it a day in court. Many citizens blamed this disaster on their monarch, whose occasional ceremonial and unavoidable wartime encounters with the kaiser had earned her the undeserved epithet "L'Allemande." As in Germany, the ruler was seen as the chief obstacle to a good peace and, as Allied records show, not entirely without reason. In response, the new socialist action program, presented to the chamber on November 10, included not only universal suffrage, already on the legislative calendar, the eight-hour workday, and the nationalization of railways and steel plants but also the abdication of the grand duchess. Workers and soldiers' councils, organized on Armistice Day in the capital and in Esch, echoed these demands. Luxemburg social-

ists, like their German counterparts, had no intention of going outside of
Parliament for help but discovered that they lacked the necessary votes in
the chamber when the dynastic issue was debated. Herschbach and Kappweiler's People's party deserted the would-be revolution at this point, and
the legislature voted instead to submit the issue to a people's referendum,
in itself a revolutionary departure. Other socialist goals fared better. The
eight-hour workday was approved on December 15, 1918, and in January
workers' councils were established in all factories employing more than
fifty persons.

After the turn of the year, Luxemburg's international position improved. France also let it be known that it would not insist on an overthrow of the dynasty, as the Allies had in Germany, as long as the grand
duchess abdicated in favor of her younger sister Charlotte. The government eagerly pursued this solution, especially since Marie Adelaide had
offered to do just that as far back as October of the previous year.

On January 8 the government announced its decision to Parliament,
with the proviso that the new ruler would not exercise authority until after
the referendum. The declaration aroused a storm which remains unique in
the annals of that body. Socialists and Liberals rejected the dynasty, and
on the following day members of the two parties proclaimed a republic.
French troops had to be summoned to clear the floor, while the government proceeded to draft documents of abdication and succession. On
January 10 a Committee of Public Safety, about whose origins and membership little is known, repeated the proclamation of a republic, without
visible effect. The occupation troops maintained order, though their intervention—without orders from Paris—resulted in the dismissal of their
commander. Five days later Princess Charlotte symbolized a more limited
revolution when she swore to uphold the constitution. Her speech from
the throne acknowledged the preeminence "of the government established
with the confidence of the nation." The accession proceeded without
incident.

On January 16 socialism's local founding father, Michael Welter, con-
soled both winners and losers among his fellow legislators that everything
had turned out for the good of the country. He accepted the monarchy as a
bulwark against absorption by Luxemburg's neighbors, "allowing us to
live our own life, to run our affairs in accordance with our character, our
customs and our usage." The government's action was supported by
nearly two-thirds of the membership.[43]

Welter's words show an understanding of reality. Rejection of revolution increased his country's credit abroad and was in tune with preferences at home. His compatriots, a majority of whom still worked and

owned land, wanted to be left alone to solve their problems peaceably. In May the chamber discharged its constituent duties by amending the constitution. It abolished all property qualifications for voting, introduced proportional representation, and made Luxemburg the first Catholic country to enfranchise women. Subject to the referendum it amended article 32 to state that "sovereignty resides in the nation," which included the dynasty, as opposed to the Socialist-Liberal formula—"Sovereignty resides in the people"—designed to exclude the house of Nassau. On the day on which Luxemburg voters vainly opted for a customs union with France, September 28, 1919, they also endorsed with an overwhelming majority Grand Duchess Charlotte's succession. Six out of every eight voters chose this outcome; fewer than 20 percent favored the republic. Esch was the only constituency with a republican majority (57 percent).

Four weeks later parliamentary elections reinforced this result by returning thirty Catholics, eleven socialists, and eight liberals. The Catholics received more than 50 percent of the vote in every district except Luxemburg and Esch. Even in those old Liberal and new Socialist strongholds, Catholic pluralities would have shut out the opposition had it not been for the new countervailing force of proportional representation. Politically, Luxemburg emerged from five years of upheaval with a weakened monarchy, a more democratic constitution, and, as far as labels went, with the most conservative government in almost half a century.

Social peace returned more slowly. Neither the buy-out of German interests nor the constitutional reforms of 1919 prevented a deep if ephemeral postwar depression in Luxemburg's steel industry. Until 1922 the population of towns like Dudelange and Differdange actually declined (by 5 and 6 percent). Only Esch kept on growing. The shift to steel production prevented a recovery in the iron foundries, while it took four years before steel production returned to those high 1913 levels by which the state of the industrial economy was measured. The only good news was employment. Thanks to the foreign exodus during the war, twice as many Luxemburgers worked in the Minette after the fighting stopped.

But as during the war, employment did not hold hunger at bay. After more than three years of peace, a kilo of bread, priced at 35 centimes in 1914, still cost 1 franc, a kilo of butter 12 francs instead of 2.50, a liter of milk sold for 83 centimes as compared to the prewar price of 25 centimes. Added to the hardship of inflation was the galling fact that farmers benefited from the country's temporary separation from customary markets and sources of supply. Only workers' wives had to stand in line to purchase meager rations at high prices.

During 1919 food riots were commonplace in the capital and the southwest. On August 14 workers stormed the chamber, demanding special salary supplements. Stagnant wages and sometimes well-founded fears of layoffs increased the number of strikes. What held revolution at bay during this volatile interim was not only French troops but divisions among the workers themselves. By the end of 1919, 15,000 workers had joined the Socialist General Federation of Labor. But the emergence of a new Catholic labor organization brought another rival into the field. The election results of 1919 indicated that it drew on a constituency as large as the Socialists, whose position was further undermined by the founding of a Communist union in January 1921.

In the middle of February some temporary plant closings were followed by more strikes in Differdange and Rodange. Fired workers occupied the HADIR plants, and the movement spread to ARBED's fief in Belval. This was to be no replay of 1917, however. Neither Catholics, nor railroaders, nor white-collar workers of any description supported the stoppage. French troops cleared the plants. The government dissolved all workers' councils, and then everybody just sat back and waited. Two weeks later on March 17, the men returned to work. One hundred local activists were fired, and sixty Germans and Italians, identified as troublemakers, were deported. Thus ended the last confrontation of the postwar period.[44]

Life among the violated neutrals thus followed the pattern of spasmodic near-revolution, coupled with constitutional reform, that marked the wartime and postwar history of other neutral countries in Europe. Socio-economic tensions in Luxemburg reached more explosive levels than in Belgium and Liechtenstein, but—unlike Belgium—a large agrarian population remained unaffected by the inroads made by the militant left in the Minette. The Catholics' timely embrace of reform contained socialism whose growth was further impeded by the emergence of a small but viable Communist movement. The Liberals were the biggest losers in this re-alignment. How much the enfranchisement of women added to the new clerical preponderance remains unclear, since it is impossible to study that new vote in isolation.

In the years that followed, none of the opposition parties, from Liberals to Communists, folded their tents and left. All participated in a working system of competitive coexistence. In that constellation the Communist party members of Luxemburg remained more visible in Parliament than their Belgian counterparts, while the Socialists played a more modest role than did the party of Emile Vandervelde. During the late 1920s the iron and steel industry operated at twice the levels of the *belle époque*, thus providing the material prerequisites for political accommodation. Twelve years after the 1921 strike, when another depression struck, the safety valve still worked. Indigenous unemployment never rose above 7.5 percent and remained far below the levels of the world's industrial great powers.[45] On the eve of World War II, Luxemburg remained the placid, prosperous microcosm it had been before 1914.

Notes

1. Quoted in Jules Ingenbleek, *Temps passeés, temps nouveaux* (Brussels, 1945), p. 168.
2. Theo Luykx, *Politieke Geschiedenis van België van 1789 tot heden*, 2d ed. (Amsterdam, 1973); John Bartier et al., *Histoire de la Belgique contemporaine, 1914–1970* (Brussels, 1975); Centrum voor Politieke Studiën, *De Belgisch Grondwet van 1831 tot heden* (Louvain, 1971); Jean Gilissen, *Le régime représentatif en Belgique depuis 1790* (Brussels, 1958). For the time after World War I, the pioneering work by the Swedish political scientist Carl-Henrik Höjer, *Le régime parlementaire belge de 1918 à 1940* (Uppsala, 1949), should be supplemented by François Perin, *La démocratie enrayée: essai sur le régime parlementaire belge de 1918 à 1958* (Brussels, 1960). Louis de Lichtervelde, De Broqueville's sometime secretary, has left a good account of the prewar years, *Avant l'orage (1911–1914)* (Brussels, 1938). There exist two aging works in English on Belgian foreign policy, Jane K. Miller, *Belgian Foreign Policy between the War* (New York, 1951), and David Owen Kieft, *Belgium's Return to Neutrality* (Oxford, 1972), now admirably supplemented in the crucial places by Sally Marks's *Innocent Abroad: Belgium at the Paris Peace Conference of 1919* (Chapel Hill, N.C., 1981). The relation between international questions and language politics is detailed in Daniel H. Thomas, *The Guarantee of Belgian Independence and Neutrality* (Kingston, R.I., 1983), and for the postwar period by Guido Provoost, *Vlanderen en het militair-politiek beleid in België tussen twee Wereld Oorlogen*, vol. 1: *Het Frans-Belgisch Militair Akkord van 1920* (Louvain, 1976). Also useful on Belgian politics since 1908 is Jacques Willequet's *Albert Ier, Roi des Belges: Un portrait politique et humain* (Paris, 1979). German policy in Belgium receives a full critical treatment in Fritz Fischer's *Griff nach der Weltmacht*, 3d ed. (Düsseldorf, 1964), pp. 125–28, 268–80, 583–92, summarized in French in the same author's "La Belgique dans les plans allemands de restructurations de l'Europe," in *Sentiment national en Allemagne et en Belgique (XIXe–XXe siècles), colloque du 25 et 26 avril 1963* (Brussels, 1973), pp. 29–49. On the ethnic conflict we have Shepherd Clough's *History of the Flemish Movement in Belgium* (New York, 1930); Harry van Velthoven, *De Vlaamse Kwestie, 1830–1914: Macht en Onmacht van de Vlaams Gezindheden* (Ancien Pays et Assembleés d'Etat, vol. 82) (Kortrijk-Herle, 1982); Arie Wolters Willemsen, *Het Vlaams Nationalisme 1914–1940*, 2d ed. (Groningen, 1969); and H. J. Elias, *Vijf en twintig Jaar Vlaamse Beweging 1914/39*, vol. 1: *De erste Wereldoorlog en zijn onmiddelijk Nasleep, Augustus 1914/November 1918* (Antwerp, Utrecht, 1971). While there seems to be no work on Belgium's Liberal party, we have Alois Simon, *Le Parti catholique belge, 1830–*

1945 (Brussels, 1958), and a rich literature on socialism, including Jean Dhondt, ed., *Geschiedenis van de socialistische Arbeidersbeweging in België* (Antwerp, 1960); Marcel Liebman, *Les socialistes belges, 1885–1914* (Histoire du mouvement ouvrier en Belgique, vol. 3) (Brussels, 1979), esp. pp. 76–116; Mieke Claeys-van Haegendoren, *25 Jaar Belgisch Socialisme* (Antwerp, 1963). On industrial and demographic change, see Guido L. De Brabander, *Regional Specialization, Employment, and Economic Growth in Belgium between 1846 and 1970* (Dissertations in Economic History) (New York, 1981), and Ph. van Praag, *Het Bevolkingsvraagstuk in België: Ontwikkeling van Standpunten en Opvattingen (1900–1917)* (Reeks, Studien en Dokumenten, vol. 12) (Antwerp, 1979). Finally, a sweeping and comprehensive look at these problems across Belgian history can be found in Val R. Lorwin, "Belgium: Religion, Class and Language in National Politics," in Richard A. Dale, ed., *Political Opposition in Western Democracies* (New Haven, 1969), pp. 147–87.

3. Hilmar Ospelt, "Liechtenstein in der Dichtung," in *Das Fürstentum Liechtenstein im Wandel der Zeit und im Zeichen seiner Souveränität: Festgabe zur 150-Jahrfeier der Souveränität* (Vaduz, 1956), pp. 127–28.

4. Cf., Georg Malin, "Zur liechtensteinischen Kulturpolitik," *Liechtenstein: Politische Schriften* 3 (1974): 38.

5. Hubert d'Havrincourt, *Liechtenstein* (Lausanne, 1964), p. 128.

6. Gerard Batliner, "Strukturelemente des Kleinstaates: Grundlagen einer liechtensteinischen Politik," *Liechtenstein, Politische Schriften* 1 (1972): 11–20; Clemens Amelunxen, "Schwierige Vaterländer: Aspekte der liechtensteinisch-deutschen Beziehungen in Vergangenheit und Gegenwart," ibid., 2 (1973): 57–74.

7. Havrincourt, *Liechtenstein*, p. 80.

8. Apart from the sources cited, the following titles reflect the standard literature. Pierre Raton, *Le Liechtenstein, histoire et institutions*, 2d ed. (Geneva, 1967), is the best and most comprehensive work on the subject. Other general monographs include the first history of the principality by Peter Kaiser, *Geschichte des Fürstentums Liechtenstein* (Chur, 1847; 2d ed. by Johann Baptist Büchel, Vaduz, 1923); Ernst Pappermann, *Die Regierung des Fürstentums Liechtenstein* (Bigge/Ruhr, 1967); Gregor Steger, *Fürst und Landtag nach liechtensteinischem Recht* (Vaduz, 1950); Herbert Wille, *Staat und Kirche im Fürstentum Liechtenstein* (Fribourg, 1972); Eduard von und zu Liechtenstein's memoirs, *Liechtenstein's Weg von Österreich zur Schweiz: Eine Rückschau auf meine Arbeit in der Nachkriegszeit, 1918–1921* (Vaduz, n.d.); Hans Zurlinden, *Liechtenstein und die Schweiz* (Bern and Leipzig, 1931); Hans J. Spillmann, *Die rechtliche und politische Lage des Fürstentums Liechtenstein nach dem Weltkriege* (Abhandlungen des Institus für Politik und ausländisches öffentliches Recht und Völkerrecht, vol. 26) (Leipzig, 1933). The domestic transformation of 1918–19 is recorded by the first *Rechenschaftsbericht der fürstlichen Regierung an den hohen Landtag, erstattet in der Landtagssitzung vom 12. Oktober 1922* (2 vols., Dornbirn, 1922–23). Important monographic treatments of special questions include: Georg Malin, "Die politische Geschichte des Fürstentums Liechtenstein in den Jahren 1800–1815," *Jahrbuch des Vereins für Geschichte des Fürstentums Liechtenstein* 53 (1953): 5–178; Rupert Quaderer, "Politische Geschichte des Fürstentums Liechtenstein von 1815 bis 1848," ibid. 69 (1969): 5–241; Arthur Hager, "Aus der Zeit der Zoll und Wirtschaftsunion zwischen Österreich und Liechtenstein von 1852–1919," ibid. 61 (1961): 25–58; Herbert Wille, "Rechtspolitischer Hintergrund

der vertraglichen Beziehungen Liechtensteins zur Schweiz in den Jahren 1918–
1934," ibid. 81 (1981): 81–109; Livia Brotschi-Zambroni, "Die Auswirkung des
ersten Weltkrieges auf die liechtensteinische Aussenpolitik," *Liechtenstein: Politische Schriften* 6 (1976): 59–118. For basic population data, see Amt für Statistik des Fürstentums Liechtenstein, *Fürstentum Liechtenstein-Wohnbevölkerung-
Volkszählungen, 1812–1930* (Vaduz, n.d.).

9. Gilbert Trausch, *Le Luxembourg à l'époque contemporaine* (Manuel d'histoire luxembourgeoise, vol. 4) (Luxemburg, 1975); and the collective work *Le
Luxembourg: Livre du centenaire*, 2d ed. (Luxembourg, 1950), originally assembled in celebration of the centennial of independence in 1939.

10. Joseph Petit, "Luxembourg et l'élection impériale de 1308," *Hémecht* 29
(1977): 501–24.

11. Jean Schoos, "Die nassauische Thronfolge in Luxemburg," *Rheinische
Vierteljahrsblätter* 19 (1954): 561–72; Albert Calmes, *Le Grand-Duché de Lux-
embourg dans la révolution belge (1830–1839)* (Brussels, 1939), pp. 406–12;
Raymond Fusilier, *Les monarchies parlementaires* (Paris, 1960), pp. 555–69.

12. Hans A. Schmitt, "Prussia's Last Fling: The Annexation of Hanover, Hesse,
Frankfurt, and Nassau, June 15–October 8, 1866," *Central European History* 8
(1975): 326–27, 336–37, 345.

13. Schoos, "Die nassauische Thronfolge in Luxemburg," 573–80; Marcel
Junod, *Die Neutralität des Grossherzogtums Luxemburg von 1867 bis 1948*
(Luxemburg, 1951), pp. 26–39.

14. Gilbert Trausch, "Structures et problèmes agraires du passé: L'agriculture
du XXIème siècle," *Hémecht* 23 (1971): 115–24; André Heiderscheid, *Aspects de
la sociologie religieuse du Diocèse de Luxembourg*, vol. 1: *L'Infrastructure de la
société religieuse: La société nationale* (Luxemburg, 1961), pp. 82–84.

15. Paul Rathgeber, *Die Wirtschaftslage Luxemburgs vor und nach dem Kriege*
(Cologne, 1936), pp. 35–52; Pierre Lecoeur, "Histoire économique, monétaire et
financière contemporaine du Grand-Duché de Luxembourg (1919–1949)" (Ph.D.
diss., Nancy, 1950), pp. 37–39. I am grateful to the Bibliothèque Nationale of
Luxemburg, its director, Gilbert Trausch, and its staff for their hospitality during a
visit which enabled me to consult this and other sources, not available elsewhere.

16. Michael Ungeheuer, *Die wirtschaftliche Entwicklung der luxemburger Eisenindustrie bis zur Gegenwart* (Luxemburg, 1910); Camille Wagner, *La sidérurgie luxembourgeoise sous les régimes du Zollverein et de l'Union Economique
belgo-luxembourgeoise* (Luxemburg, 1931), pp. 13–14, 19–26; Paul Berkenkopf,
*Die Entwicklung und die Lage der lothringisch-luxemburgischen Grosseisenin-
dustrie seit dem Weltkriege* (Schriften der volkswirtschaftlichen Vereinigung im
rheinisch-westfälischen Industriegebiet, vol. 4) (Jena, 1925), pp. 30–38, 236–42;
Rathgeber, *Die Wirtschaftslage Luxemburgs*, pp. 6–10; Rolf Bühlmann,
*Wirtschaftliche Entwicklung und Bedeutung der Gruben- und Eisenindustrie im
Grossherzogtum Luxemburg* (Luxemburg, 1949).

17. G. Calot, *La démographie du Luxembourg: Passé, présent et avenir. Rapport au Président du gouvernement* (Min. de l'Economie nationale, Cahiers économiques, no. 56) (Luxemburg, 1978), p. 21; Georges Als, *La population du Grand-
Duché de Luxembourg* (Cahiers économiques, no. 54), pp. 7–9, 43; Lecoeur,
"Histoire économique," pp. 31–39; Paul Weber, *Histoire de l'économie luxembourgeoise* (Luxemburg, 1950), 209–21.

18. *Annuaire statistique retrospectif du Luxembourg* (Luxembourg, 1973), pp.

39, 41–44; Als, *La population*, pp. 103–14; Raymond Kirsch, *La croissance de l'économie luxembourgeoise* (Cahiers économiques, no. 44) (Luxemburg, 1971), pp. 12–22.

19. Michael Braun, *Die luxemburgische Sozialversicherung bis zum zweiten Weltkrieg* (Beiträge zur Wirtschaftsgeschichte, vol. 15) (Stuttgart, 1982), pp. 97–106, 106–23, 135–45, 257–65, 385–89; and Heiderscheid, *Aspects de la sociologie*, 1:177–80.

20. Heiderscheid, *Aspects de la sociologie*, 1:303–42; Henri Koch, "Die luxemburger Arbeiterklasse und ihre Gewerkschaften," *Hémecht* 29 (1977): 473–500, esp. 492–99; Gilbert Trausch, "L'immigration italienne au Luxembourg des origines (1890) à la grande crise de 1929," ibid. 33 (1981): 443–71; Heinz Quasten, *Die Wirtschaftsformation der Schwerindustrie im Luxemburger Minett* (Arbeiten aus dem geographischen Institut der Universität des Saarlandes, vol. 13) (Saarbrücken, 1970), 162–68; Fernand Lorang, "Als die Ulanen durch Öttingen ritten," *Hémecht* 29 (1977): 94.

21. Emil Schaus, *Ursprung und Leistung einer Partei: Rechtspartei und Christlich-Soziale Volkspartei, 1914–1974* (Luxemburg, 1974), pp. 24, 138–39; Dieter Nohlen, "Luxemburg," in Dolf Sternberger and Dieter Nohlen, eds., *Die Wahl der Parlamente und anderer Staatsorgane*, vol. 1: *Europa* (Berlin, 1969), pp. 812–17. On the dynastic question, see Schoos, "Die nassauische Thronfolge in Luxemburg," 586–91; Schoos, "Wilhelm, Grossherzog von Luxemburg, Herzog von Nassau, 1852–1912," *Hémecht* 5 (1954): 2–53; Schoos, "Die nassauischen Herzöge als Grossherzöge von Luxemburg," *Nassauische Annalen* 95 (1984): 173–85; August Collart, *Sturm um Luxemburgs Thron* (Luxemburg, 1959), pp. 64–95. For a somewhat one-sided view of Luxemburg's "mixed" civilization, see Josef Meyers, "Die Sonderstellung Luxemburgs im deutschen Kulturverband," *Rheinische Vierteljahrsblätter* 1–2 (1931): 105–11.

22. Paul Weber, *Histoire de l'économie*, pp. 9–11; Gilbert Trausch, "Contributions à l'histoire sociale de la question du Luxembourg 1914–1922," *Hémecht* 26 (1974): 10–11; Christian Calmes, "Août 1914: Les protestations officielles luxembourgeoises contre l'invasion allemande," ibid. 28 (1976): 408–10.

23. Calmes, "Août 1914," pp. 416–34; Junod, *Die Neutralität des Grossherzogtums*, pp. 42–55; E. T. Melchers, *Kriegsschauplatz Luxemburg, August 1914–Mai 1940*, 4th ed. (Luxemburg, 1979), pp. 67–114; Edith O'Shaugnessy, *Marie-Adelaide, Grand Duchess of Luxemburg, Duchess of Nassau* (New York, 1932), pp. 122–29; Collart, *Sturm um Luxemburgs Thron*, pp. 118–27.

24. Christian Calmes, *Le Luxembourg au centre de l'annexionisme belge* (Luxemburg, 1976); Gilbert Trausch, "Le Luxembourg entre la France et la Belgique," *Hémecht* 27 (1975): 7–32; Trausch, "L'Accesion au trône de la Grand-Duchesse Charlotte en janvier 1919 . . . dans sa signification historique," ibid. 31 (1979): 149–72; Pierre Renouvin, "Les buts de guerre du gouvernement francais, 1914–1918," *Revue historique* 223 (1966): 1–38.

25. Lecoeur, "Histoire économique," pp. 62–63, 68; Trausch, "Contributions à l'histoire sociale," pp. 20–33. See also the informative contemporary account by the secretary of the Luxemburg Chamber of Commerce, Joseph P. Sevening, "Luxemburgs Volkswirtschaft im Kriege," *Weltwirtschaftliches Archiv* 12 (1918): 1–8, as well as Emile Erpelding, "Luxemburger Verhältnisse im Kriegsjahr 1916," *An der Ucht* 20 (1968): 181–88; and Erpelding, "Luxemburger Ereignisse im Kriegsjahr 1917," ibid. 21 (1967): 115–23.

26. Paul M. Kennedy, "The First World War and the International Power System," in Steven E. Miller, ed., *Military Strategy and the Origins of the First World War* (Princeton, N.J., 1985), p. 22.

27. Lacoeur, "Histoire économique," p. 65.

28. *Annuaire statistique retrospectif*, pp. 198, 202. For a year-by-year contemporary analysis of these fluctuations, see Joseph P. Sevening, *Luxemburgisches Erwerbsleben im Kriege* (Luxemburg, 1917), pp. 5–10; and Gerald D. Feldman, *Iron and Steel in the German Inflation, 1916–1923* (Princeton, N.J., 1977), p. 52. Iron and steel production figures are available from a number of sources: Sevening, *Luxemburger Erwerbsleben*, pp. 12–13; Sevening, "Die Beeinflussung der Luxemburger Wirtschaft durch die Kriegswirren," *Weltwirtschaftliches Archiv* 5 (1915): 143–45; Sevening, "Luxemburger Wirtschaft im Kriege," pp. 3–4; Wagner, *La sidérurgie luxembourgeoise*, pp. 187, 194; Berkenkopf, *Entwicklung und Lage der lothringisch-luxemburgischen Grosseisenindustrie*, pp. 265–66.

29. Braun, *Die luxemburgische Sozialversicherung*, p. 605.

30. Lacoeur, "Histoire économique," p. 76.

31. Ben Fayot, "Das Jahr 1916," *Le Phare*, no. 214 (1966); Christian Calmes, *Une banque raconte son histoire: Histoire de la Banque Internationale* (Luxemburg, 1981), pp. 276–83; Sevening, *Luxemburgs Volkswirtschaft im Kriege*, pp. 6–8, 52–53.

32. Collart, *Sturm um Luxemburgs Thron*, pp. 140–69; Nikolaus Welter's memoirs, *Im Dienste: Erinnerungen aus verworrener Zeit* (Luxemburg, 1925), pp. 217–21; Schaus, *Ursprung und Leistung*, pp. 37–64.

33. Koch, "Die luxemburger Arbeiterklasse," pp. 306–8; Trausch, "Contributions à l'histoire sociale," pp. 34–50. The figures on ARBED dividends come from Berkenkopf, *Entwicklung und Lage der lothringisch-luxemburgischen Grosseisenindustrie*, p. 245.

34. ARBED, *Un demi siècle d'histoire industrielle, 1911–1964* (Luxemburg, 1972), p. 335.

35. Koch, "Die luxemburger Arbeiterklasse," pp. 308–11; Trausch, "Contributions à l'histoire sociale," pp. 51–67; Collart, *Sturm um Luxemburgs Thron*, pp. 187–91.

36. Welter, *Im Dienste*, pp. 15–19; Koch, "Die luxemburger Arbeiterklasse," pp. 311–12; Collart, *Sturm um Luxemburgs Thron*, pp. 202–8.

37. Gilbert Trausch, "Le Luxembourg entre la France et la Belgique 1914–1922," *Hémecht* 27 (1975): 24–26; Sally Marks, "The Luxemburg Question at the Paris Peace Conference and After," *Revue belge d'histoire contemporaine* 2 (1970): 1–20; Marks, *Innocent Abroad*, pp. 206–16, 222–43.

38. Wagner, *La sidérurgie luxembourgeoise*, pp. 32–36; Junod, *Die Neutralität des Grossherzogtums*, pp. 56–58.

39. Rathgeber, *Die Wirtschaftslage Luxemburgs*, pp. 79–80; Berkenkopf, *Entwicklung und Lage der lothringisch-luxemburgischen Grosseisenindustrie*, pp. 189–93; Max Suetens, *Histoire de la politique commerciale de la Belgique depuis 1830 à nos jours* (Brussels, 1955), pp. 170–77; Trausch, "Le Luxembourg entre la France et la Belgique," pp. 21–23, 26–30; Trausch, "Du Zollverein à l'Union Economique Belgo-Luxembourgeoise (1914–1922): Un virage difficile pour un petit pays," *Hémecht* 36 (1984): 343–90; J. E. Meade, *Case Studies in European Economic Union, the Mechanics of Integration* (London, New York, Toronto, 1962), pp. 15–57.

40. Wagner, *La sidérurgie luxembourgeoise*, pp. 9–10, 31–36, 40–42; Berkenkopf, *Entwicklung und Lage der lothringisch-luxemburgischen Grosseisenindustrie*, pp. 263–64; Rathgeber, *Die Wirtschaftslage Luxemburgs*, pp. 69–74.

41. Rathgeber, *Die Wirtschaftslage Luxemburgs*, pp. 84–90, lists the membership of the new boards, while Berkenkopf, *Entwicklung und Lage*, pp. 56–62, 196–206, provides the most detailed summary and graphic portrayal of these transactions.

42. Quasten, *Die Wirschaftsformation der Schwerindustrie in Luxemburg*, pp. 239–44; Wagner, *La sidérurgie luxembourgeoise*, pp. 40–45, 129–31; Berkenkopf, *Entwicklung und Lage*, pp. 222–25, 236–42; and Jacques Bariéty, "Le rôle d'Emile Mayrisch entre les sidérurgies allemandes et françaises après la première guerre mondiale," *Relations Internationales*, no. 1 (May 1974): 123–34.

43. Welter, *Im Dienste*, pp. 22–61, 71–76, 96–105, 111–36; Luc Hommel, "Quarante-huit heures de république à Luxembourg," *La revue générale* 60 (1927): 513–37, 661–75. For a French report of the army's role, see Serge Bonnet, "La tentative d'instaurer la république à Luxembourg en 1919," *Hémecht* 26 (1974): 169–86. Other treatments include O'Shaughnessy, *Marie-Adelaide*, pp. 135–51; Collart, *Sturm um Luxemburgs Thron*, pp. 217–48, 276–81; Trausch, "Contributions à l'histoire sociale," pp. 73–80; Dto., "L'accession au trône de la Grande-Duchesse Charlotte," pp. 159–71; Jean Schoos, *Thron und Dynastie*, 2d ed. (Luxemburg, 1978), p. 85; Henri Wehenkel, "10. November 1918: Der Anfang der revolutionären Bewegung in Luxemburg," in *Centre Jean Kill, 1921–1981: Beiträge zur Geschichte der kommunistischen Partei Luxemburgs* (Luxemburg, 1981), pp. 11–20.

44. *Annuaire statistique retrospectif*, pp. 38, 198, 202, 338; Welter, *Im Dienste*, pp. 186–89; Koch, "Die Luxemburger Arbeiterklasse," pp. 319–27; Trausch, "Contributions à l'histoire sociale," pp. 82–110; Berkenkopf, *Entwicklung und Lage*, pp. 227–30. Paul Weber's "La situation éonomique du Luxembourg au lendemain de la première guerre mondiale," *Echo de l'industrie* 11 (1970): 51–61, surveys only entrepreneurial activities.

45. Braun, *Die luxemburgische Sozialversicherung*, pp. 78–81.

8

Crisis, War, and Revolution in Europe, 1917–23

STEPHEN C. MACDONALD

The chapters in this book provide a welcome and instructive departure from the usual itinerary taken by students of revolution in Europe at the close of the First World War. We have in the past trod again and again the streets of Petrograd and Berlin, of Budapest and Vienna. There was much to be learned in those interesting cities. But what we learned there can be better understood if we travel, at least briefly, to places on the periphery, places seldom visited in connection with the great seismic shocks of revolution which seemed, for an instant, about to bring down the edifice of the national polity, the "steel frame" of the state, from North Cape to Gibraltar and from Ireland to the vastness of European Russia. This was a compelling and important moment in European history. It may seem in retrospect that the shape of the melancholy decades to come was forged in the fires of the Great War's last year and the first eighteen months of the peace that temporarily followed, but it is not true that what happened or did not happen between 1917 and 1920 determined ineluctably the history of the next generation. Men and women remained free to choose their own history. Yet the war and its wake of revolutions— equally those that succeeded and those that failed—exerted a powerful influence over the minds of Europeans and lent exaggerated and sometimes lurid features to their collective anxieties and aspirations.

One is struck by the variety of the European revolutionary and near-revolutionary episodes in the years 1917–23. A bewildering pattern emerges from a survey of the social dislocations that erupted among belligerents and neutrals as the war drew to a close. In no two countries did things happen in quite the same way. This variety need not, however, blind us to the essential unities. As in 1848, the supranational character of revolution in 1917–23 asserts the Continent's historical identity. Amid all the contingencies and accidents and the European tribes' resolute parochialism we can detect the outlines of general processes. The inclusion of the neutrals in this analysis does more than expand the field of inquiry; without them a true measure of the European-wide character of the period is impossible. If we are to employ the hypothesis that it was the Great War that triggered revolution, we must examine those states which did not participate in the war. We need to visit the neutrals even if our interest in probing the origins of revolutions brings us back once again to those belligerents where revolutions occurred.

The scale and extent of the revolutionary and near-revolutionary outbursts of 1917–23 are unprecedented. At no other moment in Europe's history did so many almost simultaneous irruptions of domestic disquiet threaten to sweep away the old order. One authority counts twenty-seven violent transfers of political power in Europe between the February revolution and the coup in Vilna in October 1920.[1] This number does not include revolutionary efforts that were defeated. Everywhere, it seemed, there was insurrection. Everywhere variations on the themes of governmental collapse and popular revolt assumed visible and dramatic form: restive breadlines, general strikes, mutinous garrisons, sullen mass demonstrations, the charge of mounted soldiery, gunfire across ministerial gardens, martyrs' funerals, and endless orations. Thrones toppled and venerable empires dissolved. Even where the forces of order prevailed against halfhearted revolutionary excitations—as in the neutrals—wounds were inflicted on the body politic and confidence in the powers of the state's centripetal influence was shaken.

This blizzard of rebellion warrants our joining Gerald Meaker in speaking of a "general crisis" of European civilization in the second decade of the twentieth century. It was just such a storm of simultaneous revolutions across Europe in the 1640s which prompted historians one generation ago to identify a general crisis of the seventeenth century. We concede that "crisis" is an easily abused, imprecise word—a "lay term in search of a scholarly meaning."[2] Observers notoriously discover incipient crises in all but the most tranquil landscapes. Still, the ubiquitousness and simultaneity of the outbreaks of 1917–20 insist we adopt a conceptual framework sufficiently broad to account for, or at least to describe, the general incidence of insurrection. Randolph Starn argues that "crisis" suggests an "intermediate zone between 'revolution' and 'continuity.'"[3] Given the occurrence of so much civil violence and insurrection and the ultimate triumph, in most places, of the antirevolutionary forces, this seems a fair description of Europe as a whole in the period 1917-23.

If there was a general crisis in Europe in the early twentieth century, what was the relationship of this crisis to the First World War? Did the crisis produce the war, the war the crisis, or was it precisely the war and its attendant public and private calamities that constituted the crisis? These same questions have been asked of the general crisis of the seventeenth century and the Thirty Years' War. The answers proposed are instructive for our own inquiry. To Hugh Trevor-Roper the revolutions of the 1640s marked the political demise of the Renaissance: the inefficient and expensive Renaissance court proved itself unable to govern effectively and was pushed aside by new political forms and forces. The Thirty Years' War neither precipitated the crisis nor resulted from it.[4] J. H. Elliott, in contrast, argued that the "imperious demands" of the new scale of warfare in the seventeenth century produced the crisis by imposing novel financial burdens on the states of Europe. When these states sought to meet the burdens by raising new taxes and by otherwise tapping previously privileged sources of wealth, they ignited revolts by classes and provinces determined to resist any extensions of the central authorities' prerogatives.[5] The revolutions of the 1640s were only one element, by no means a central one, in the general crisis described by E. J. Hobsbawm, for whom the real crisis stemmed from deep, architectonic fractures of European society as the Continent shifted from a feudal, inland-sea economy to a capitalist, Atlantic one. War may have exacerbated this crisis. But Hobsbawm dismissed as "perhaps too speculative to be worth pursuing" the notion that this economic crisis might itself have caused the war or prolonged it.[6]

One acute observer of modern European history has not hesitated to pursue this speculation. Arno J. Mayer asserts that there was indeed a general crisis in Europe in the twentieth century analogous to that of the seventeenth, and he declares emphatically that this crisis produced the great wars of our time. The crisis was, in Mayer's words, "the preconditon and cause rather than the consequence of foreign wars."[7] This twentieth-century crisis lasted from Russia's defeat in 1904-5 to about 1950 when the Cold War imposed an exogenous stability on European affairs. This crisis, which triggered both world wars (the "Thirty Years' War of the twentieth century"), was reactionary in nature: it was created not by the stirrings of rebellious proletarians and frustrated democrats asserting social and political claims but by a besieged "hegemonic bloc" of agrarians and nobles, allied with elements from the middle classes, which mounted a counterrevolutionary offensive in order to preserve its preeminence and power. This was a "crisis of *over*-reaction," a "revolt from the right," like the aristocratic resurgence of the ancien regime in decline.[8] Conservative "ultras," fearful of modernity and all forms of change, contrived to destroy their domestic foes by demagogic appeals to nationalism and by confrontational foreign adventures that courted an acknowledged risk of general war. The total wars of the twentieth century are thus in no way accidental; the statesmen did not stumble into hostilities in 1914. General organic crisis produced general total war.

Mayer is right to stress the powerfully antirevolutionary tenor of European politics in the first half of the twentieth century. The outbreaks described in this volume did not, after all, bring down existing society. Despite the singular and spectacular success of the Bolsheviks—and to some extent because of it—socialists, syndicalists, communists, and left-radicals elsewhere in Europe were nowhere able to achieve a wholesale destruction of the old order. Not that they always sought to destroy it. But the explanation of the continuity of European society in the face of the revolutionary wave of 1917–23 must be sought at least as much in the resilience and energy of the forces of order as in the putative failures and omissions of the revolutionary parties. It is the particular merit of Mayer's schema that it directs our attention to and requires an explanation of the accomplishments of the antirevolutionaries rather than laments the inadequacies of the revolutionaries. And the schema proffers an attractive coherence as well. It joins with Ernst Nolte's "Era of Fascism" of the interwar years to produce an inclusive construct that presents fascism as one aspect of a general reactionary phenomenon—a reactionary phenomenon, however, that does not react to the shock of revolution but provokes crisis by attacking the ideological and social antagonist before the revolution.

Is Mayer's thesis correct? Did domestic political crisis produce war? Were the statesmen of 1914—and 1939—ready to seek war, or at least unready to seek peace, in order to further the resurgence of their hegemonic blocs at home? Did Berchtold strike at Pašić in order to destroy Adler? Was Bethmann's real target Sazonov or Liebknecht? Did Paléologue issue his blank check to strengthen Nicholas II or weaken Jaurès? Put so baldly, these alternatives reduce a complex situation to a simple-minded either/or. But these unrealistically harsh alternatives require that we confront the fundamental question. That the states of Europe were beset with serious, even profound, political and social problems in 1914 is true. Yet it is a banal truth. It had always been so. That some statesmen in Europe would consider foreign wars a useful stratagem to employ against their enemies at home is certain. But it is far from certain that the decisions they made for war in the summer of 1914 followed from this. Today there may be a consensus among Western historians that the German Empire pursued an aggressive foreign policy after 1897 in order to throttle social democracy in the Reich. But in July 1914 Bethmann-Hollweg did not expect war to strengthen the conservative cause. *Primat der Innenpolitik* notwithstanding, Bethmann inexpertly led his country into war for reasons fully explicable in terms of traditional Great Power rivalry.[9] What was true for Germany—the "ideal-type reservoir for politically motivated external war," in Mayer's view[10]—was all the more true for Austria and Russia, to say nothing of Britain and France.

The origins of the First World War need not detain us long here. Perhaps it was the calculations of domestic counterrevolution, masked—as decency required—by conventional expressions of concern with diplomatic advantage and the requirements of national prestige, that actually motivated the actors of 1914. Perhaps not. We can establish no irrefutable causal link between a prewar conservative resurgence and the consequences of Princip's crime. The hypothesis that general crisis produced general war cannot be demonstrated. As far as the neutrals are concerned, the hypothesis is irrelevant. Whatever deep-seated societal tensions simmered in them, however frayed their social and political fabrics by the processes of modernization, however strident the temper of the conflict between their parties of order and parties of movement, the neutrals did not go to war. The imperatives of organic crisis passed them by. Unencumbered by international obligations that could have drawn them into the war, the neutrals evidenced no irresistable domestic compulsion to join the fray. All the more noteworthy, then, that they too should have been buffeted by the revolutionary storm after 1917.

It was war that brought general crisis to the European states, belligerents and neutrals alike. To be more precise, it was war that created conditions fostering the development of many discrete but closely related crises which together constituted a moment of extraordinary peril for the established order and a moment of exceptional opportunity for those opposed to that order. This moment is unthinkable without World War I. As war in the seventeenth century confounded and bewildered statesmen by its unexpected cost, ferocity, and duration, the First World War rapidly assumed proportions exceeding the imaginative powers of participants and onlookers. "A hideous embarrassment," Paul Fussell calls it.[11] Embarrassing and destructive. The war acted as a solvent on the mortar of European civilization; it exacerbated latent conflicts and laid bare in cruel fashion the inadequacies of the Continent's political arrangements. The war accelerated the pace of change by making imminent ideological and social conflicts which, long extant but regarded more leisurely in the days of peace, acquired a furious urgency from 1916 on. The war was unforgiving. For those who accepted its implacable terms, failure to master them meant ignominy and eclipse. This was as true for Nivelle and almost for France as it was for Brussilov and Kerensky and for Ludendorff and the Hohenzollerns. More surprising, as the chapters in the present volume show, it was true as well for some who stood apart from the conflict, for Arvid Lindman and Crown Prince Gustav Adolf and nearly true for Count Romanones and Alfonso XIII.

Two central questions emerge from this survey of the neutrals in the midst of general European crisis. First, why did the neutrals, spared the full effect of the war's destructive forces, nonetheless experience serious manifestations of social and political disorder in 1917–23? Second, why did these manifestations not develop into full-scale revolutions? Or to phrase the second question as Mayer would have it, why were the forces of counterrevolution successful in preventing this development?

The most obvious cause of popular unrest in the neutrals was economic distress brought about by the war. There was much hunger in Europe by 1917, and it made people impolite. The hunger was not experienced by everyone; this made those who were hungry all the more unwilling to endure their suffering in silence. The hunger march and the bread riot thus became recurring leitmotivs throughout the neutrals and the belligerents after the war's third winter. James Cronin has given us a general description of the course of the economic developments in the European neutrals that produced these conditions.[12] After the initial flurry of dislocations triggered by the outbreak of hostilities in 1914, the neutrals settled into a comfortable and prosperous two-year period when they turned their productive capacities to the service of the belligerents. Then in the winter of 1916–17 things went sour. Shortages of raw materials closed down key industries; domestic inflation, already worrisome, accelerated and rapidly outpaced wages; the Allied blockade produced critical food shortages; a neglected industrial and communications infrastructure began to creak from the strains of overuse. Allowing for local differences, this is an accurate picture of events in most of the countries we have studied. There are significant departures from the pattern: Luxemburg, closely integrated into the German war economy, did not suffer the increased unemployment—and consequent stagflation—of the war's last year. There were winners and losers in all this. Some people—farmers, entrepreneurs, certain industrialists, and certain workers—did very well indeed during the war. Most workers and most salaried employees did not. We are faced with evidence of misery from an unexpected quarter when Swiss bank clerks go on strike.

Inflation, unemployment, food shortages, and a conspicuous inequality in the distribution of economic hardship all combined to create incendiary public moods. These phenomena constitute what Crane Brinton called "prodromal symptoms of revolution."[13] They were unquestionably necessary preconditions, but they evidently were not sufficient ones. The acute privations produced by the war do not, in themselves, explain the public violence, strikes, and revolutions of the war years. For one thing, as Cronin points out, some of the principal actors among the insurrectionists—the metalworkers—were among the highly paid labor elite which did not suffer materially during the war.[14] And the pattern of strikes, revolts, and revolutions does not coincide with the rhythms of the worst-felt economic distress. The German Empire endured the terrible turnip winter of 1916–17 without noteworthy domestic disturbances, and when it succumbed in the autumn of 1918 the food situation had actually improved. Csarist Russia collapsed not because of its demonstrable inability to distribute bread efficiently, but because it lacked the moral energy to restore order once bread riots had broken out. It is true that one of the causes of the Spanish officers' revolt was these young men's displeasure at the debasement of their pay due to wartime inflation. But good economic news, as well as bad, could evidently contribute to rebellion. Cambó and his allies in Barcelona dared challenge Madrid in 1917 in part because war-induced prosperity had emboldened them and the Catalonian middle classes they represented.

The general and inchoate misery of important segments of the urban working population assumed effective forms of political protest—forms transcending the hunger march—when the socialist parties and their union allies mobilized resentment at living conditions and transformed this into formal claims against the state. This did not occur everywhere. Where it did occur, the character of the claims made, the violence of their formulation, depended upon the relative strengths of the moderate and radical elements within the socialist camp. At the very least, demands were made for better working conditions, increased pay, the introduction of— or improvement in—unemployment and health benefits, the establishment of the eight-hour workday and the forty-eight-hour workweek. As we have seen, the claims often went beyond these modest categories and took on explicitly political, sometimes revolutionary, dimensions. Whatever specific form these demands assumed, their goal was the general democratization of society and, if not the elimination of private wealth and property, at least the melioration of the most glaring social and economic inequities. In this respect, the revolutions and proto-revolutions of 1917–23 represent not the breakdown of society but the maturation of a coherent and articulate opposition to the old order. These revolutions and near-revolutions illustrate Charles Tilly's "solidarity theory," which rejects the Durkheimian view that traces the roots of revolution back to the collective pathologies of inadequately socialized anomic individuals. Rather, says Tilly, social conflict results from the coalescing of competing interest groups which quite naturally compete for power. Unlike the "reactive" revolutions of the 1640s when groups and regions asserted negative claims—essentially the wish to be left alone—against the pretensions of the centralizing state, Tilly sees the revolutionary disturbances of the second decade of the twentieth century as "proactive" in nature, for they accepted the existence of the modern state but presented positive demands for special political and economic prerogatives.[15]

The tinder of economic distress in the neutrals was often ignited by sparks from foreign conflagrations. The Russian revolutions in 1917, those of February and October, excited admiration and fear and suggested to some the possibility of emulation. The situation obviously invites comparison with the period of the French Revolution. France had served as the center of gravity of the revolutionary epoch after the 1780s not only because of the stunning success of the revolutionaries in that country but because France was in material and spiritual terms the center of the Continent. To a much greater extent than the distant American colonies, France and its revolutionary experience determined the language and fashioned the concept of political revolution. This remained true throughout much of the nineteenth century even after the geographical reality and ideological content of revolution in France had been narrowed in successive revolutionary episodes. From a relatively early point—and with unmistakable clarity in 1848 and 1871—it was no longer France but Paris that engaged in revolution. And with each wave of insurrection after the great summer of 1789, the universality of the revolutionary message yielded to an ever more stridently expressed class doctrine. Revolution spoke less and less to "man" and more and more to particular men and women in particular circumstances. This had happened already in 1792 when republicans pushed aside their erstwhile moderate and monarchist allies.

Russia could not play the role after 1917 that France had played after 1789 though there were many who hoped and feared it would. Russia was too much on the periphery, its conditions too atypical, its history too anomalous for it to become a plausible revolutionary paradigm for the rest of the Continent. Moreover, France in 1789 had been the strongest power on the Continent; Russia in 1917 was among the most feeble. How different the results of Budenny's expedition to Warsaw in 1920 from Napoleon's march to Milan in 1796! Lenin knew this. His expectations of Russia were limited: continent-wide revolution must await events in Berlin and the West where the preconditions for a true proletarian revolution had ripened. If thousands of workers and intellectuals outside Russia welcomed the Bolshevik autumn with fervor and anticipations of general revolution, many others among the ranks of the socialist parties and unions regarded the Soviet experiment with skepticism and suspicion. Russia was simply too unlikely a setting for the inauguration of the new age. It required not only a substantial modification of Marxist doctrine to accept the legitimacy of the events unfolding in Russia; more difficult still, it required of western European socialists an uncomfortable adjustment of their attitudes toward the primitive East. Torgeir Vraa in Norway was not alone in sneering at Russian "barbarism." If there was no Age of Communist Revolutions after 1917 comparable to the Age of Democratic Revolutions at the end of the eighteenth century, it was in part because communism lodged first in a disadvantageous place where history imposed grotesque forms upon it and where—unlike France—the host country's political weaknesses and distance from the center of the Continent's cultural life rendered it incapable either of exporting the revolution by force or of stimulating general imitation.

More than events in Russia, it was the revolution in Germany in November 1918 that fired the imaginations and rhetoric of socialists in the neutrals. There was good reason for this. The German Revolution brought spontaneous and victorious rebellion to the borders of the Danes and Dutch; the Luxemburgers found themselves in the center of insurrection as the ubiquitous soldiers' councils sprang up amid the occupying army. Even those states not contiguous to Germany had to be impressed by the uprising of November 9. Precisely because Germany was a great industrial state in the heart of Europe and a leader of Western culture—precisely because Germany was not Russia—revolution in the Reich could be interpreted as an avatar of unusual significance. Pieter Troelstra and the mayor of Rotterdam may be forgiven for supposing that with the fall of the house of Hohenzollern there only remained to arrange an orderly transfer of power to the proletariat in the rest of Europe. Lenin, more astute than

Troelstra, never believed things would happen as quickly as that, but he shared the latter's estimation of Germany's importance in any European-wide revolutionary development.

Curiously, among all the neutrals studied here, only in Spain did the question of neutrality itself figure significantly in the clash between the defenders of the old order and the partisans of change. For the other nonbelligerent nations the advantages of neutrality were so obvious, the absence of compelling moral issues among the warring states sufficiently clear, that there was no occasion for a general debate between interventionists and noninterventionists. Not so in Spain. The "civil war of words," as Meaker calls the impassioned exchange between Germanophiles and Ententophiles, indicated the profound gulf separating reactionary and progressive forces in Spanish life. This gulf was not caused by war, but as the war took on the aspects of a grand international morality play, it mobilized the partisans of authoritarian and democratic Spain and provoked an ominous verbal preview of 1936–39. Despairing of the monarchy's willingness to bring Spain into the war on the Allied side—the only course, as they saw it, which could align Spain with the forces of modernity and counter the symptoms of national decadence—the Ententophiles moved toward revolution in 1917. Spain's socialists could not remain aloof from this debate. Whereas they had originally adopted an orthodox antiwar position in 1914—like Italy's socialists—they drifted toward interventionism by 1917—like France's socialists in 1914—and came to view the war as a crusade against the principles of imperialism and autocracy. Once again, the reality of socialism's operative particularism belied its internationalist pose.

Why did these "spasmodic near-revolutions," as Hans Schmitt calls them, not develop into full-blown revolutionary episodes? Why was the existing order in the neutrals able to maintain itself in the face of apparently serious challenges? The most obvious answer is that in most places there was no concerted effort to overturn society. It is an exaggeration, but not much of an exaggeration, to say that these "revolutions" failed because no one tried to make them succeed. Nearly everywhere among the neutrals the socialist parties were dominated by a functionally revisionist ideology and by leaders who entertained no expectations of a sudden collapse of capitalist society. In those places where something like a conscious revolutionary effort was undertaken—as in Spain by means of the general strike—the socialist leadership showed itself unable to master the techniques of revolution. Pablo Iglesias was no more the man to engineer a seizure of power than Robert Grimm or Hjalmar Branting.

These men were ideologically and temperamentally unprepared for violent insurrection. It is not recorded whether they "hated revolution like the plague," but like Friedrich Ebert they were, at most, ready to accept the consequences of revolution if someone else made it. We expect moderates to act moderately. It is more surprising to observe that a syndicalist like Christian Christensen was also unprepared to countenance revolution in 1918. And in the one country where avowed radicals were in the majority in the socialist camp—Norway after the spring of 1918—the radicals themselves judged the prospects of a successful revolution to be so inauspicious that they did not even try. If this was pusillanimity, it was also wisdom.

It is easy to point to the divisions between moderate and radical socialists as one source of weakness in the potentially revolutionary parties. In fact, it is not clear why a united left, unwilling to contemplate revolution, should have represented a more formidable danger to the status quo than splintered socialist parties with widely varying views on the desirability of violent revolution. The fractious state of Russian social democracy proved no hindrance to the Bolsheviks. Regional and ethnic differences among the socialist parties and their memberships were certainly more injurious to the socialist cause. Catalonian particularism moved the middle classes in Barcelona to seek autonomy from Madrid; the same particularism made it exceedingly difficult for socialist leaders to speak authoritatively for the working classes of all Spain. Most dramatically, the Swiss general strike of 1918 was crippled by the failure of Italian-speaking and French-speaking Swiss workers to join their German-speaking comrades. In this instance the war—specifically the way it ended—evoked contrasting emotions among the constituent linguistic groups of the Swiss state; working-class solidarity was undermined. And there was an additional factor militating against the prospects of revolution in Switzerland: a clear expression of Allied disapproval of soviet experiments and an implied threat of intervention should such experiments be undertaken.

A satisfactory explanation for the absence of revolutions in the neutrals cannot be provided by the moderate political dispositions of the socialist parties in these countries. The German left was similarly dominated by a revisionist, reformist socialist party whose cautious leaders eschewed rebellion. The German Social Democratic party (SPD) did not start and could not stop revolution in Germany in November 1918. It was seldom the intentions and resources of the left that counted in 1917–23; it was the will and the capacity of the center and right to act that really mattered. Where the existing order retained its confidence, where it was prepared to initiate events rather than await them, it easily defeated its opponents. In Denmark and Sweden governments averted more serious public challenges by an adept mixture of toughness and conciliation. Syndicalist and Socialist ringleaders were arrested, demonstrators bloodied by enthusiastic police, and sulking soldiers sent home, while at the same time social democratic officials were coopted by entrusting them with increased public responsibilities. In Spain the Dato government maneuvered the Socialists into a premature general strike which the regime then crushed with relish. The Swiss Federal Council stunned the leaders of the country's labor movement by the call-up of troops in early November 1918. Thrown into confusion by this unexpected provocation, the Swiss Social Democrats stumbled into a general strike which, though imprecisely conceived as a truly revolutionary device to trigger the downfall of the capitalist order, amounted under the circumstances to little more than the reflexive, ineffectual kick of a downed and defeated prey.

The forces of order in the neutrals kept their nerve. They retained confidence in their own legitimacy, they were prepared to use force to demonstrate their will to power, and they continued to command the logistical and technical means to coerce their antagonists. They prevailed, but it was by no means a sure thing; people and institutions wavered. Mutinies, desertions, and other isolated but disquieting indications of declining morale appeared in the armies of Denmark, Sweden, Switzerland, and Holland. As the German admirals discovered in the fall of 1918, the cumulative privations and routine idiocies of garrison life could be more injurious to discipline than the terrors of combat. The Spanish officers who had themselves defied their government only a few months earlier performed a sanguinary act of contrition when they turned their peasant recruits against the unions in August 1917. Marie Adelaide had discredited her dynasty in the eyes of many Luxemburgers by her political maladroitness during the German occupation; this presented a brief opening to republicans and socialists. The opportunity was fleeting, and the presence of Allied troops ill-disposed to local revolutions ensured the survival of the old order. Only in Sweden did something like a collapse of will occur among the antirevolutionary parties. In 1914 Swedish Conservatives had faced down the left over the issue of the latter's demand for the introduction of responsible parliamentary government. When the socialists and their allies raised their demands in 1917, the Conservatives did not have the stomach for a fight. Dispirited by the parliamentary gains of their opponents—gains which Steven Koblik tells us were more apparent than real—and unnerved by the whiff of foreign rebellion, the Conservatives retired and left the field to their foes.

We have not explained the continuity of political life in the neutrals in 1917-23 when we observe that the parties of order kept their heads— figuratively and literally–in the face of revolutionary disturbances. Which was cause and which effect? Did the neutral governments retain their composure and their capacity to act because the revolutionary forces opposing them were weak? Or were genuine revolutionary situations defused by the forceful intervention of the state? Put another way, we may ask whether the preconditions of revolution existed in the neutrals in 1917-23.

The contributors to this volume conclude that truly revolutionary conditions did not exist in the neutrals in the last years of the war. Clearly much depends upon one's definition, what one requires as the prerevolutionary minimum. If, like Gerald Meaker (and Rosa Luxemburg), one expects mass popular discontent poised for a more or less spontaneous eruption, then the necessary preconditions did not exist in Spain or in any other neutral. But then, according to this criterion, neither did they exist in Petrograd in the autumn of 1917. On the other hand, if one is prepared to join the Bolsheviks and bestow the name revolution on a coup, there was also a critical revolutionary ingredient lacking in the neutrals because there were no leaders of significance among the parties of the left possessing the ruthlessness and recklessness needed to attempt a seizure of power. The tragicomic character of the Spanish general strike, the pitiable discrepancy between its brave designs and its timorous execution, testifies to this, as does the defensive character of the Swiss general strike.

Clearly there is a relationship between the apparent strength and volatility of proto-revolutionary popular discontent and a state's resolve to oppose the revolutionary tide. This relationship is dynamic and contingent, not mechanistic. A visible increase in revolutionary disturbances may harden the state's determination to fight, or it may trigger a collapse of will and the flight of the guardians of the old order. Bellicose displays by the state may frighten its opponents into retreat or summon new recruits to the revolutionary cause. To see how this can occur in practice, we may consider the case of a successful revolution. To do this, we need to return to the belligerents. Let us tread one more time those familiar Berlin streets and observe the flow of popular unrest and official response which ended in revolution in the first weeks of November 1918.

The revolution of 1918 has not been much esteemed by the Germans. The government of the Federal Republic saw fit to commemorate the 150th anniversary of the birth of Bismarck in 1965 and the centennial of the founding of the Second Empire in 1971, but it let pass uncelebrated the 50th anniversary of the revolutionary birth of German democracy in

1968–69. Until recently the revolution fared little better in scholarly circles where it was, in the words of one observer, "widely-ignored, often despised, and half-forgotten."[16] This has changed. Prompted in part by the polemical uses to which the subject of the 1918 revolution lent itself in fratricidal ideological debates within the Social Democratic party, the revolution has emerged as a central motif of recent German historiography. The revolution was once portrayed as no real revolution at all, merely a military collapse and a subsequent limited reordering of the state's political structure.[17] According to this view, the new German state had to conform to one of two incompatible alternatives: a Western-style parliamentary democracy or a soviet dictatorship with workers' and soldiers' councils serving as the organs of class rule. Beginning in the 1960s a new generation of German historians challenged this interpretation, and from their collective studies there developed a new orthodoxy regarding 1918.[18] These historians argued that there had existed in 1918–19 a "third way" beyond parliamentary democracy and soviet democracy, a real—and missed—opportunity to implement a fundamental democratization of German society by retaining the workers' and soldiers' councils as grass-roots buttresses to the edifice of a traditional parliamentary system. This opportunity was squandered, they claimed, by the unimaginative and timid leaders of the SPD, who rejected the proferred assistance of the councils in the mistaken belief that these were "Bolshevist." Instead, the Social Democratic leaders placed their trust, foolishly, in the workings of a parliamentary system without having first broken the economic and social power of their temporarily paralyzed reactionary foes. The new orthodoxy in turn found its critics. Karl Dietrich Bracher has labeled the thesis of the "third way" of council democracy a "partly nostalgic, partly agitational, historical legend."[19]

Our interest is in the course of events leading to the outbreak of the revolution. We see in Germany between January and November 1918 the evolution from what Meaker describes as a nonrevolutionary situation—planned strikes by organized workers—to an unambiguously revolutionary one—spontaneous mass demonstrations everywhere filling the streets with an irresistible tide of workers, soldiers, artisans, farmers, even people from the middle classes. The German labor unions had staged the strikes of late January and early February 1918 to protest the continuation of the war and the annexations claimed at Brest-Litovsk. The strike leaders also called for an end to martial law and for the democratization of the state— an end, in short, to the old order. The strikes spread over most of industrial Germany and drew more than one million workers into demonstrations against their goverment. This was an impressive achievement in wartime. But there was no revolution. The workers were not joined by other elements of the population which continued to express wary confidence in the monarchy and high command. The apparatus of coercion—the police, the army, the bureaucracy—continued to do its duty. The government itself did not flinch; it struck with force against the demonstrators and quickly broke the back of the movement.

Autumn brought a change. In the last days of October the enlisted ranks of the High Seas Fleet demonstrated their sanity and mutinied. Within a fortnight the authority of the imperial government and of the governments in the empire's constituent states vanished. People stopped obeying; their disobedience instantly and fatally punctured the sacerdotal aura of the regime's sovereignty, and almost at once people stopped giving orders. In one convulsive shrug, the nation tossed aside its dynasties. Hardly anyone tried to save them. The police and administration watched; the army officers suffered their epaulets to be torn off by the crowds. Everywhere there appeared, unbeckoned, the characteristic revolutionary form of the period—soldiers' and workers' councils—which took up the for them novel enterprise of running a great state.

Whereas the German government had defeated its domestic enemies in February 1918, nine months later it was easily destroyed. What had happened in the interim? The Allied blockade had had additional time to drain the physical resources of the German people. But the food situation was probably better in the fall of 1918 than in the previous winter. Bolshevik propaganda had had further opportunities to win adherents among laborers and troops; there had been fraternization on the eastern front. With the help of the Soviet embassy in Berlin, Emil Barth and others among the radical wing of the Independent Socialists had purchased weapons and plotted a coup by the "revolutionary shop stewards." It was scheduled for November 11, but the plotters were overtaken by the naval mutinies and the collapse of the old regime.

What happened, of course, between February and November 1918 was that Germany lost the war. In the spring Ludendorff could still promise victory; for a moment in April it appeared he might keep his word. By July the promise had proved hollow and the truth could not be concealed for long. If, as we have suggested, the war produced crisis, the lost war produced revolution. All the belligerents suffered terribly on the battlefield. It was not "Passchendaeles" that destroyed regimes; the real Passchendaele toppled neither the English government nor the crown. Pyrrhic victories evidently could be borne. "Passchendaele" plus defeat could not, and this is what brought down William II, Nicholas II, and Charles I. Not all the defeated succumbed to revolution as the quieter course of events in Sofia demonstrated. Yet in Bulgaria, too, defeat cost a monarch his throne: Ferdinand I abdicated, and the coming of the Agrarian party under Alexander Stamboliski constituted, if not revolution, at least a marked discontinuity in Bulgarian affairs. Again, there were contingencies. But where there was revolution, there was also defeat.

The neutrals were spared these defeats. There is good reason to suppose that had they not been spared them, they would also not have escaped subsequent revolution. Spain was already fragile; the fissures that would open in 1936 were plainly visible one-quarter century earlier. Indeed, so fragile was Spain that one wonders if it could have endured a major bloodletting even on the victorious side. Would the Spanish army and state have dissolved under the crush of total war as the French army, if not state, almost did in the summer of 1917? If Switzerland, Holland, and the Scandinavian countries appear models of stability beside the Spanish example, they were hardly more cohesive and immune to shocks than the German Empire. It is, in fact, the coming of revolution to Germany—no enfeebled Habsburg contrivance or Romanov pasture—that testifies to military defeat's corrosive effect.

The storm passed over the neutrals. They were buffeted by its chilling drafts, and their houses shook. At times it seemed they might give way. But the center held; the forces of order did not yield. Unburdened by war making and unembarrassed by defeat, they prevailed in peace.

Notes

1. Peter Calvert, *A Study of Revolution* (Oxford, 1970), pp. 183–84.
2. *Encyclopedia of the Social Sciences,* 1968 ed., s.v. "Crisis," by James A. Robinson.
3. Randolph Starn, "Historians and 'Crisis,'" *Past and Present* 52 (1971): 17.
4. H. R. Trevor-Roper, "The General Crisis of the Seventeenth Century," in Trevor Aston, ed., *Crisis in Europe* (New York, 1965), pp. 59–95.
5. J. H. Elliott, "Trevor-Roper's 'General Crisis': Symposium," ibid., pp. 104–10.
6. E. J. Hobsbawm, "The Crisis of the Seventeenth Century," ibid., p. 14.
7. Arno J. Mayer, "International Crisis and War since 1870," in Charles L. Bertrand, ed., *Revolutionary Situations in Europe, 1917–1920: Germany, Italy, Austria-Hungary* (Quebec, 1977), p. 212.
8. Ibid., pp. 201, 211. Emphasis in original.
9. See David E. Kaiser, "Germany and the Origins of the First World War," *Journal of Modern History* 55 (1983): 442–74.

10. Mayer, "International Crisis and War," p. 229.

11. Paul Fussell, *The Great War and Modern Memory* (New York, 1975), p. 8.

12. James E. Cronin, "Labor Insurgency and Class Formation: Comparative Perspectives on the Crisis of 1917–1920 in Europe," *Social Science History* 4 (1980): 125–47.

13. Crane Brinton, *The Anatomy of Revolution* (New York, 1965), p. 250.

14. Cronin, "Labor Insurgency," pp. 134–35.

15. Charles Tilly, Louise Tilly, Richard Tilly, *The Rebellious Century, 1830–1930* (Cambridge, Mass., 1975), pp. 252–62.

16. Gerhard P. Bassler, "The Communist Movement in the German Revolution, 1918–1919: A Problem of Historical Typology?" *Central European History* 6 (1973): 240.

17. See Karl Dietrich Erdmann, "Die Geschichte der Weimarer Republik als Problem der Wissenschaft," *Vierteljahrshefte für Zeitgeschichte* 3 (1955): 1–19.

18. See, among others, Eberhard Kolb, *Die Arbeiterräte in der deutschen Innenpolitik, 1918–1919* (Düsseldorf, 1962); Erich Matthias, *Zwischen Räten und Geheimräten: Die deutsche Revolutionsregierung, 1918–1919* (Düsseldorf, 1970); Ulrich Kluge, *Soldatenräte und Revolution: Studien zur Militärpolitik in Deutschland, 1918/1919* (Göttingen, 1975); Peter von Oertzen, *Betriebsräte in der Novemberrevolution* (Düsseldorf, 1963); Reinhold Rürup, ed., *Arbeiter- und Soldatenräte im rheinisch-westfälischen Industriegebiet: Studien zur Geschichte der Revolution 1918/19* (Wuppertal, 1975).

19. Karl Dietrich Bracher, review of Karl Dietrich Erdmann's *Die Zeit der Weltkriege* in *Historische Zeitschrift* 225 (1977): 644. See also Allan Mitchell, "The German Revolution and the Fallacy of Misplaced Concreteness," in Bertrand, *Revolutionary Situations,* pp. 51–55.

Index

Contributors

Carol Gold	University of Alaska, Anchorage, Alaska
Erik Hansen	Union College, Schenectady, New York
Steven Koblik	Pomona College, Claremont, California
Stephen MacDonald	Dickinson College, Carlisle, Pennsylvania
Gerald H. Meaker	Emeritus, Long Beach State University, Long Beach, California
Heinz K. Meier	Old Dominion University, Norfolk, Virginia
Sten S. Nilson	University of Oslo, Oslo, Norway
Hans A. Schmitt	University of Virginia, Charlottesville, Virginia

/D723.N48>C1/